MARVEL
ULTIMATE
SPIDER-MAN™

GREAT POWER

D0953854

W. ..DRAWN

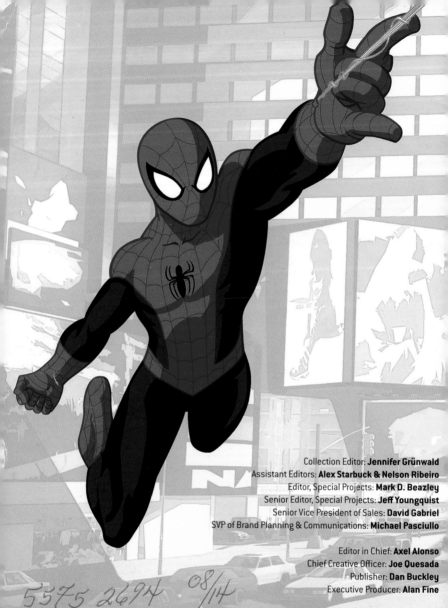

Collection Editor: **Jennifer Grünwald**
Assistant Editors: **Alex Starbuck & Nelson Ribeiro**
Editor, Special Projects: **Mark D. Beazley**
Senior Editor, Special Projects: **Jeff Youngquist**
Senior Vice President of Sales: **David Gabriel**
SVP of Brand Planning & Communications: **Michael Pasciullo**

Editor in Chief: **Axel Alonso**
Chief Creative Officer: **Joe Quesada**
Publisher: **Dan Buckley**
Executive Producer: **Alan Fine**

5575 2694 · 08/14

MARVEL UNIVERSE ULTIMATE SPIDER-MAN: GREAT POWER. First printing 2012. ISBN# 978-0-7851-6494-4. Published by MARVEL WORLDWIDE, INC., a subsidiary of MARVEL ENTERTAINMENT, LLC. OFFICE OF PUBLICATION: 135 West 50th Street, New York, NY 10020. Copyright © 2012 Marvel Characters, Inc. All rights reserved. $ 9.99 per copy in the U.S. and $10.99 in Canada (GST #R127032852); Canadian Agreement #40668537. All characters featured in this issue and the distinctive names and likenesses thereof, and all related indicia are trademarks of Marvel Characters, Inc. No similarity between any of the names, characters, persons, and/or institutions in this magazine with those of any living or dead person or institution is intended, and any such similarity which may exist is purely coincidental. **Printed in the U.S.A.** ALAN FINE, EVP - Office of the President, Marvel Worldwide, Inc. and EVP & CMO Marvel Characters B.V.; DAN BUCKLEY, Publisher & President - Print, Animation & Digital Divisions; JOE QUESADA, Chief Creative Officer; TOM BREVOORT, SVP of Publishing; DAVID BOGART, SVP of Operations & Procurement, Publishing; RUWAN JAYATILLEKE, SVP & Associate Publisher, Publishing; C.B. CEBULSKI, SVP of Creator & Content Development; DAVID GABRIEL, SVP of Publishing Sales & Circulation; MICHAEL PASCIULLO, SVP of Brand Planning & Communications; JIM O'KEEFE, VP of Operations & Logistics; DAN CARR, Executive Director of Publishing Technology; SUSAN CRESPI, Editorial Operations Manager; ALEX MORALES, Publishing Operations Manager; STAN LEE, Chairman Emeritus. For information regarding advertising in Marvel Comics or on Marvel.com, please contact John Dokes, SVP Integrated Sales and Marketing, at jdokes@ marvel.com. For Marvel subscription inquiries, please call 800-217-9158. **Manufactured between 5/7/2012 and 5/28/2012 by SHERIDAN BOOKS, INC., CHELSEA, MI, USA.**

10 9 8 7 6 5 4 3 2 1

MARVEL ULTIMATE SPIDER-MAN™

GREAT POWER

ADAPTED BY
CHRIS ELIOPOULOS

BASED ON
EPISODE 1: "GREAT POWER"
BY PAUL DINI

EPISODE 2: "GREAT RESPONSIBILITY"
BY PAUL DINI

EPISODE 3: "DOOMED"
BY MAN OF ACTION

EPISODE 4: "VENOM"
BY MAN OF ACTION AND JAMES FELDER

EDITOR: JORDAN D. WHITE
SENIOR ART DIRECTOR: JEFF SUTER
DIRECTOR OF SALES: JIM NAUSEDAS
DIRECTOR OF MERCHANDISING & PROMOTIONS: TIM DILLON
DIRECTOR OF COMMUNICATIONS: ARUNE SINGH
ASSOCIATE PUBLISHER: RUWAN JAYATILLEKE
HEAD OF MARVEL TV: JEPH LOEB

GREAT POWER

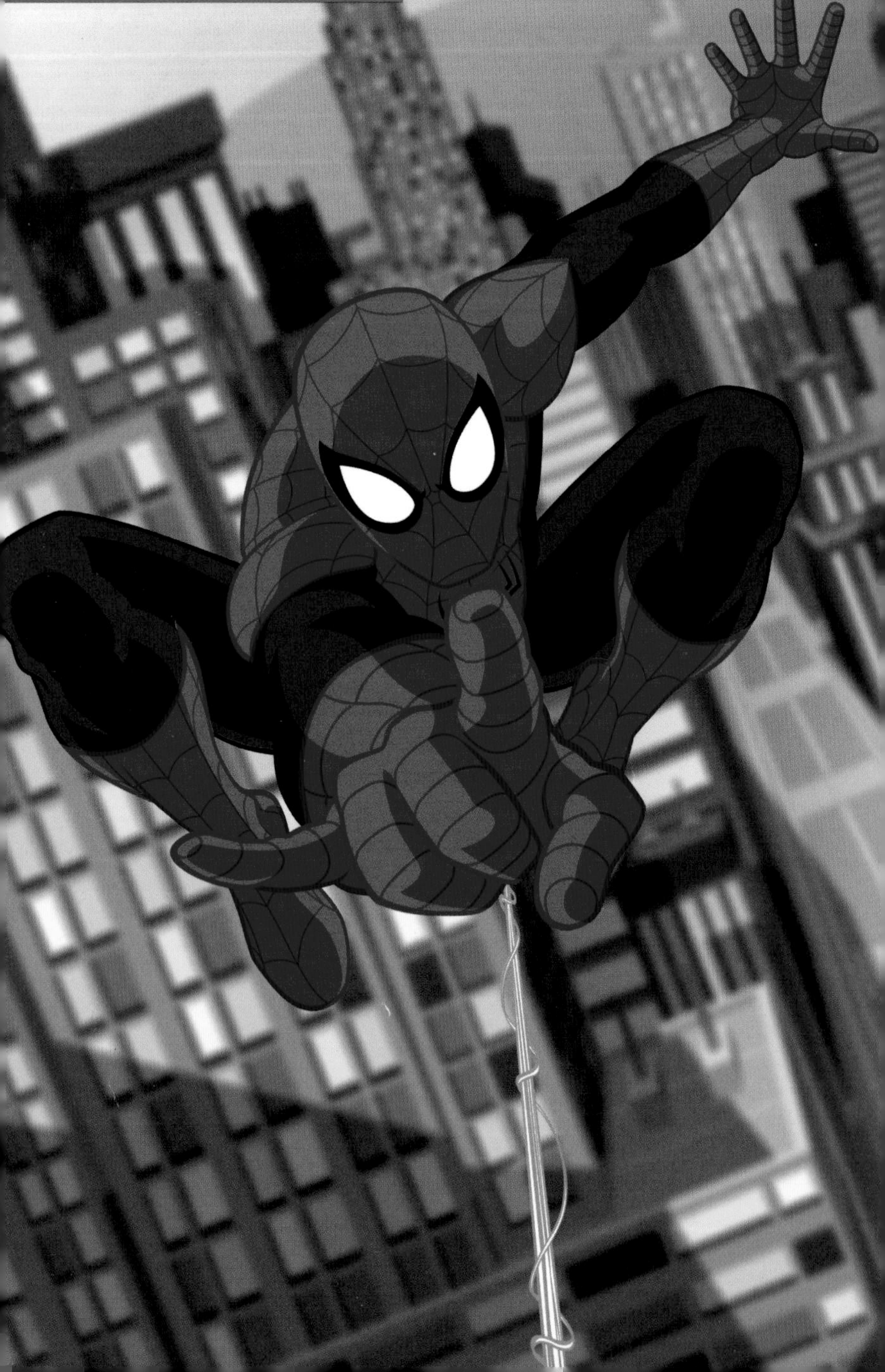

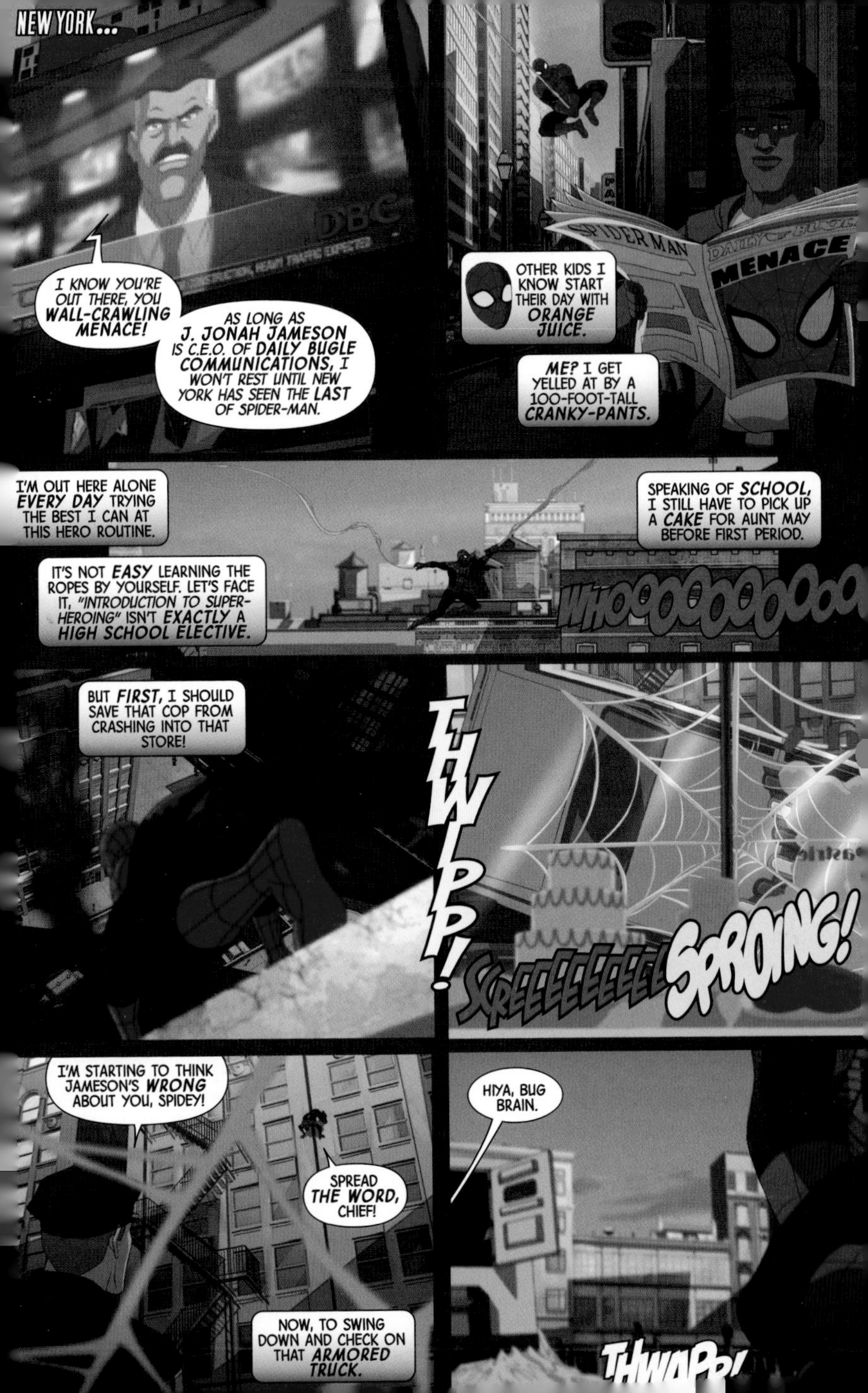
NEW YORK...
I KNOW YOU'RE OUT THERE, YOU WALL-CRAWLING MENACE!
AS LONG AS J. JONAH JAMESON IS C.E.O. OF DAILY BUGLE COMMUNICATIONS, I WON'T REST UNTIL NEW YORK HAS SEEN THE LAST OF SPIDER-MAN.
DBC
OTHER KIDS I KNOW START THEIR DAY WITH ORANGE JUICE.
ME? I GET YELLED AT BY A 100-FOOT-TALL CRANKY-PANTS.
SPIDER MAN
MENACE
I'M OUT HERE ALONE EVERY DAY TRYING THE BEST I CAN AT THIS HERO ROUTINE.
IT'S NOT EASY LEARNING THE ROPES BY YOURSELF. LET'S FACE IT, "INTRODUCTION TO SUPER-HEROING" ISN'T EXACTLY A HIGH SCHOOL ELECTIVE.
SPEAKING OF SCHOOL, I STILL HAVE TO PICK UP A CAKE FOR AUNT MAY BEFORE FIRST PERIOD.
WHOOOOOOOOOO
BUT FIRST, I SHOULD SAVE THAT COP FROM CRASHING INTO THAT STORE!
THWIPP!
SCREEEEEEEEEL
SPROING!
I'M STARTING TO THINK JAMESON'S WRONG ABOUT YOU, SPIDEY!
SPREAD THE WORD, CHIEF!
NOW, TO SWING DOWN AND CHECK ON THAT ARMORED TRUCK.
HIYA, BUG BRAIN.
THWAPP!

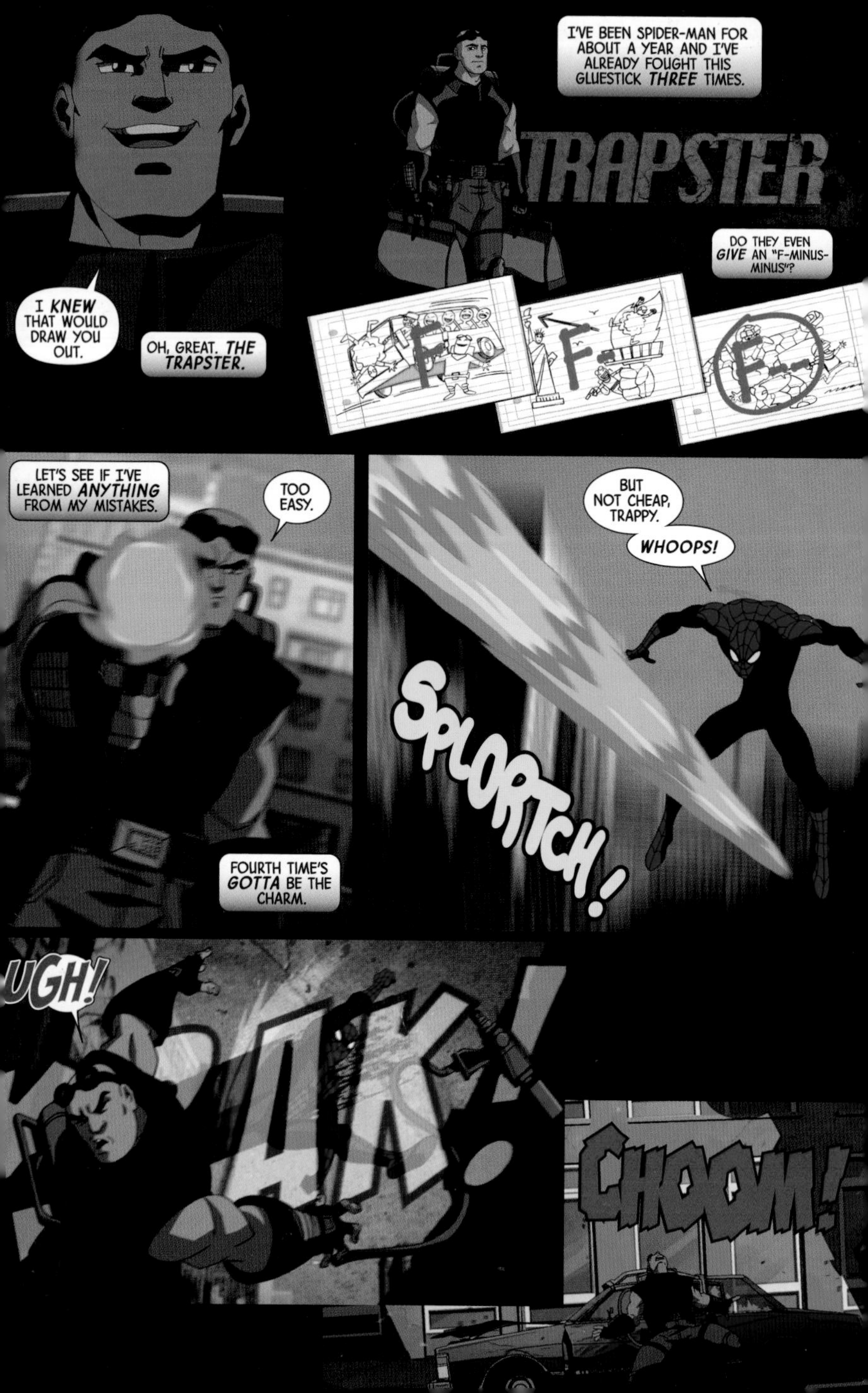
I'VE BEEN SPIDER-MAN FOR ABOUT A YEAR AND I'VE ALREADY FOUGHT THIS GLUESTICK THREE TIMES.
TRAPSTER
I KNEW THAT WOULD DRAW YOU OUT.
OH, GREAT. THE TRAPSTER.
DO THEY EVEN GIVE AN "F-MINUS-MINUS"?
F
F-
F--
LET'S SEE IF I'VE LEARNED ANYTHING FROM MY MISTAKES.
TOO EASY.
FOURTH TIME'S GOTTA BE THE CHARM.
BUT NOT CHEAP, TRAPPY.
WHOOPS!
SPLORTCH!
UGH!
CHOOM!

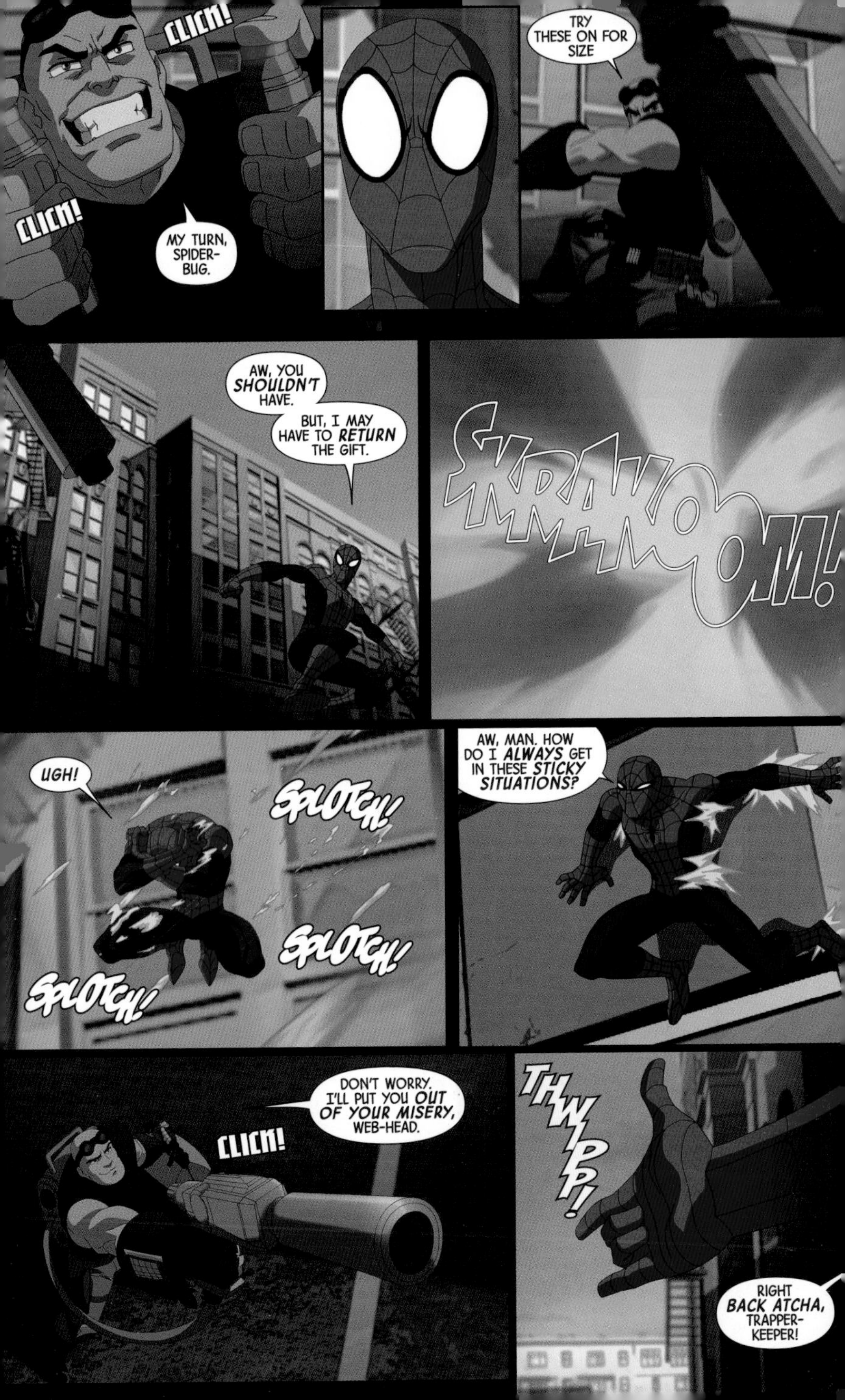
CLICK!
CLICK!
MY TURN, SPIDER-BUG.
TRY THESE ON FOR SIZE
AW, YOU SHOULDN'T HAVE.
BUT, I MAY HAVE TO RETURN THE GIFT.
SKRAKOOM!
UGH!
SPLOTCH!
SPLOTCH!
SPLOTCH!
AW, MAN. HOW DO I ALWAYS GET IN THESE STICKY SITUATIONS?
DON'T WORRY. I'LL PUT YOU OUT OF YOUR MISERY, WEB-HEAD.
CLICK!
THWIP!
RIGHT BACK ATCHA, TRAPPER-KEEPER!

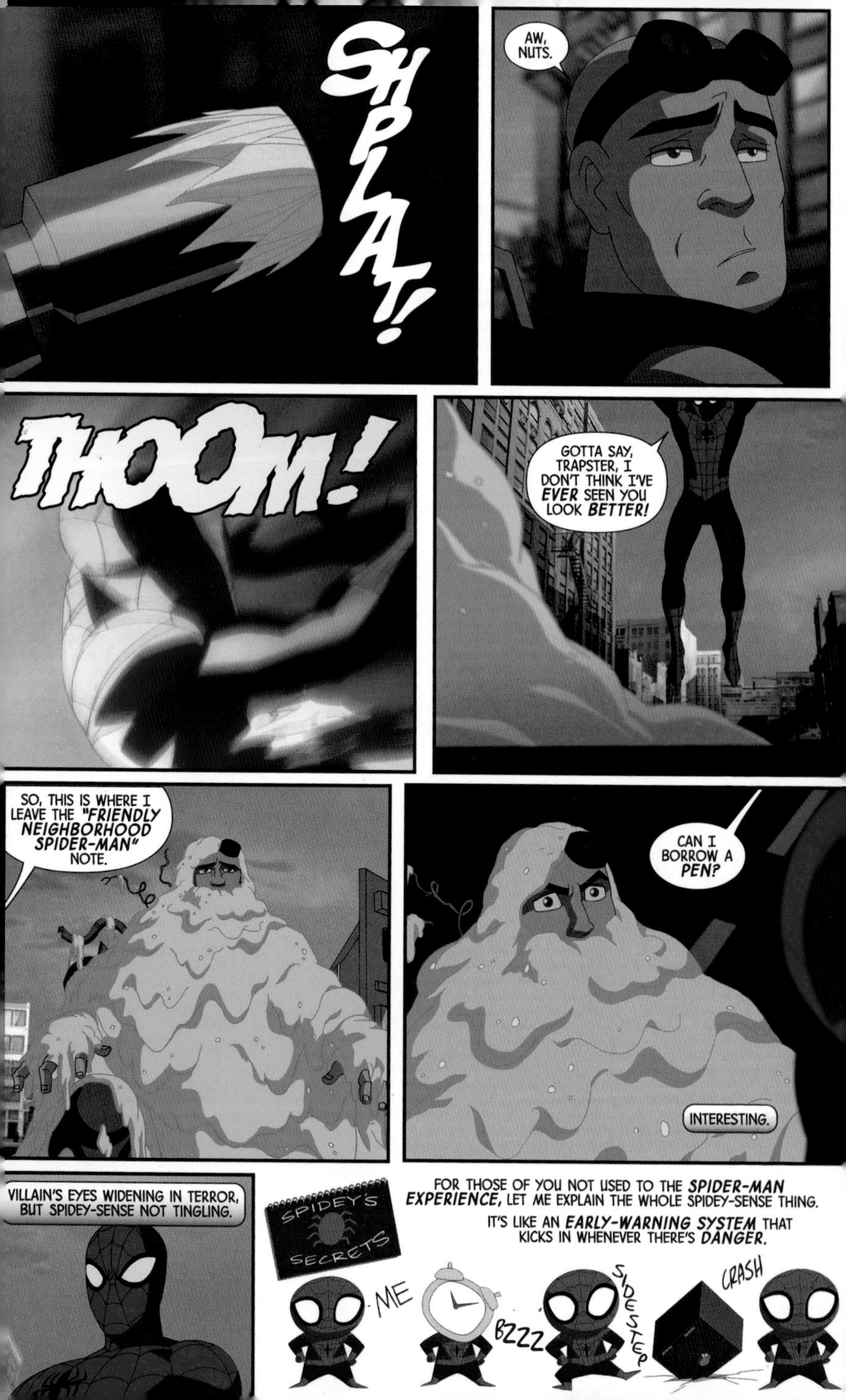
SHPLAT!
AW, NUTS.
THOOM!
GOTTA SAY, TRAPSTER, I DON'T THINK I'VE EVER SEEN YOU LOOK BETTER!
SO, THIS IS WHERE I LEAVE THE "FRIENDLY NEIGHBORHOOD SPIDER-MAN" NOTE.
CAN I BORROW A PEN?
INTERESTING.
VILLAIN'S EYES WIDENING IN TERROR, BUT SPIDEY-SENSE NOT TINGLING.
SPIDEY'S SECRETS
FOR THOSE OF YOU NOT USED TO THE SPIDER-MAN EXPERIENCE, LET ME EXPLAIN THE WHOLE SPIDEY-SENSE THING.
IT'S LIKE AN EARLY-WARNING SYSTEM THAT KICKS IN WHENEVER THERE'S DANGER.
ME
BZZZ
SIDESTEP
CRASH

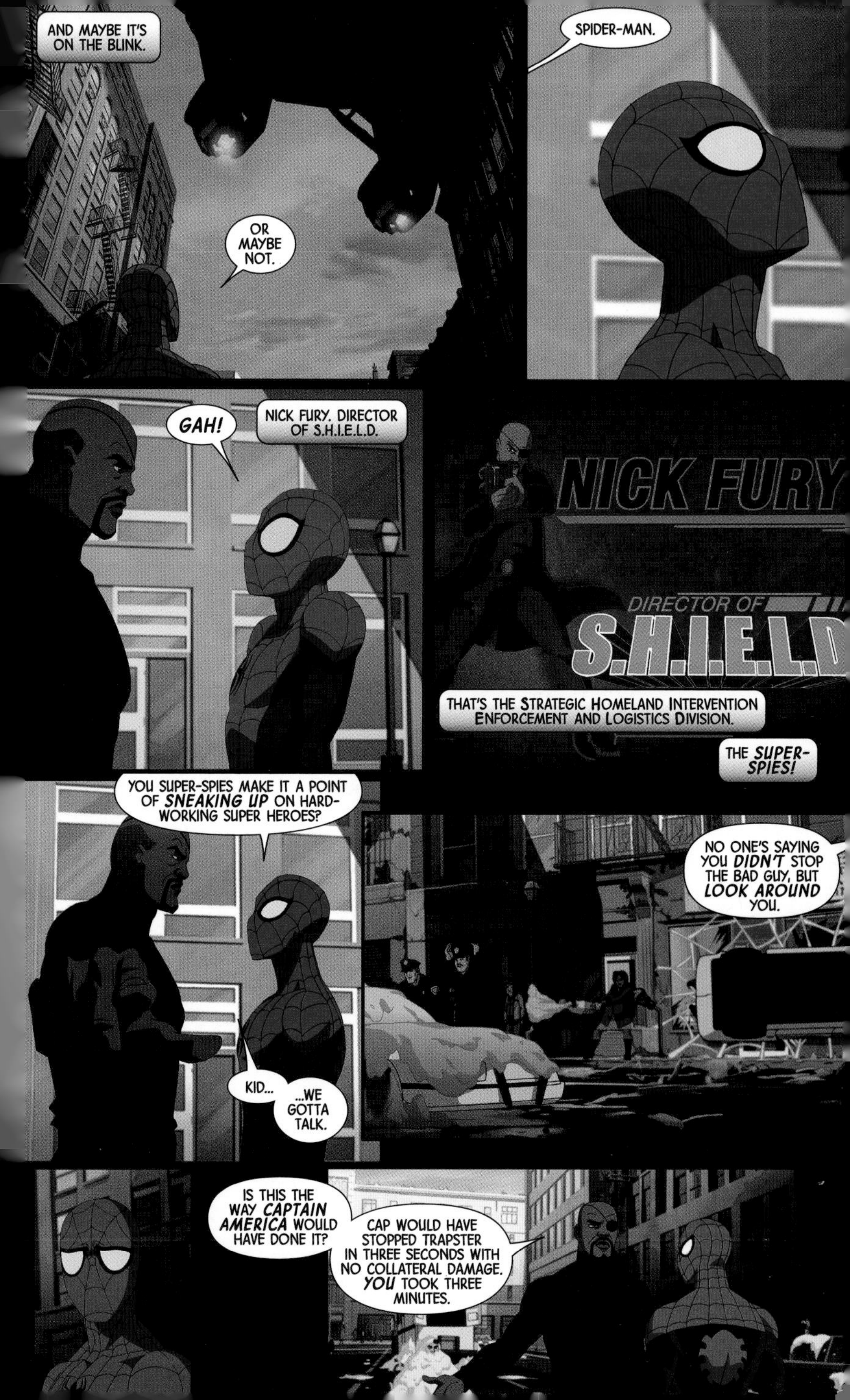
AND MAYBE IT'S ON THE BLINK.
OR MAYBE NOT.
SPIDER-MAN.
GAH!
NICK FURY. DIRECTOR OF S.H.I.E.L.D.
NICK FURY
DIRECTOR OF
S.H.I.E.L.D
THAT'S THE STRATEGIC HOMELAND INTERVENTION ENFORCEMENT AND LOGISTICS DIVISION.
THE SUPER-SPIES!
YOU SUPER-SPIES MAKE IT A POINT OF SNEAKING UP ON HARD-WORKING SUPER HEROES?
KID...
...WE GOTTA TALK.
NO ONE'S SAYING YOU DIDN'T STOP THE BAD GUY, BUT LOOK AROUND YOU.
IS THIS THE WAY CAPTAIN AMERICA WOULD HAVE DONE IT?
CAP WOULD HAVE STOPPED TRAPSTER IN THREE SECONDS WITH NO COLLATERAL DAMAGE. YOU TOOK THREE MINUTES.

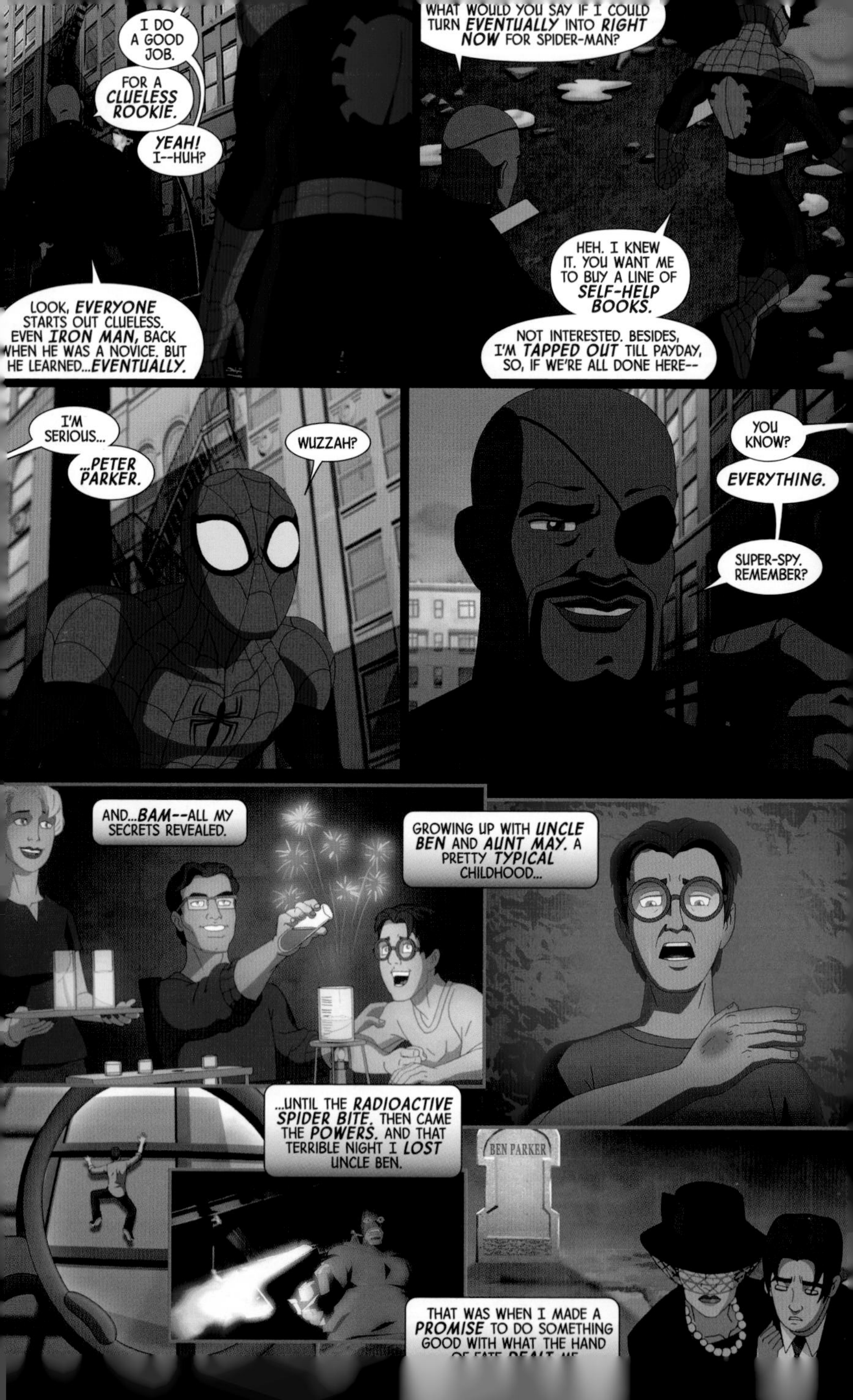
I DO A GOOD JOB.
FOR A CLUELESS ROOKIE.
YEAH! I--HUH?
LOOK, EVERYONE STARTS OUT CLUELESS. EVEN IRON MAN, BACK WHEN HE WAS A NOVICE. BUT HE LEARNED...EVENTUALLY.
WHAT WOULD YOU SAY IF I COULD TURN EVENTUALLY INTO RIGHT NOW FOR SPIDER-MAN?
HEH. I KNEW IT. YOU WANT ME TO BUY A LINE OF SELF-HELP BOOKS.
NOT INTERESTED. BESIDES, I'M TAPPED OUT TILL PAYDAY, SO, IF WE'RE ALL DONE HERE--
I'M SERIOUS...
...PETER PARKER.
WUZZAH?
YOU KNOW?
EVERYTHING.
SUPER-SPY. REMEMBER?
AND...BAM--ALL MY SECRETS REVEALED.
GROWING UP WITH UNCLE BEN AND AUNT MAY. A PRETTY TYPICAL CHILDHOOD...
...UNTIL THE RADIOACTIVE SPIDER BITE. THEN CAME THE POWERS. AND THAT TERRIBLE NIGHT I LOST UNCLE BEN.
BEN PARKER
THAT WAS WHEN I MADE A PROMISE TO DO SOMETHING GOOD WITH WHAT THE HAND

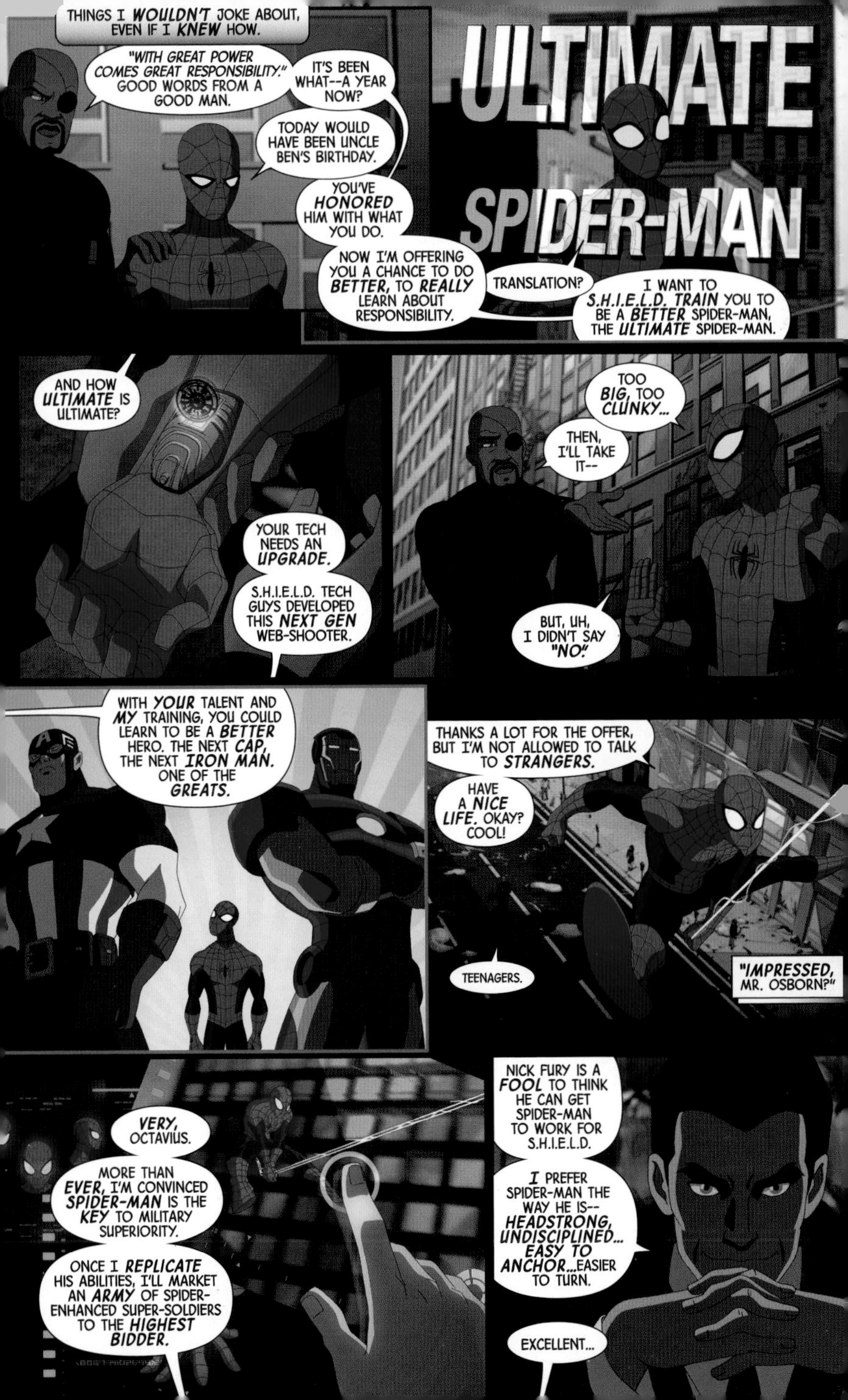
THINGS I WOULDN'T JOKE ABOUT, EVEN IF I KNEW HOW.
"WITH GREAT POWER COMES GREAT RESPONSIBILITY." GOOD WORDS FROM A GOOD MAN.
IT'S BEEN WHAT--A YEAR NOW?
TODAY WOULD HAVE BEEN UNCLE BEN'S BIRTHDAY.
YOU'VE HONORED HIM WITH WHAT YOU DO.
NOW I'M OFFERING YOU A CHANCE TO DO BETTER, TO REALLY LEARN ABOUT RESPONSIBILITY.
TRANSLATION?
I WANT TO S.H.I.E.L.D. TRAIN YOU TO BE A BETTER SPIDER-MAN, THE ULTIMATE SPIDER-MAN.
ULTIMATE SPIDER-MAN
AND HOW ULTIMATE IS ULTIMATE?
YOUR TECH NEEDS AN UPGRADE.
S.H.I.E.L.D. TECH GUYS DEVELOPED THIS NEXT GEN WEB-SHOOTER.
TOO BIG, TOO CLUNKY...
THEN, I'LL TAKE IT--
BUT, UH, I DIDN'T SAY "NO."
WITH YOUR TALENT AND MY TRAINING, YOU COULD LEARN TO BE A BETTER HERO. THE NEXT CAP, THE NEXT IRON MAN. ONE OF THE GREATS.
THANKS A LOT FOR THE OFFER, BUT I'M NOT ALLOWED TO TALK TO STRANGERS.
HAVE A NICE LIFE. OKAY? COOL!
TEENAGERS.
"IMPRESSED, MR. OSBORN?"
VERY, OCTAVIUS.
MORE THAN EVER, I'M CONVINCED SPIDER-MAN IS THE KEY TO MILITARY SUPERIORITY.
ONCE I REPLICATE HIS ABILITIES, I'LL MARKET AN ARMY OF SPIDER-ENHANCED SUPER-SOLDIERS TO THE HIGHEST BIDDER.
NICK FURY IS A FOOL TO THINK HE CAN GET SPIDER-MAN TO WORK FOR S.H.I.E.L.D.
I PREFER SPIDER-MAN THE WAY HE IS--HEADSTRONG, UNDISCIPLINED... EASY TO ANCHOR...EASIER TO TURN.
EXCELLENT...

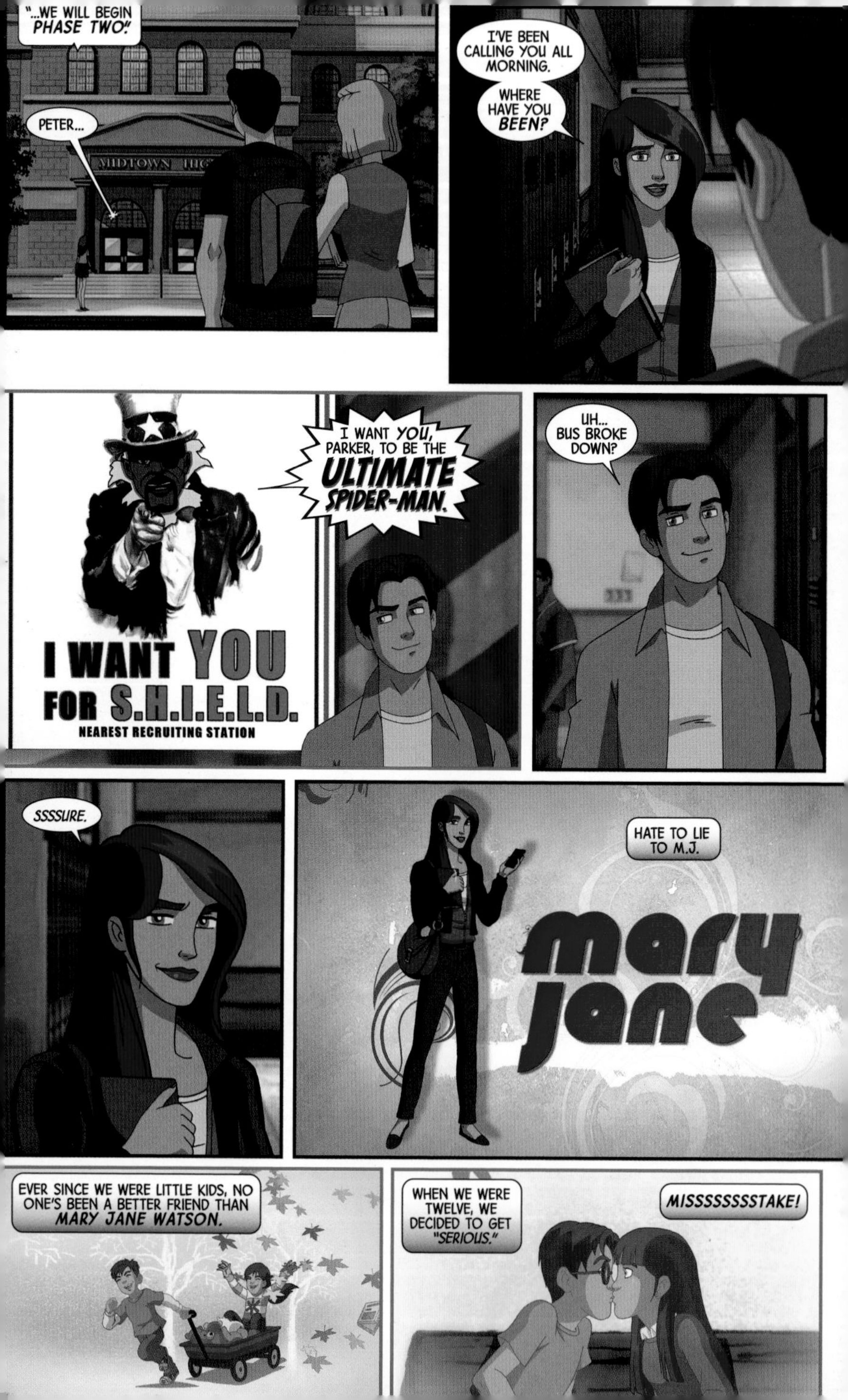
"...WE WILL BEGIN PHASE TWO!"
PETER...
MIDTOWN HIGH
I'VE BEEN CALLING YOU ALL MORNING.
WHERE HAVE YOU BEEN?
I WANT YOU FOR S.H.I.E.L.D.
NEAREST RECRUITING STATION
I WANT YOU, PARKER, TO BE THE ULTIMATE SPIDER-MAN.
UH... BUS BROKE DOWN?
SSSSURE.
HATE TO LIE TO M.J.
mary jane
EVER SINCE WE WERE LITTLE KIDS, NO ONE'S BEEN A BETTER FRIEND THAN MARY JANE WATSON.
WHEN WE WERE TWELVE, WE DECIDED TO GET "SERIOUS."
MISSSSSSSSTAKE!

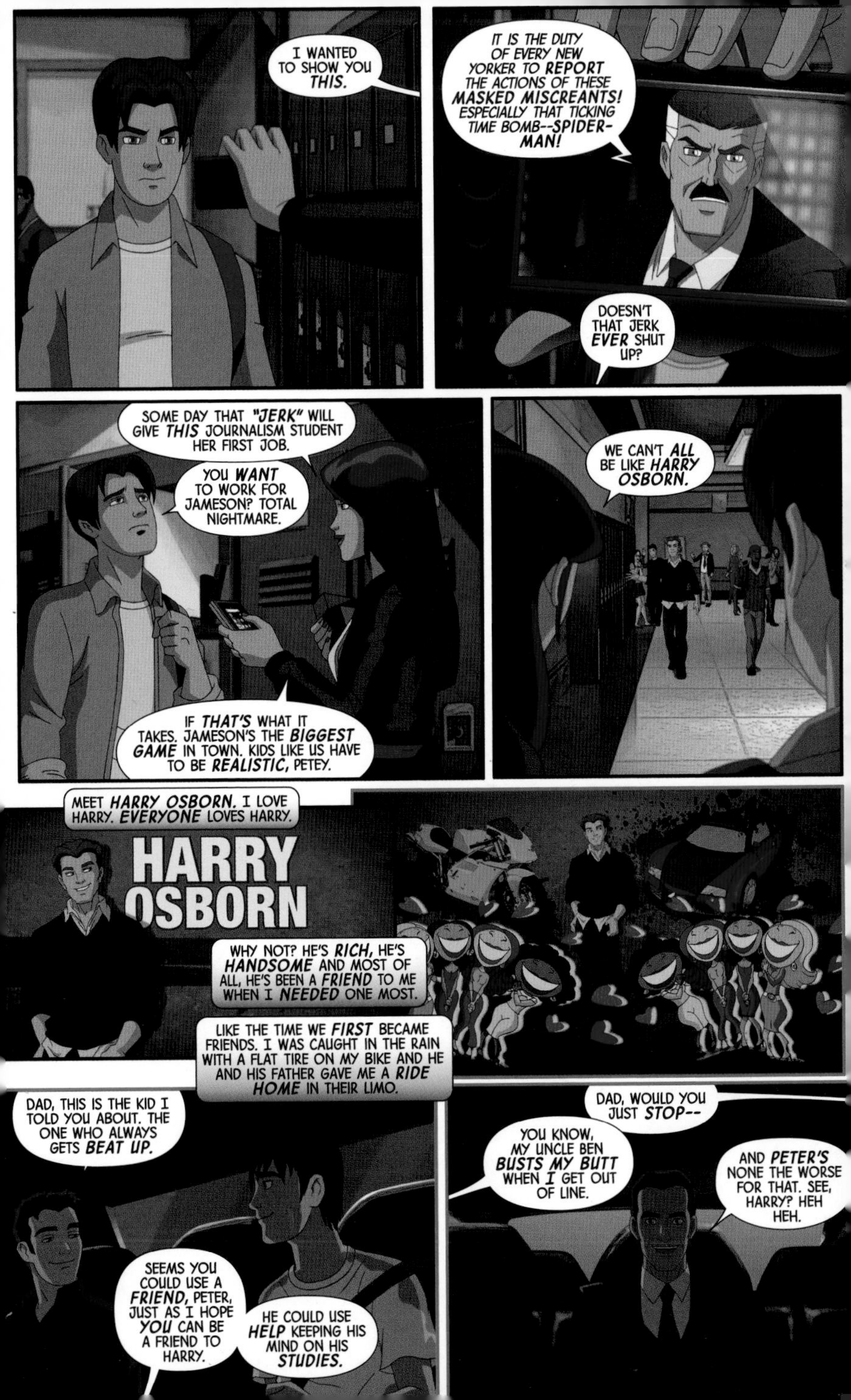
I WANTED TO SHOW YOU THIS.
IT IS THE DUTY OF EVERY NEW YORKER TO REPORT THE ACTIONS OF THESE MASKED MISCREANTS! ESPECIALLY THAT TICKING TIME BOMB--SPIDER-MAN!
DOESN'T THAT JERK EVER SHUT UP?
SOME DAY THAT "JERK" WILL GIVE THIS JOURNALISM STUDENT HER FIRST JOB.
YOU WANT TO WORK FOR JAMESON? TOTAL NIGHTMARE.
IF THAT'S WHAT IT TAKES. JAMESON'S THE BIGGEST GAME IN TOWN. KIDS LIKE US HAVE TO BE REALISTIC, PETEY.
WE CAN'T ALL BE LIKE HARRY OSBORN.
MEET HARRY OSBORN. I LOVE HARRY. EVERYONE LOVES HARRY.
HARRY OSBORN
WHY NOT? HE'S RICH, HE'S HANDSOME AND MOST OF ALL, HE'S BEEN A FRIEND TO ME WHEN I NEEDED ONE MOST.
LIKE THE TIME WE FIRST BECAME FRIENDS. I WAS CAUGHT IN THE RAIN WITH A FLAT TIRE ON MY BIKE AND HE AND HIS FATHER GAVE ME A RIDE HOME IN THEIR LIMO.
DAD, THIS IS THE KID I TOLD YOU ABOUT. THE ONE WHO ALWAYS GETS BEAT UP.
SEEMS YOU COULD USE A FRIEND, PETER, JUST AS I HOPE YOU CAN BE A FRIEND TO HARRY.
HE COULD USE HELP KEEPING HIS MIND ON HIS STUDIES.
DAD, WOULD YOU JUST STOP--
YOU KNOW, MY UNCLE BEN BUSTS MY BUTT WHEN I GET OUT OF LINE.
AND PETER'S NONE THE WORSE FOR THAT. SEE, HARRY? HEH HEH.

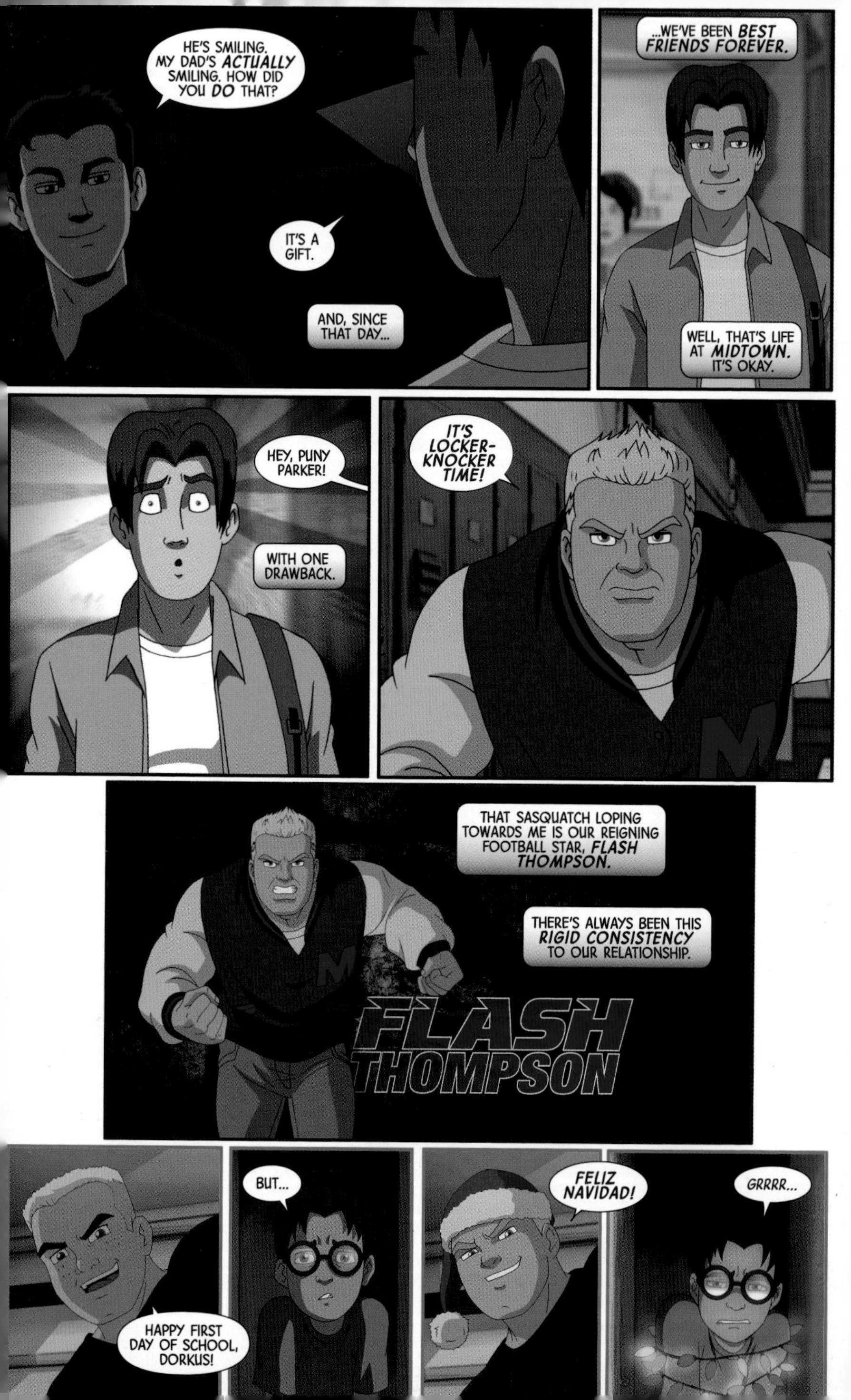
HE'S SMILING. MY DAD'S ACTUALLY SMILING. HOW DID YOU DO THAT?
IT'S A GIFT.
AND, SINCE THAT DAY...
...WE'VE BEEN BEST FRIENDS FOREVER.
WELL, THAT'S LIFE AT MIDTOWN. IT'S OKAY.
HEY, PUNY PARKER!
WITH ONE DRAWBACK.
IT'S LOCKER-KNOCKER TIME!
THAT SASQUATCH LOPING TOWARDS ME IS OUR REIGNING FOOTBALL STAR, FLASH THOMPSON.
THERE'S ALWAYS BEEN THIS RIGID CONSISTENCY TO OUR RELATIONSHIP.
FLASH THOMPSON
HAPPY FIRST DAY OF SCHOOL, DORKUS!
BUT...
FELIZ NAVIDAD!
GRRRR...

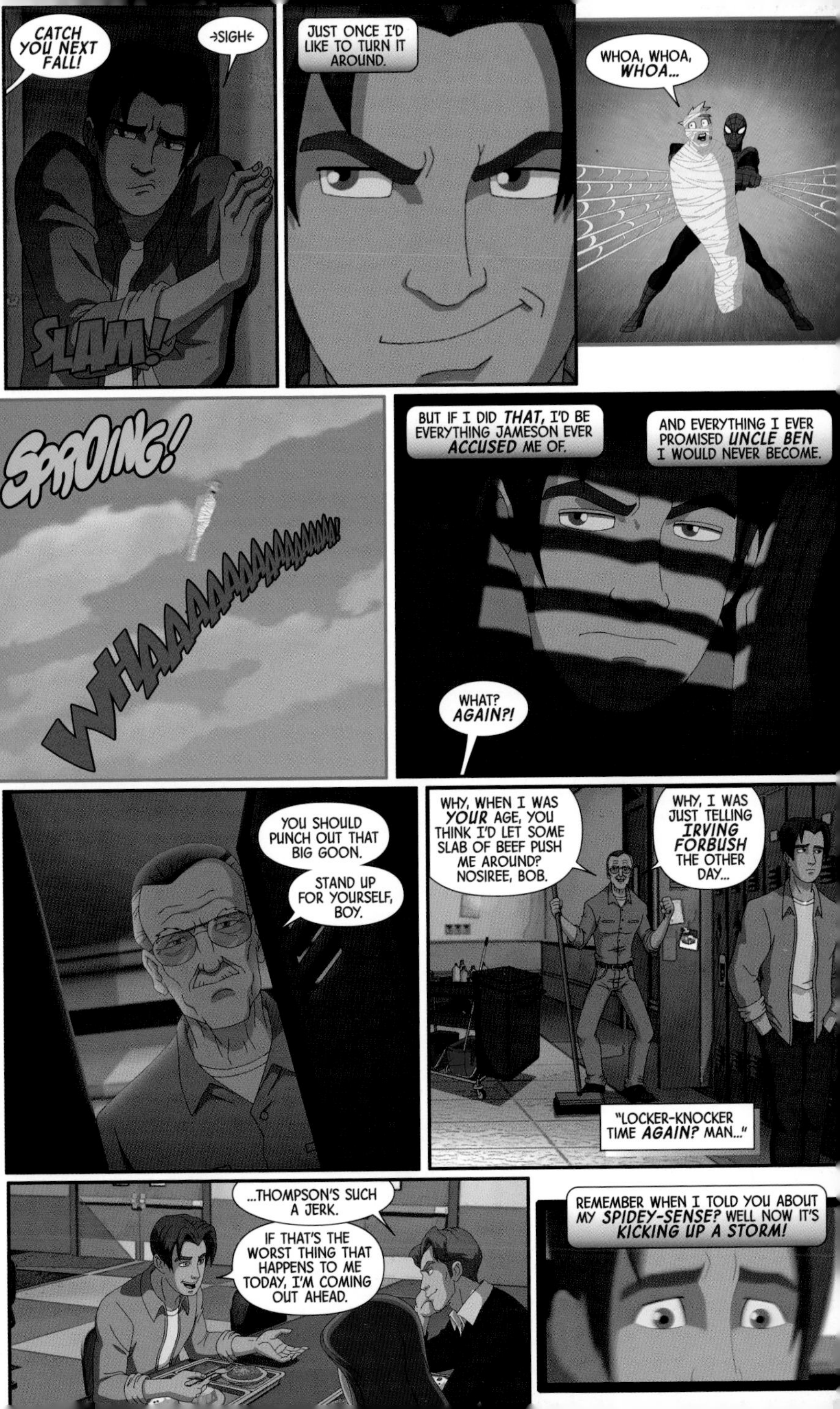
CATCH YOU NEXT FALL!
→SIGH←
SLAM!
JUST ONCE I'D LIKE TO TURN IT AROUND.
WHOA, WHOA, WHOA...
SPROING!
WHAAAAAAAAAAAAAAAAA!
BUT IF I DID THAT, I'D BE EVERYTHING JAMESON EVER ACCUSED ME OF.
AND EVERYTHING I EVER PROMISED UNCLE BEN I WOULD NEVER BECOME.
WHAT? AGAIN?!
YOU SHOULD PUNCH OUT THAT BIG GOON.
STAND UP FOR YOURSELF, BOY.
WHY, WHEN I WAS YOUR AGE, YOU THINK I'D LET SOME SLAB OF BEEF PUSH ME AROUND? NOSIREE, BOB.
WHY, I WAS JUST TELLING IRVING FORBUSH THE OTHER DAY...
"LOCKER-KNOCKER TIME AGAIN? MAN..."
...THOMPSON'S SUCH A JERK.
IF THAT'S THE WORST THING THAT HAPPENS TO ME TODAY, I'M COMING OUT AHEAD.
REMEMBER WHEN I TOLD YOU ABOUT MY SPIDEY-SENSE? WELL NOW IT'S KICKING UP A STORM!

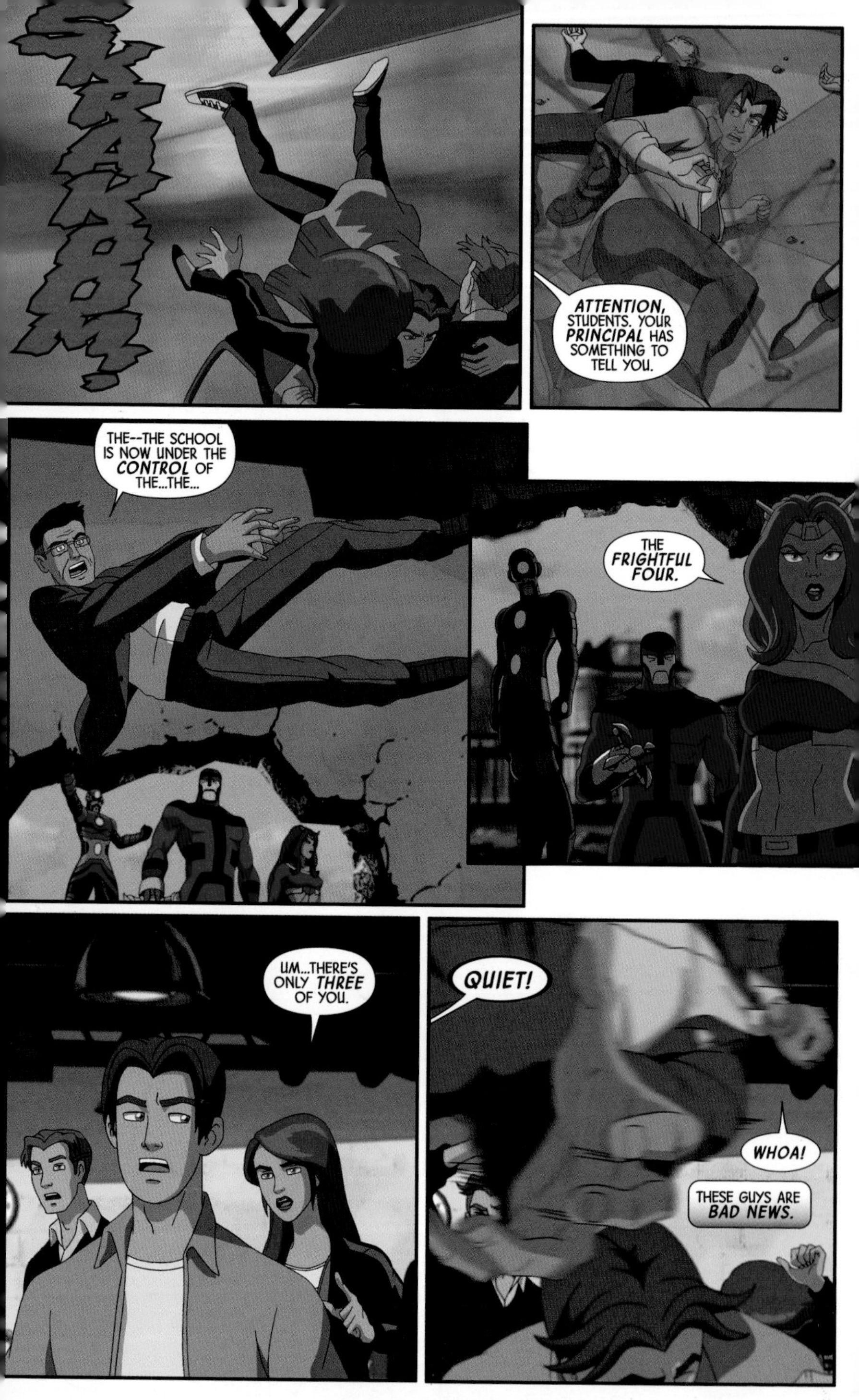
SKRAKOOM!
ATTENTION, STUDENTS. YOUR PRINCIPAL HAS SOMETHING TO TELL YOU.
THE--THE SCHOOL IS NOW UNDER THE CONTROL OF THE...THE...
THE FRIGHTFUL FOUR.
UM...THERE'S ONLY THREE OF YOU.
QUIET!
WHOA!
THESE GUYS ARE BAD NEWS.

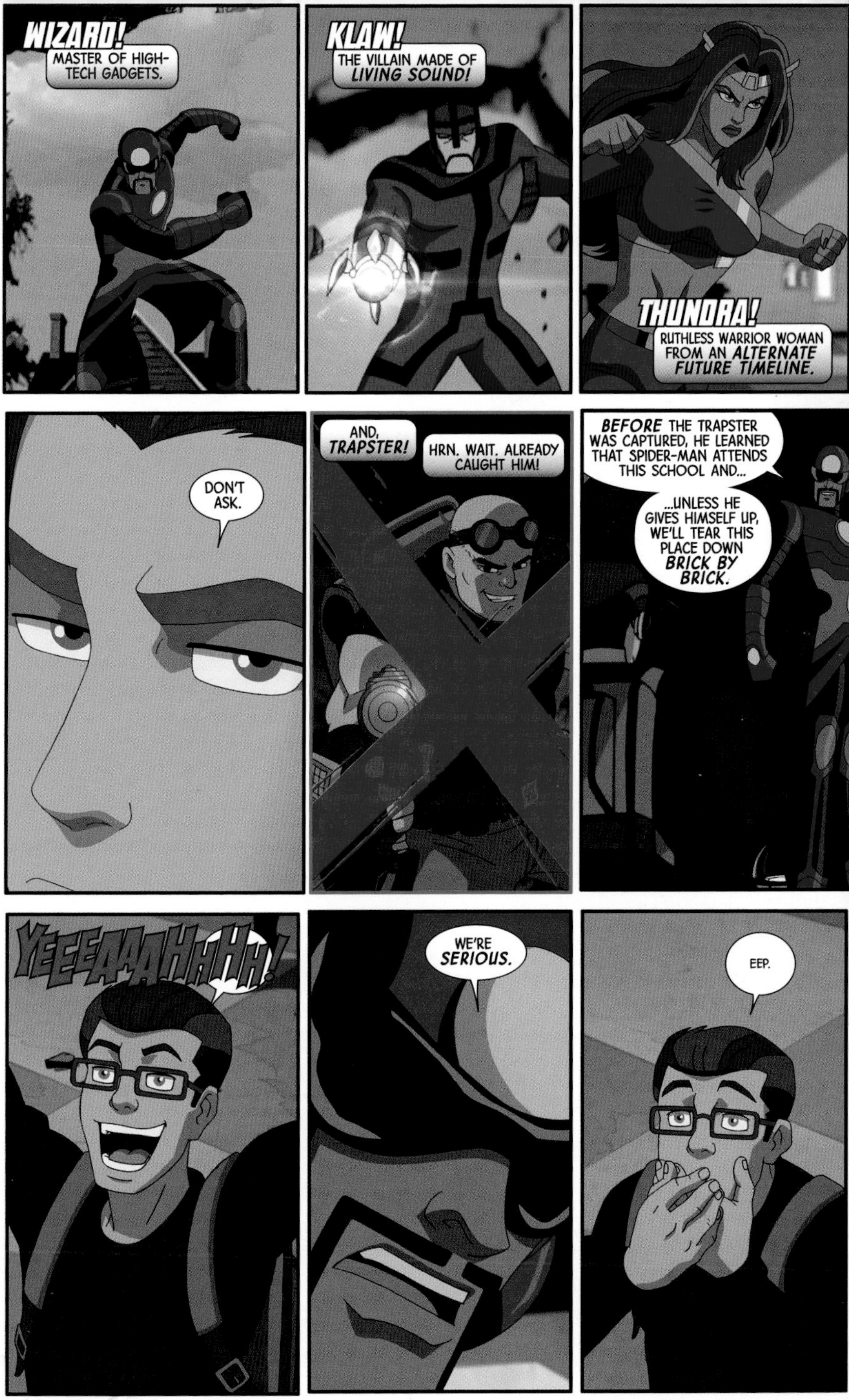
WIZARD!
MASTER OF HIGH-TECH GADGETS.
KLAW!
THE VILLAIN MADE OF LIVING SOUND!
THUNDRA!
RUTHLESS WARRIOR WOMAN FROM AN ALTERNATE FUTURE TIMELINE.
DON'T ASK.
AND, TRAPSTER!
HRN. WAIT. ALREADY CAUGHT HIM!
BEFORE THE TRAPSTER WAS CAPTURED, HE LEARNED THAT SPIDER-MAN ATTENDS THIS SCHOOL AND...
...UNLESS HE GIVES HIMSELF UP, WE'LL TEAR THIS PLACE DOWN BRICK BY BRICK.
YEEEAAAHHHH!
WE'RE SERIOUS.
EEP.

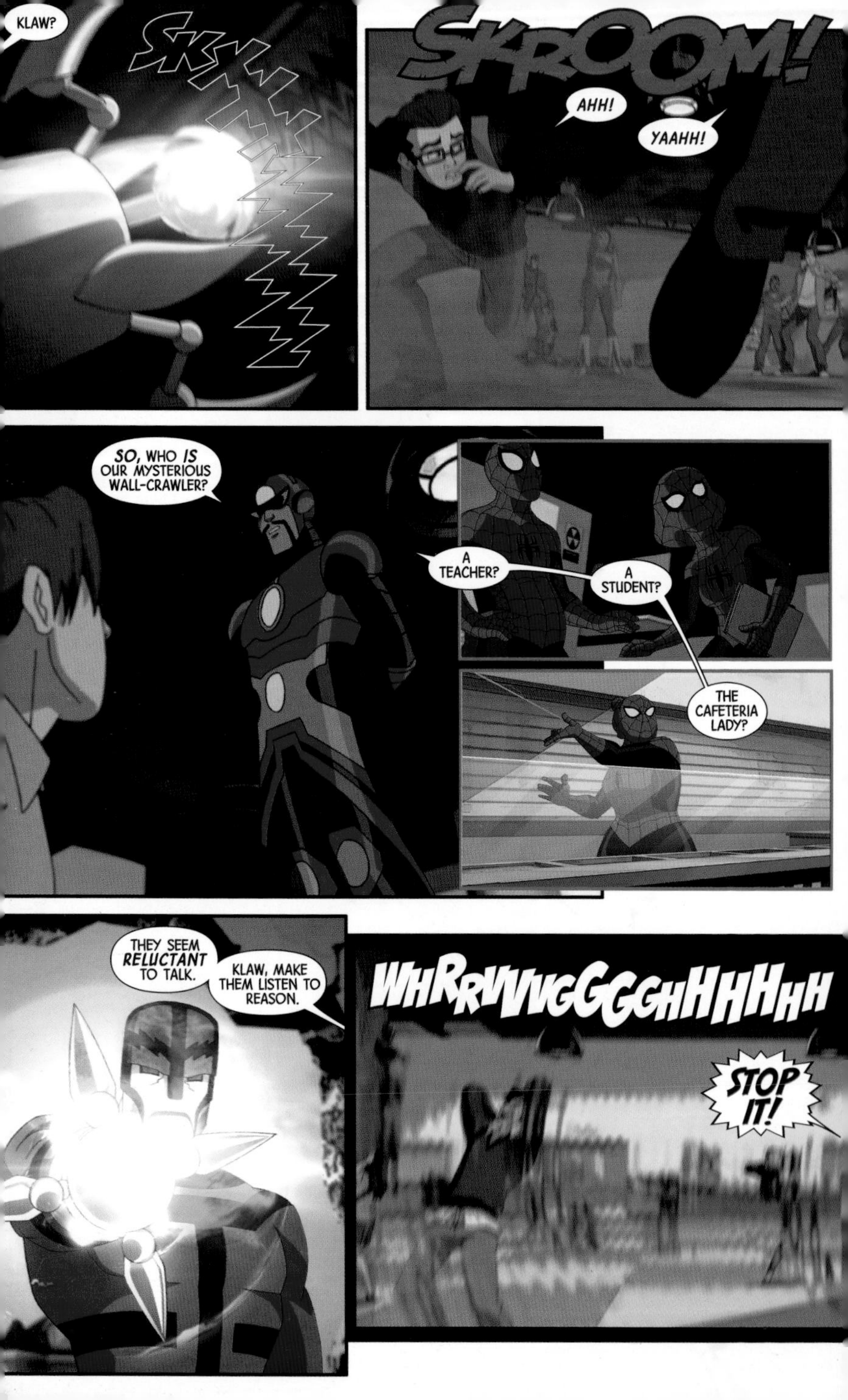

KLAW?
SKXXZZZZZ
SKROOOM!
AHH!
YAAHH!
SO, WHO IS OUR MYSTERIOUS WALL-CRAWLER?
A TEACHER?
A STUDENT?
THE CAFETERIA LADY?
THEY SEEM RELUCTANT TO TALK.
KLAW, MAKE THEM LISTEN TO REASON.
WHRRVVVGGGGHHHHHH
STOP IT!

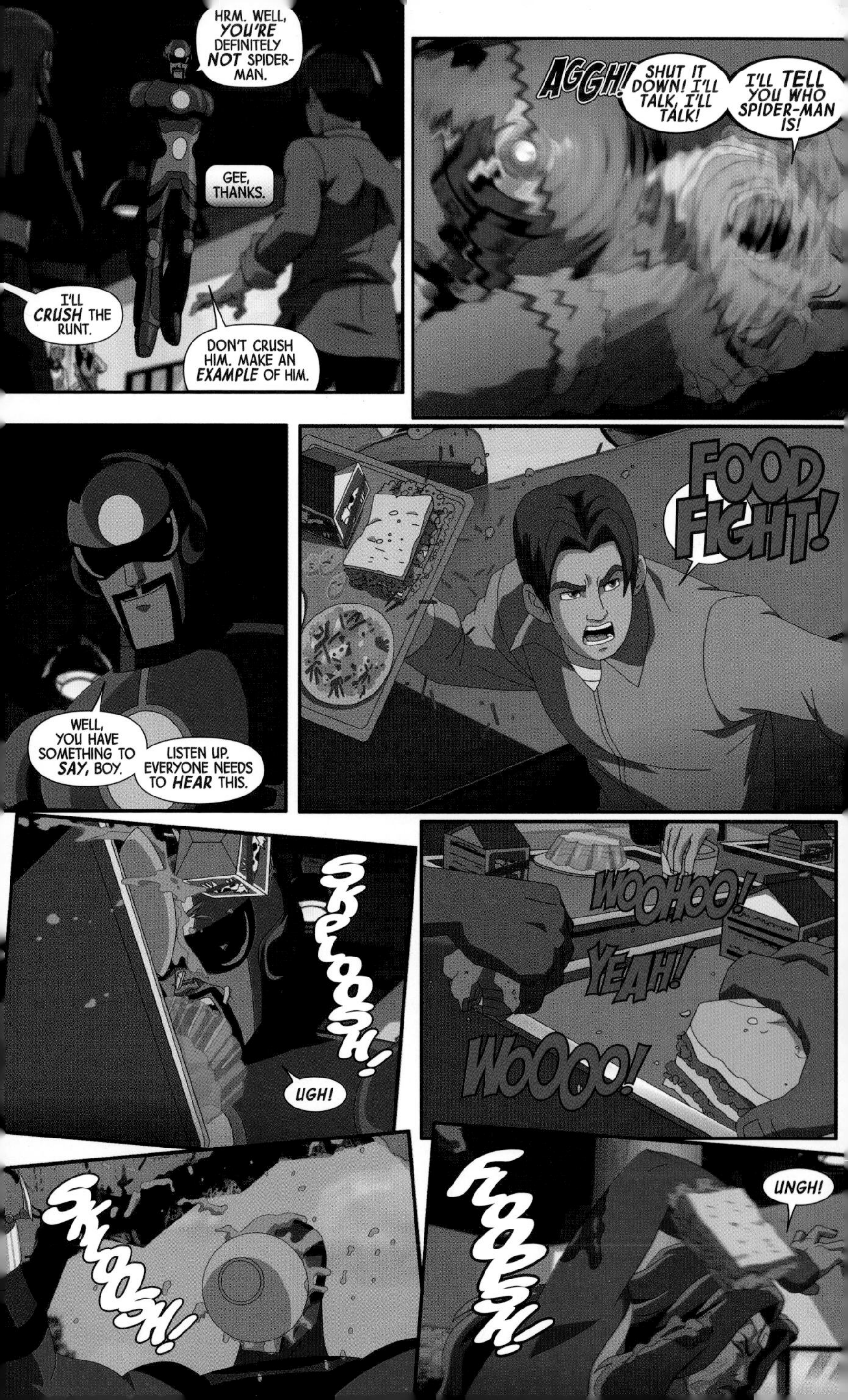

HRM. WELL, YOU'RE DEFINITELY NOT SPIDER-MAN.
GEE, THANKS.
I'LL CRUSH THE RUNT.
DON'T CRUSH HIM. MAKE AN EXAMPLE OF HIM.
AGGH!
SHUT IT DOWN! I'LL TALK, I'LL TALK!
I'LL TELL YOU WHO SPIDER-MAN IS!
WELL, YOU HAVE SOMETHING TO SAY, BOY.
LISTEN UP. EVERYONE NEEDS TO HEAR THIS.
FOOD FIGHT!
SHPLOOSH!
UGH!
WOOHOO!
YEAH!
WOOOO!
SKLOOSH!
FLOOSH!
UNGH!

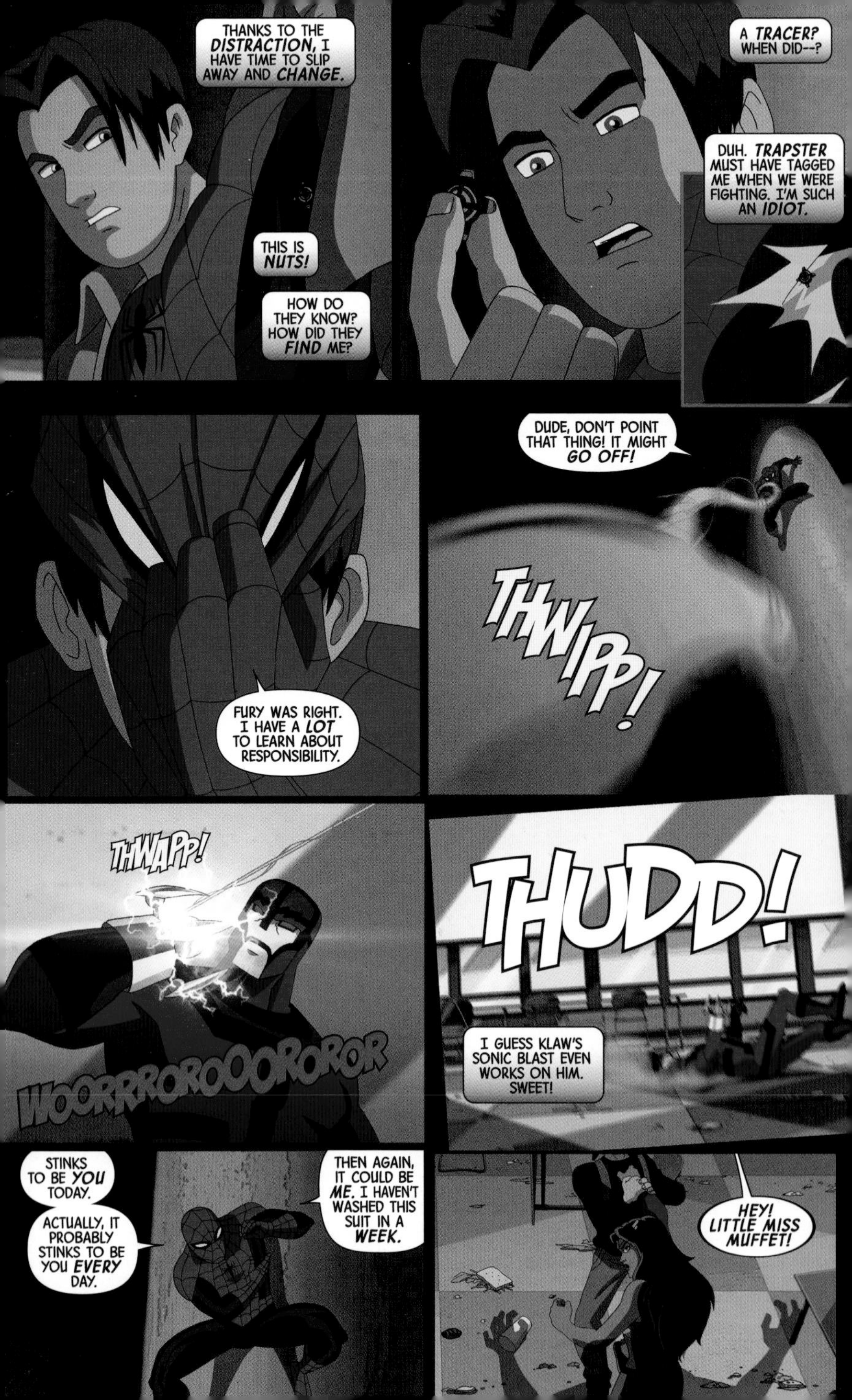
THANKS TO THE DISTRACTION, I HAVE TIME TO SLIP AWAY AND CHANGE.
THIS IS NUTS!
HOW DO THEY KNOW? HOW DID THEY FIND ME?
A TRACER? WHEN DID--?
DUH. TRAPSTER MUST HAVE TAGGED ME WHEN WE WERE FIGHTING. I'M SUCH AN IDIOT.
FURY WAS RIGHT. I HAVE A LOT TO LEARN ABOUT RESPONSIBILITY.
DUDE, DON'T POINT THAT THING! IT MIGHT GO OFF!
THWIPP!
THWAPP!
WOORRROROOORORОR
THUDD!
I GUESS KLAW'S SONIC BLAST EVEN WORKS ON HIM. SWEET!
STINKS TO BE YOU TODAY.
ACTUALLY, IT PROBABLY STINKS TO BE YOU EVERY DAY.
THEN AGAIN, IT COULD BE ME. I HAVEN'T WASHED THIS SUIT IN A WEEK.
HEY! LITTLE MISS MUFFET!

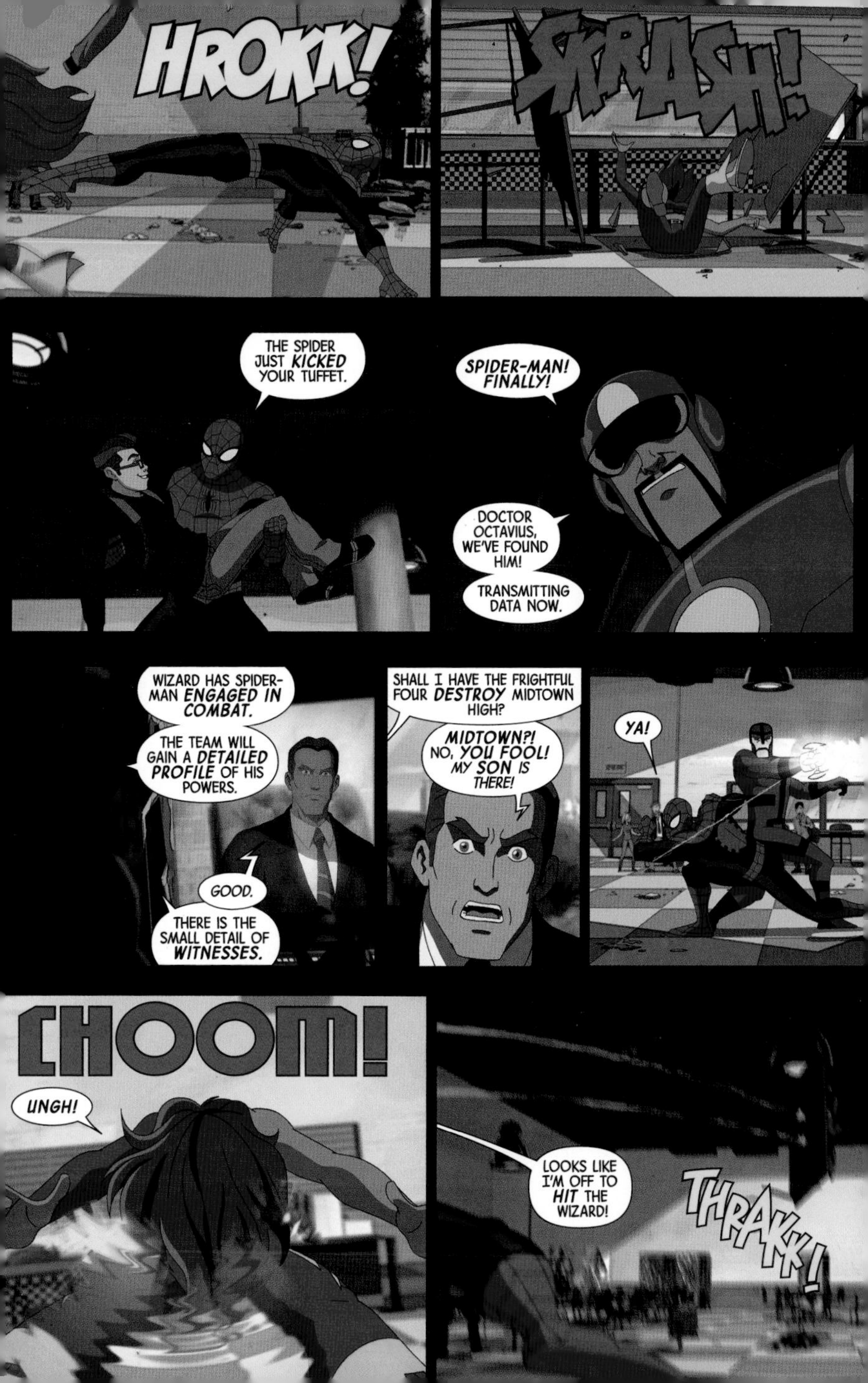
HROKK!
SKRASH!
THE SPIDER JUST KICKED YOUR TUFFET.
SPIDER-MAN! FINALLY!
DOCTOR OCTAVIUS, WE'VE FOUND HIM!
TRANSMITTING DATA NOW.
WIZARD HAS SPIDER-MAN ENGAGED IN COMBAT.
THE TEAM WILL GAIN A DETAILED PROFILE OF HIS POWERS.
GOOD.
THERE IS THE SMALL DETAIL OF WITNESSES.
SHALL I HAVE THE FRIGHTFUL FOUR DESTROY MIDTOWN HIGH?
MIDTOWN?! NO, YOU FOOL! MY SON IS THERE!
YA!
CHOOM!
UNGH!
LOOKS LIKE I'M OFF TO HIT THE WIZARD!
THRAKK!

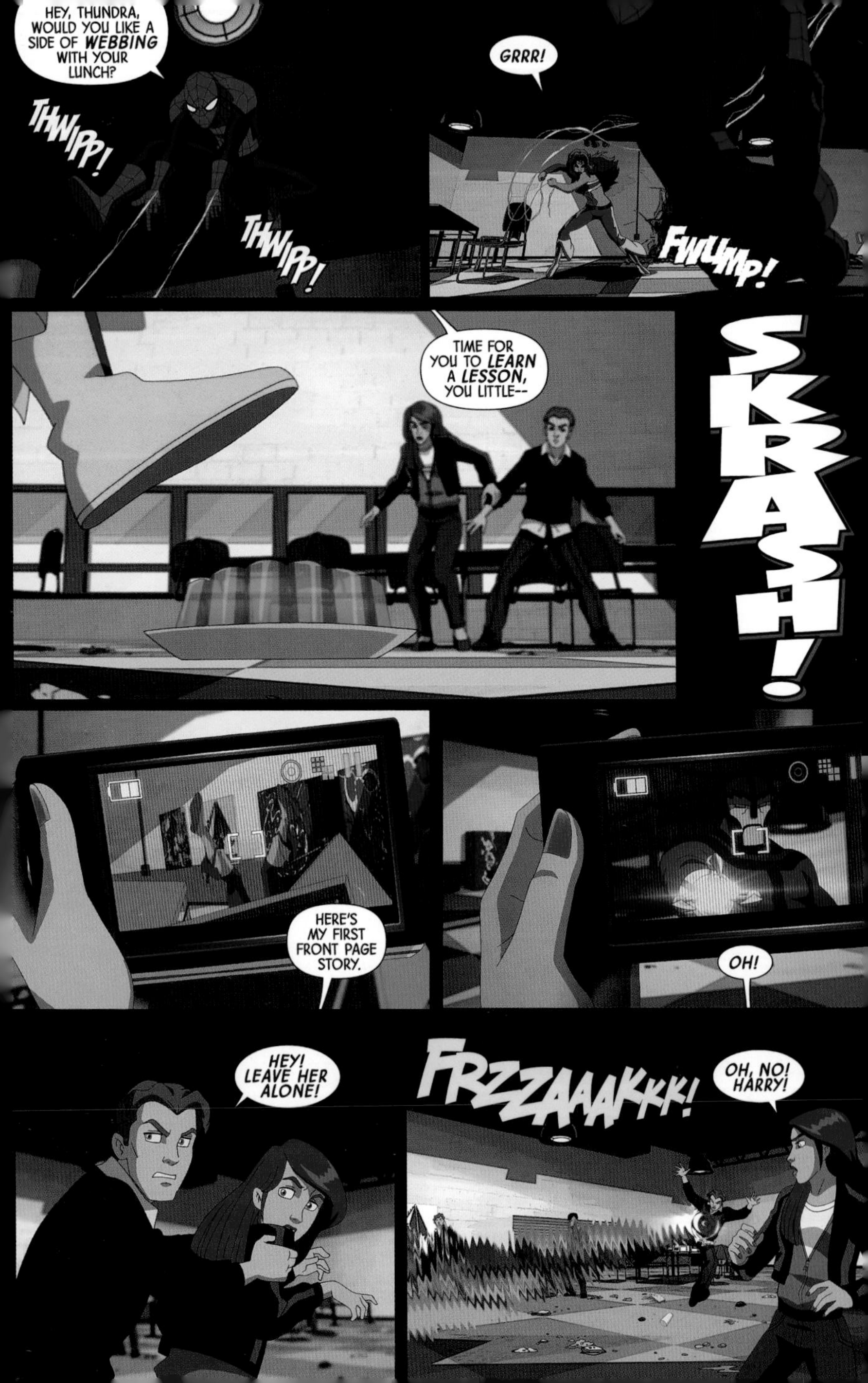
HEY, THUNDRA, WOULD YOU LIKE A SIDE OF WEBBING WITH YOUR LUNCH?
THWIPP!
THWIPP!
GRRR!
FWUMP!
TIME FOR YOU TO LEARN A LESSON, YOU LITTLE--
SKRASH!
HERE'S MY FIRST FRONT PAGE STORY.
OH!
HEY! LEAVE HER ALONE!
FRZZAAAKKK!
OH, NO! HARRY!

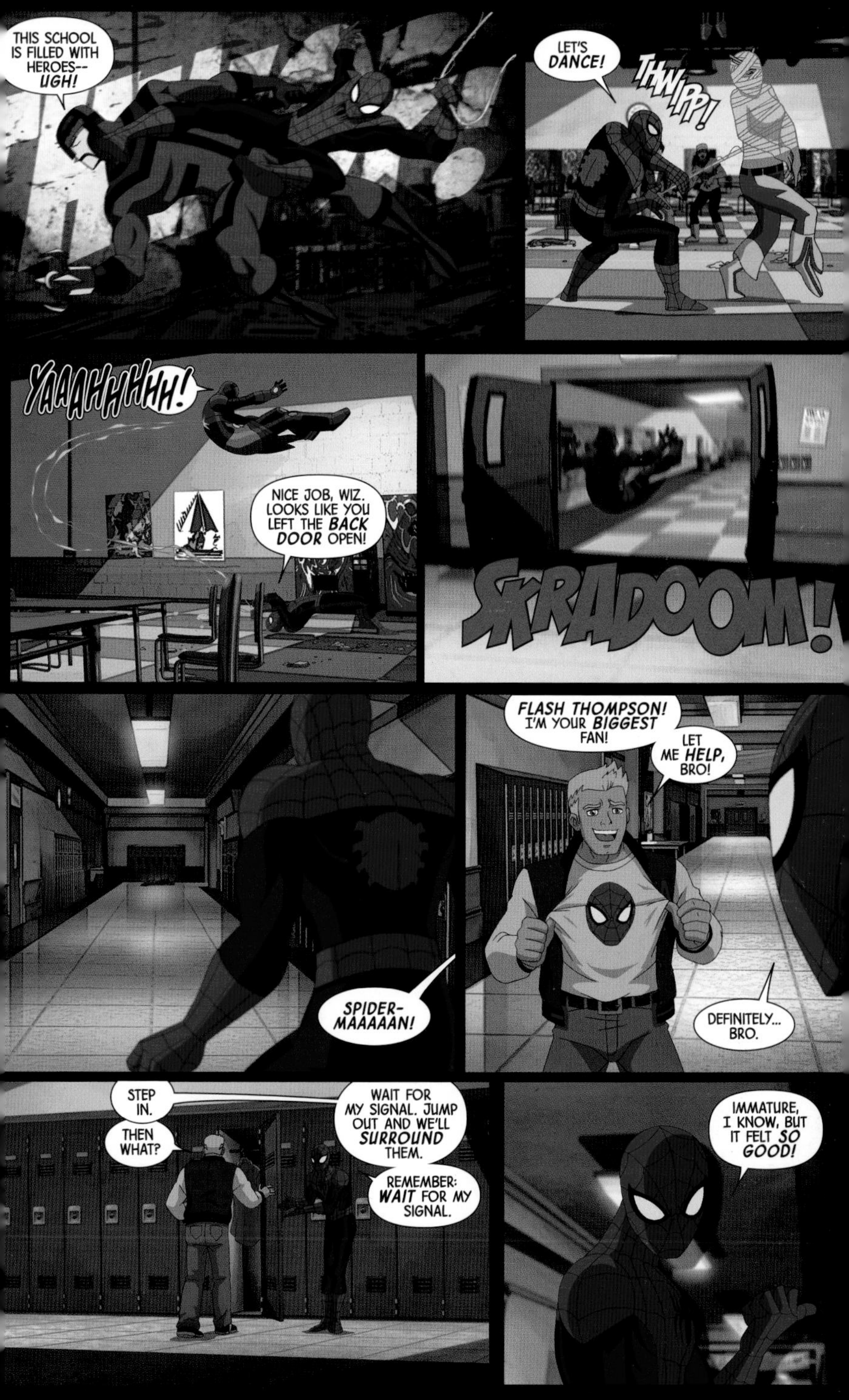
THIS SCHOOL IS FILLED WITH HEROES-- UGH!
LET'S DANCE!
THWIPP!
YAAAHHHHH!
NICE JOB, WIZ. LOOKS LIKE YOU LEFT THE BACK DOOR OPEN!
SKRADOOM!
SPIDER-MAAAAAN!
FLASH THOMPSON! I'M YOUR BIGGEST FAN!
LET ME HELP, BRO!
DEFINITELY... BRO.
STEP IN.
THEN WHAT?
WAIT FOR MY SIGNAL. JUMP OUT AND WE'LL SURROUND THEM.
REMEMBER: WAIT FOR MY SIGNAL.
IMMATURE, I KNOW, BUT IT FELT SO GOOD!

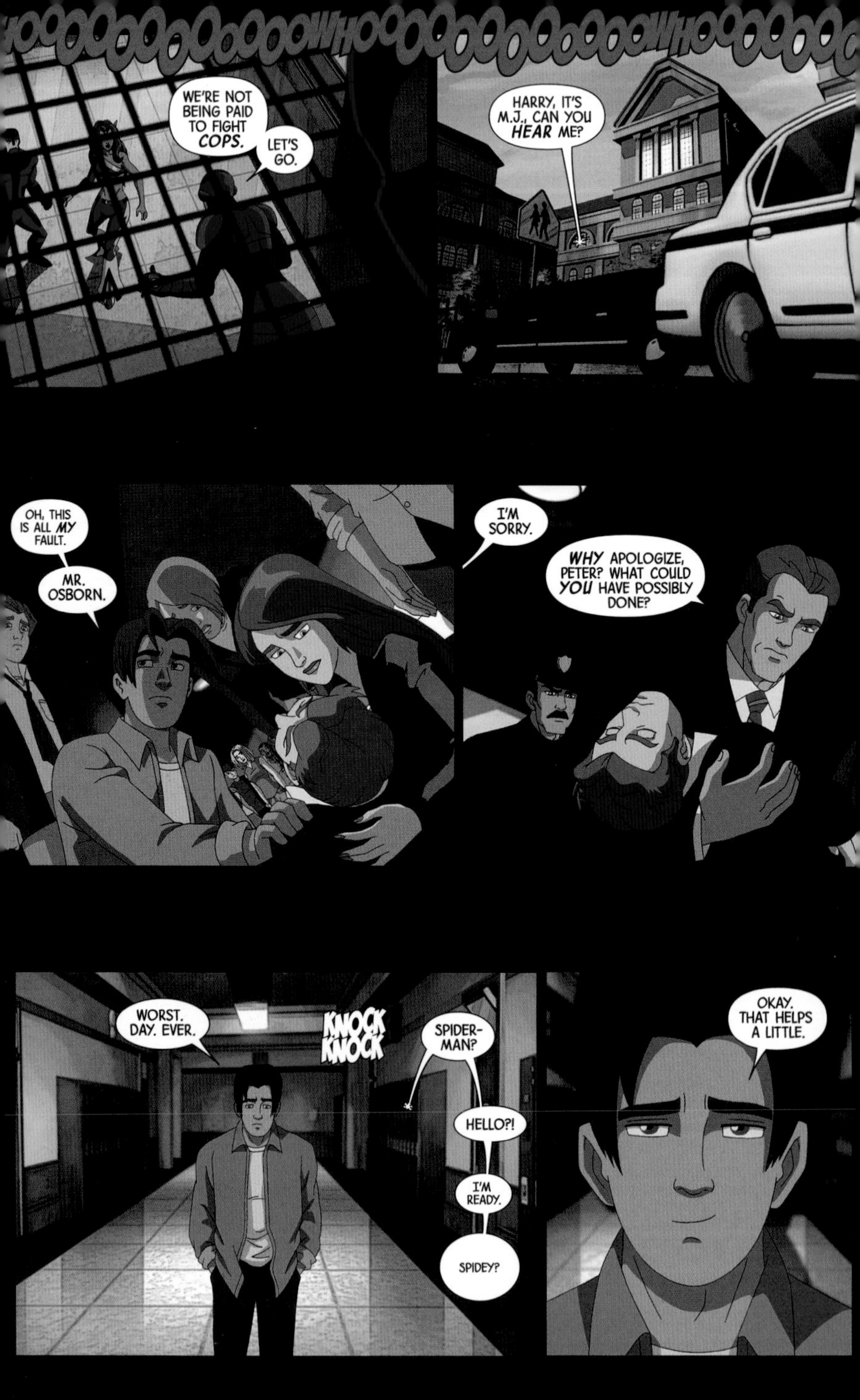
HOOOOOOOOOOOOOOWHOOOOOOOOOOOOOOWHOOOOOOOO
WE'RE NOT BEING PAID TO FIGHT COPS.
LET'S GO.
HARRY, IT'S M.J., CAN YOU HEAR ME?
OH, THIS IS ALL MY FAULT.
MR. OSBORN.
I'M SORRY.
WHY APOLOGIZE, PETER? WHAT COULD YOU HAVE POSSIBLY DONE?
WORST. DAY. EVER.
KNOCK KNOCK
SPIDER-MAN?
HELLO?!
I'M READY.
SPIDEY?
OKAY. THAT HELPS A LITTLE.

IN A *SHOCKING BETRAYAL* OF THE JUSTICE SYSTEM HE CLAIMS TO UPHOLD, SPIDER-MAN TODAY LED *KNOWN* SUPER-CRIMINALS ON AN ATTACK ON *INNOCENT* SCHOOL CHILDREN!

BELIEVE ME, IT GIVES THIS HUMBLE COMMENTATOR *NO PLEASURE* IN SAYING, "I TOLD YOU SO."

IT IS THE OPINION OF *DAILY BUGLE COMMUNICATIONS* THAT THE POLICE SHOULD ISSUE A *WARRANT* FOR SPIDER-MAN'S ARREST!

PETER!

HI, AUNT MAY.

ARE YOU *OKAY?* I HEARD THERE WAS *TROUBLE* AT YOUR SCHOOL.

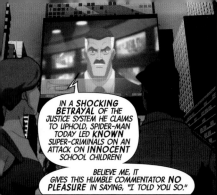

I KNOW WHAT YOU'RE THINKING.

"SPIDER-MAN LIVES AT *HOME* WITH HIS DOTING OLD AUNT? *LOSER!*"

THINK AGAIN. MY AUNT IS *PRETTY COOL.* SHE WORKS ALL DAY, THEN MONDAY NIGHTS SHE'S AT *YOGA.*

TUESDAY IS *FRENCH COOKING,* THURSDAY IS *BOWLING.* HER FULL SCHEDULE LETS ME COME AND GO AS I PLEASE.

OF COURSE, I HAVE TO KEEP THE SPIDEY STUFF ON THE *DOWN-LOW.* SHE'D NEVER APPROVE OF HER *"LITTLE PETEY"* MIXING IT UP WITH *SUPER VILLAINS.*

THOSE PSYCHOS *NEVER* TOUCHED ME, AUNT MAY.

I WISH I COULD SAY THE *SAME* FOR HARRY.

...JUST A LITTLE RINGING IN MY EARS. BUT I'LL BE *FINE.*

STRANGE, PETER, THOSE VILLAINS SEEMED TO BELIEVE SPIDER-MAN GOES TO YOUR *SCHOOL.* DO YOU KNOW ANYTHING *ABOUT* THAT?

I THINK HE SITS NEXT TO ME IN *SPANISH.*

¡HOLA! ¿DONDE ESTA LA BIBLIOTECA?

DINNER'S ALMOST READY. PUT THE *CANDLES* ON THE CAKE.

CAKE?

THE CAKE YOU WERE *SUPPOSED* TO GET IN THE CITY. DID YOU GET *DISTRACTED* AGAIN?

OH, THAT'S ALL RIGHT. WITH ALL THAT HAPPENED AT *SCHOOL* TODAY...

"...I COULDN'T *EXPECT* YOU TO REMEMBER."

UNCLE BEN, I'M SO SORRY.

I CAN'T BELIEVE I LET HER DOWN.

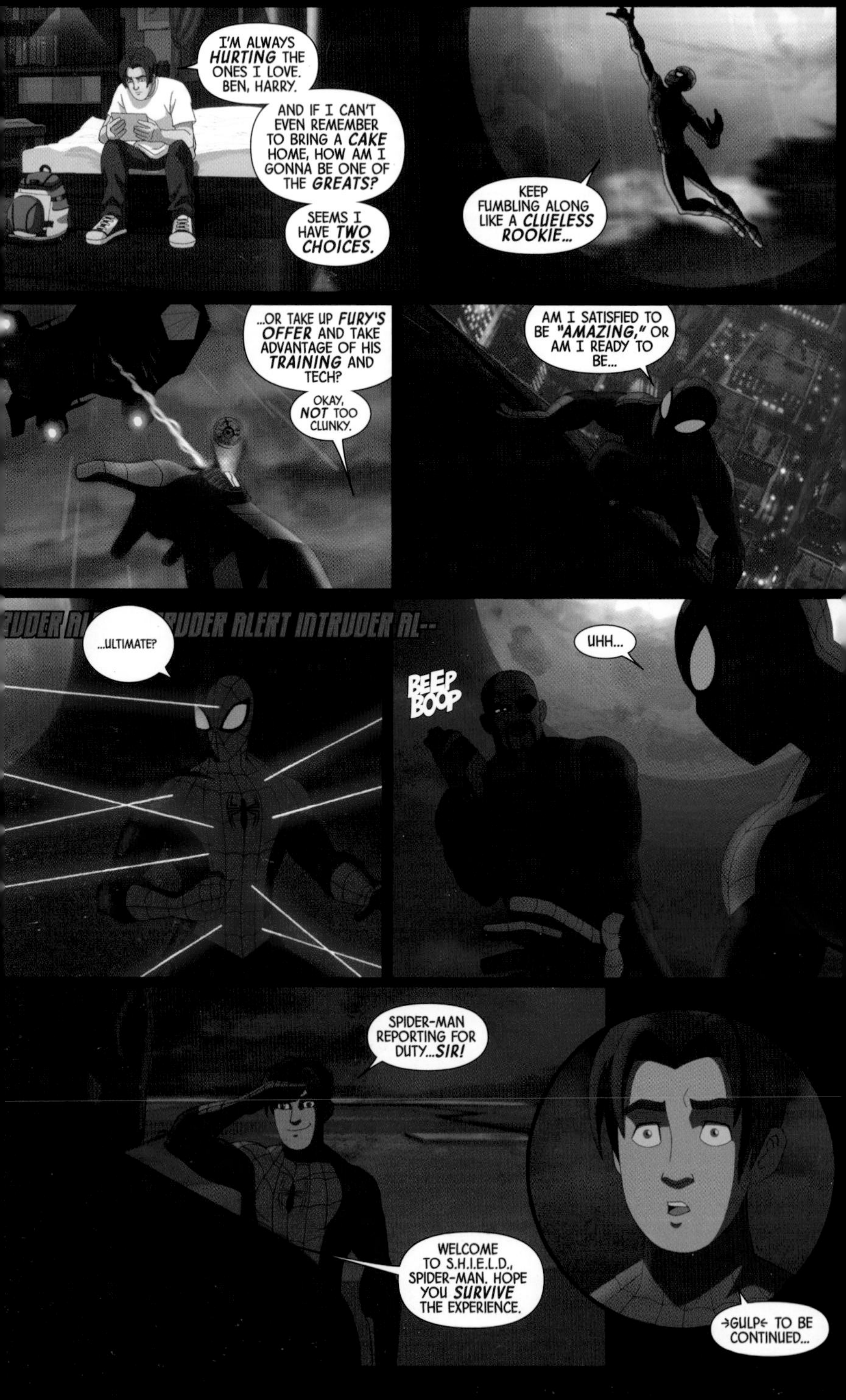
I'M ALWAYS HURTING THE ONES I LOVE. BEN, HARRY.
AND IF I CAN'T EVEN REMEMBER TO BRING A CAKE HOME, HOW AM I GONNA BE ONE OF THE GREATS?
SEEMS I HAVE TWO CHOICES.
KEEP FUMBLING ALONG LIKE A CLUELESS ROOKIE...
...OR TAKE UP FURY'S OFFER AND TAKE ADVANTAGE OF HIS TRAINING AND TECH?
OKAY, NOT TOO CLUNKY.
AM I SATISFIED TO BE "AMAZING," OR AM I READY TO BE...
...ULTIMATE?
UHH...
BEEP BOOP
SPIDER-MAN REPORTING FOR DUTY...SIR!
WELCOME TO S.H.I.E.L.D., SPIDER-MAN. HOPE YOU SURVIVE THE EXPERIENCE.
→GULP← TO BE CONTINUED...

GREAT RESPONSIBILITY

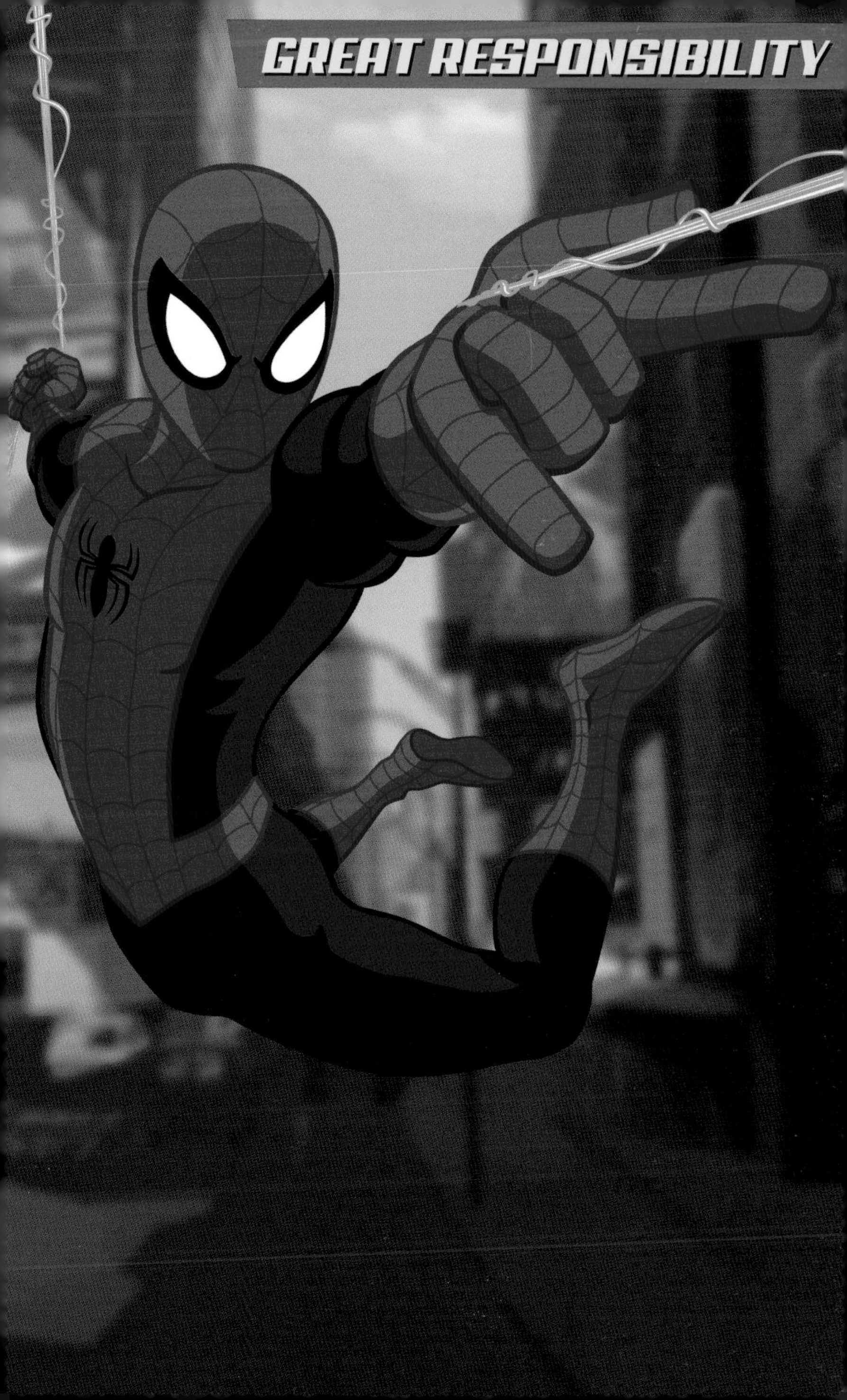

NEW YORK...

THIS IS IT--THE TEST TO SEE IF I CAN *MAKE IT* IN THE SUPER HERO BIG LEAGUES.

THIS EXCERCISE WILL GAUGE YOUR *EFFICIENCY* AGAINST *SUPERIOR NUMBERS.*

EASY-PEASY, DIRECTOR FURY, SIR.

DISABLE ALL ATTACKERS. YOU HAVE *THIRTY SECONDS.* F.Y.I., CAPTAIN AMERICA DID IT IN *TEN.*

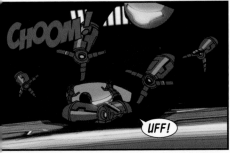

CHOOM!

UFF!

THIS IS MORE *HUMILIATING* THAN *PARKER FAMILY GAME NIGHT!*

KO

HULK SMASH!

WOO! OH YEAH! I GOT YOU! IT'S MY BIRTHDAY! IT'S MY BIRTHDAY!

HOW WEAK IS *THIS?* I'M GONNA LAND ON THE SUPER HERO *WALL OF SHAME* FOR DYING TEN MINUTES AFTER JOINING S.H.I.E.L.D.

SHIELD WALL OF SHAME

I REALLY THOUGHT HE'D MAKE IT.

MAYBE IF I CAN JUST *SNAP* THEIR *TENTACLES,* I CAN--

BABOOM!

SCORE! YEAH!

HUH?

KLANG!

OW.

HEH HEH.

HEY...

...WHY IS FURY TESTING A NEW CANDIDATE? I DIDN'T *APPROVE* OF THIS!

LOOK WHO THINKS HE'S STILL IN CHARGE. THAT'S *SO CUTE.*

SPIDER-MAN IS ROUGH AROUND THE EDGES, BUT NOT WITHOUT *POTENTIAL.*

POTENTIAL?

THERE'S NO *DISCIPLINE* TO HIS FIGHTING TECHNIQUE.

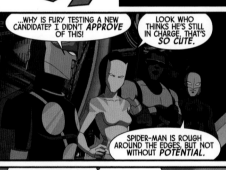

HE'S JUST *THRASHING AROUND* HITTING THINGS.

I'LL CLEAN THE HELICARRIER FOR A *MONTH* IF HE MAKES IT.

TOILETS, TOO?

TOILETS TOO.

YOU'RE ON.

I'M IN.

ME TOO.

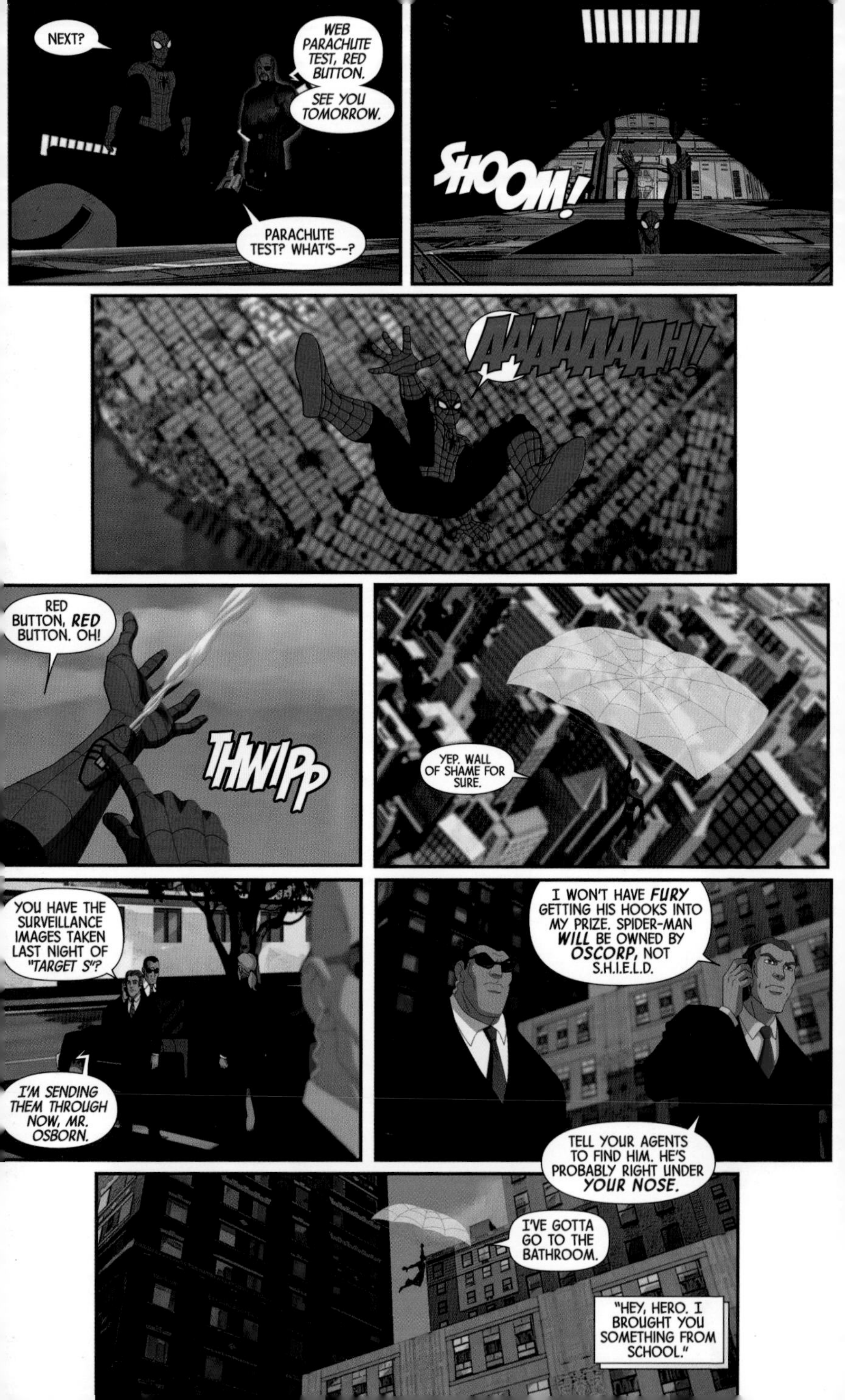
NEXT?
WEB PARACHUTE TEST, RED BUTTON.
SEE YOU TOMORROW.
PARACHUTE TEST? WHAT'S--?
SHOOM!
AAAAAAAH!!
RED BUTTON, RED BUTTON. OH!
THWIPP
YEP. WALL OF SHAME FOR SURE.
YOU HAVE THE SURVEILLANCE IMAGES TAKEN LAST NIGHT OF "TARGET S"?
I'M SENDING THEM THROUGH NOW, MR. OSBORN.
I WON'T HAVE FURY GETTING HIS HOOKS INTO MY PRIZE. SPIDER-MAN WILL BE OWNED BY OSCORP, NOT S.H.I.E.L.D.
TELL YOUR AGENTS TO FIND HIM. HE'S PROBABLY RIGHT UNDER YOUR NOSE.
I'VE GOTTA GO TO THE BATHROOM.
"HEY, HERO. I BROUGHT YOU SOMETHING FROM SCHOOL."

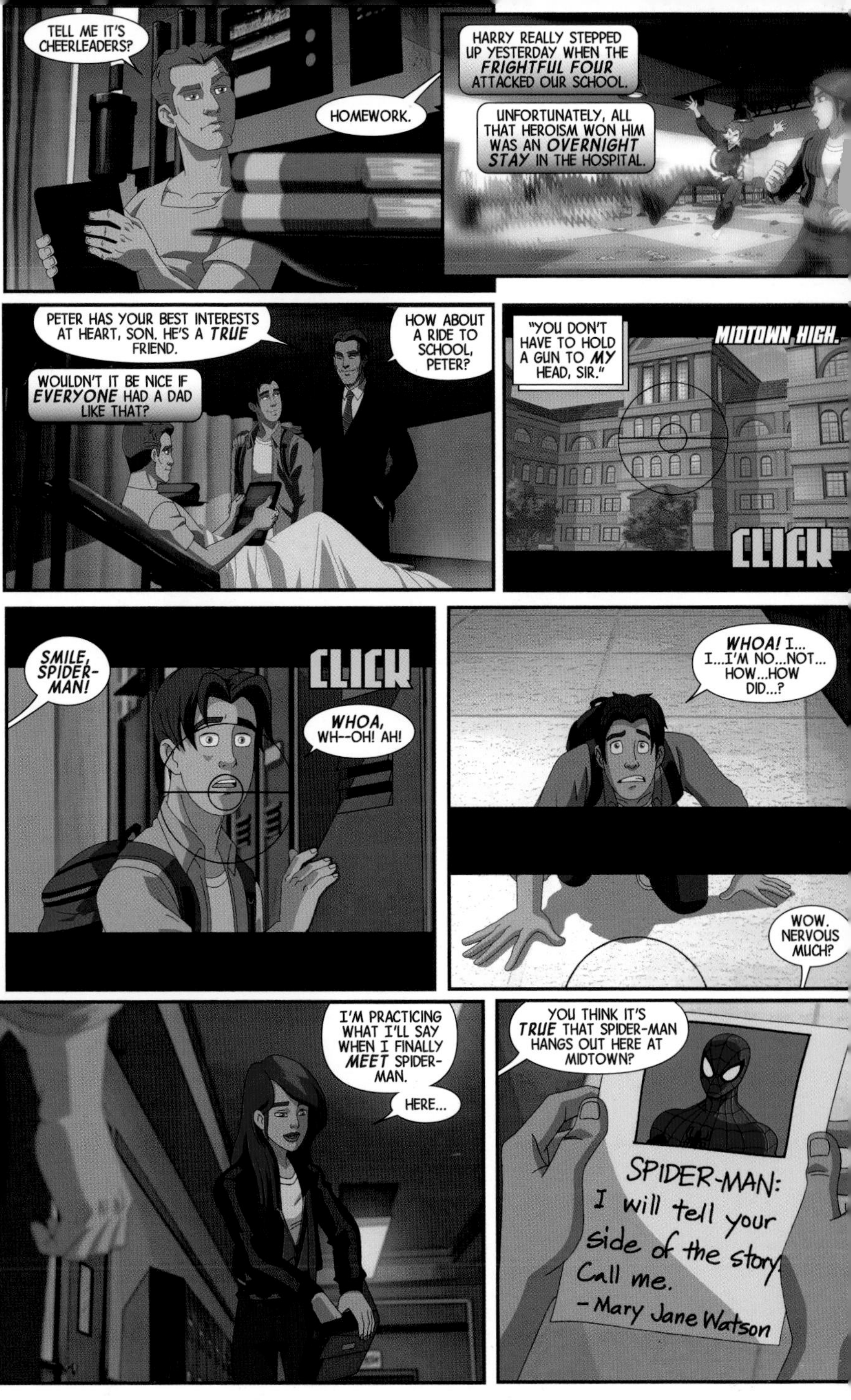
TELL ME IT'S CHEERLEADERS?
HOMEWORK.
HARRY REALLY STEPPED UP YESTERDAY WHEN THE FRIGHTFUL FOUR ATTACKED OUR SCHOOL.
UNFORTUNATELY, ALL THAT HEROISM WON HIM WAS AN OVERNIGHT STAY IN THE HOSPITAL.
PETER HAS YOUR BEST INTERESTS AT HEART, SON. HE'S A TRUE FRIEND.
HOW ABOUT A RIDE TO SCHOOL, PETER?
WOULDN'T IT BE NICE IF EVERYONE HAD A DAD LIKE THAT?
"YOU DON'T HAVE TO HOLD A GUN TO MY HEAD, SIR."
MIDTOWN HIGH.
CLICK
SMILE, SPIDER-MAN!
CLICK
WHOA, WH--OH! AH!
WHOA! I... I...I'M NO...NOT... HOW...HOW DID...?
WOW. NERVOUS MUCH?
I'M PRACTICING WHAT I'LL SAY WHEN I FINALLY MEET SPIDER-MAN.
HERE...
YOU THINK IT'S TRUE THAT SPIDER-MAN HANGS OUT HERE AT MIDTOWN?
SPIDER-MAN: I will tell your side of the story! Call me. - Mary Jane Watson

HE'S BEEN ON CAMPUS OFTEN ENOUGH.

HE COULD BE ANYBODY, A *STUDENT*, A *TEACHER*, OR...

THWIP-THWIP!

SPIDER-MAN
I will tell your side of the story. Call me.
— Mary Jane Watson

WELL, MAYBE NOT *ANYBODY.*

I KNOW HOW MUCH IT MEANS FOR MJ TO GET THAT REPORTER JOB WITH THE *BUGLE*, AND I'D *LOVE* TO HELP HER OUT.

I'M AFRAID I'D *BLOW* IT ONCE I STARTED TALKING TO HER. I MEAN, MJ KNOWS ME *SO WELL.*

GOOD EVENING, MISS WATSON. I HEAR YOU'VE BEEN *LOOKING* FOR ME.

PETER! WHAT ARE YOU DOING IN THAT *SILLY COSTUME?* AND WHAT'S UP WITH THAT *STUPID VOICE?*

D'OH!

EVEN IF SPIDER-MAN *IS* A STUDENT, HE'S GOING TO KEEP IT ON THE DOWN LOW. THERE'S NO WAY HE'D LET *ANYONE* KNOW WHO HE REALLY IS.

MAYBE. BUT I'M *NOT* GIVING UP.

LATER.

SIR.

MA'AM.

YO!

WHAT UP?

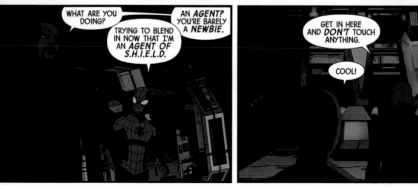

WHAT ARE YOU DOING?

TRYING TO BLEND IN NOW THAT I'M AN *AGENT OF S.H.I.E.L.D.*

AN *AGENT?* YOU'RE BARELY A *NEWBIE.*

GET IN HERE AND *DON'T* TOUCH ANYTHING.

COOL!

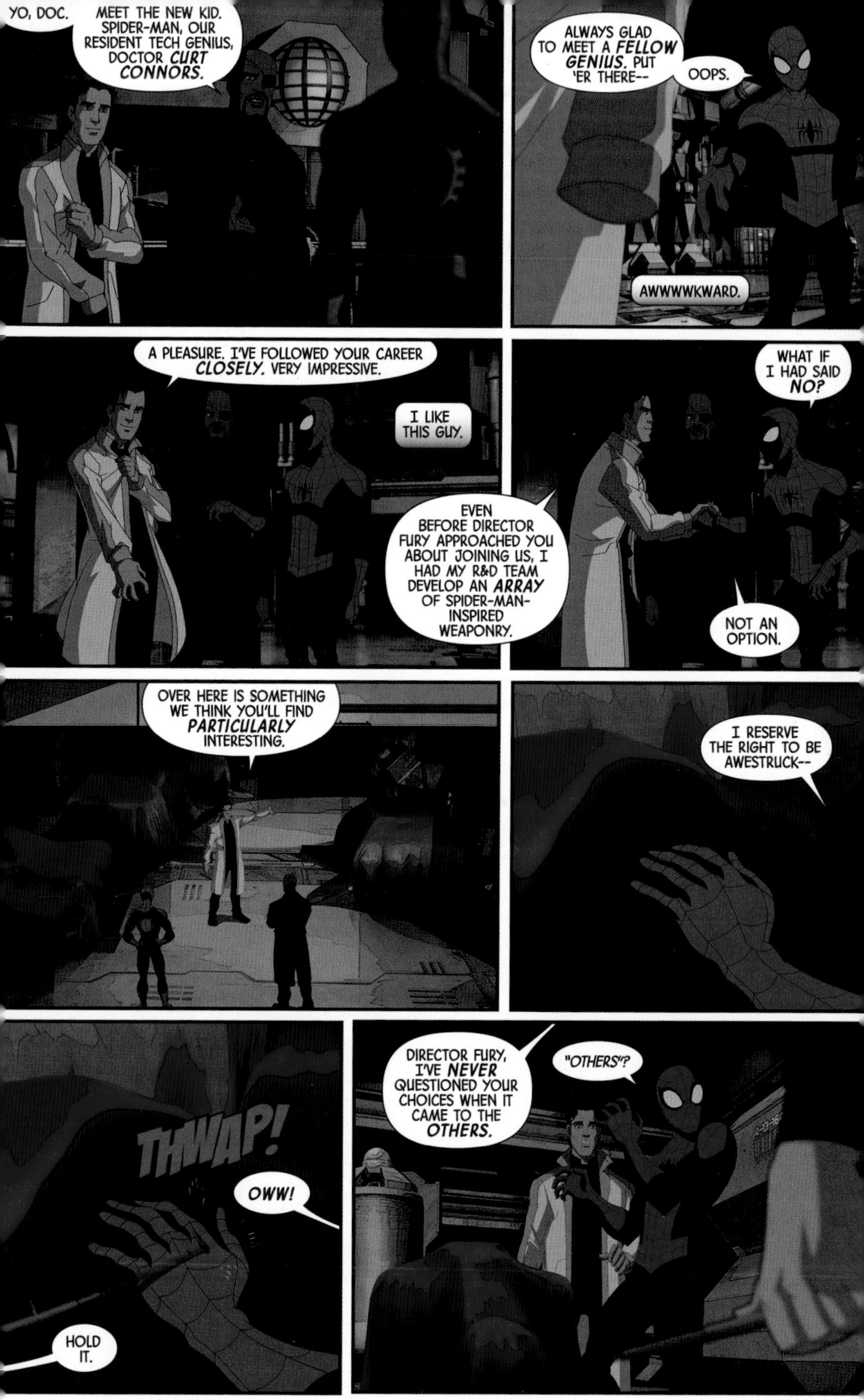
YO, DOC.
MEET THE NEW KID. SPIDER-MAN, OUR RESIDENT TECH GENIUS, DOCTOR CURT CONNORS.
ALWAYS GLAD TO MEET A FELLOW GENIUS. PUT 'ER THERE--
OOPS.
AWWWWKWARD.
A PLEASURE. I'VE FOLLOWED YOUR CAREER CLOSELY. VERY IMPRESSIVE.
I LIKE THIS GUY.
EVEN BEFORE DIRECTOR FURY APPROACHED YOU ABOUT JOINING US, I HAD MY R&D TEAM DEVELOP AN ARRAY OF SPIDER-MAN-INSPIRED WEAPONRY.
WHAT IF I HAD SAID NO?
NOT AN OPTION.
OVER HERE IS SOMETHING WE THINK YOU'LL FIND PARTICULARLY INTERESTING.
I RESERVE THE RIGHT TO BE AWESTRUCK--
THWAP!
OWW!
HOLD IT.
DIRECTOR FURY, I'VE NEVER QUESTIONED YOUR CHOICES WHEN IT CAME TO THE OTHERS.
"OTHERS"?

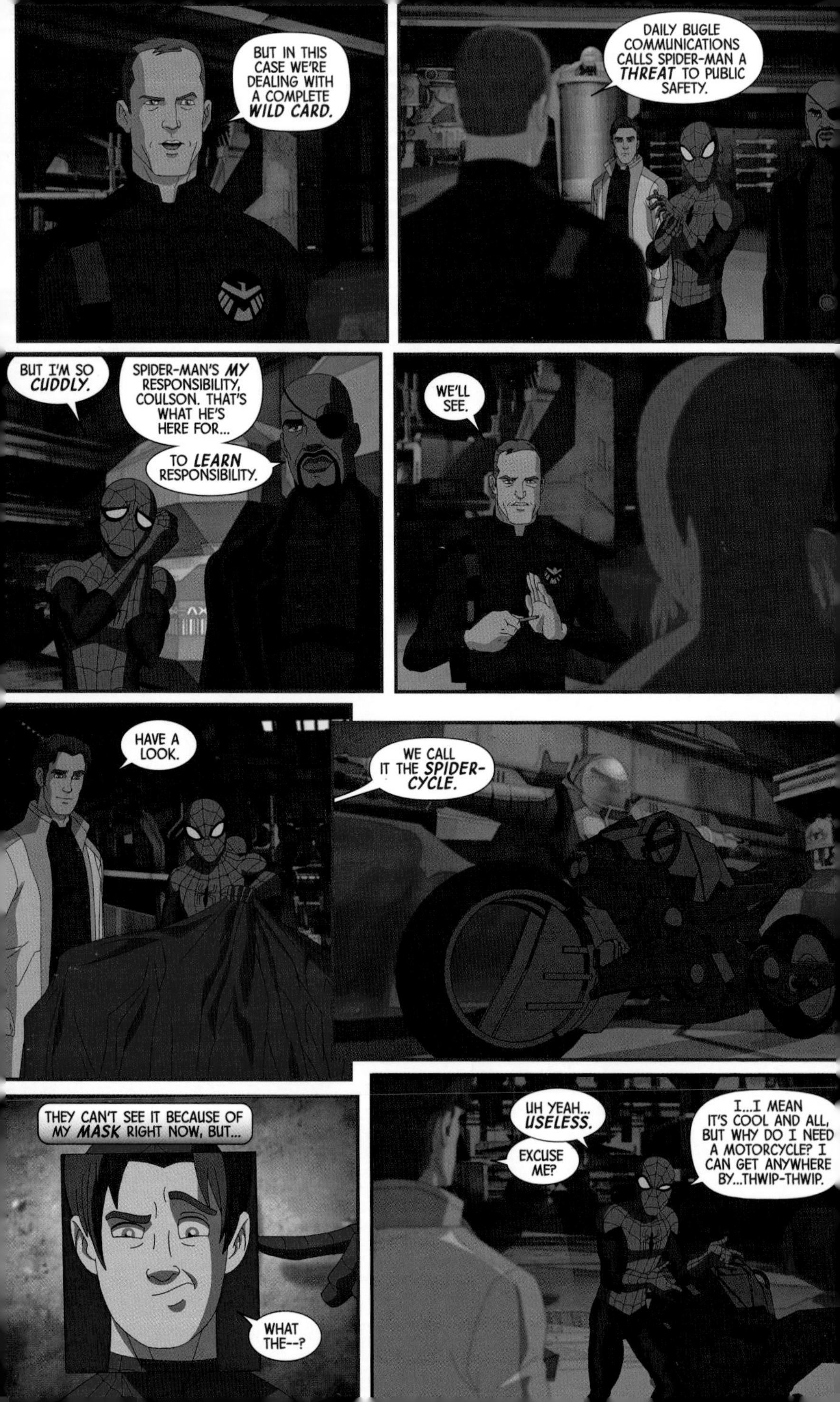
BUT IN THIS CASE WE'RE DEALING WITH A COMPLETE WILD CARD.
DAILY BUGLE COMMUNICATIONS CALLS SPIDER-MAN A THREAT TO PUBLIC SAFETY.
BUT I'M SO CUDDLY.
SPIDER-MAN'S MY RESPONSIBILITY, COULSON. THAT'S WHAT HE'S HERE FOR...
TO LEARN RESPONSIBILITY.
WE'LL SEE.
HAVE A LOOK.
WE CALL IT THE SPIDER-CYCLE.
THEY CAN'T SEE IT BECAUSE OF MY MASK RIGHT NOW, BUT...
WHAT THE--?
I...I MEAN IT'S COOL AND ALL, BUT WHY DO I NEED A MOTORCYCLE? I CAN GET ANYWHERE BY...THWIP-THWIP.
UH YEAH... USELESS.
EXCUSE ME?

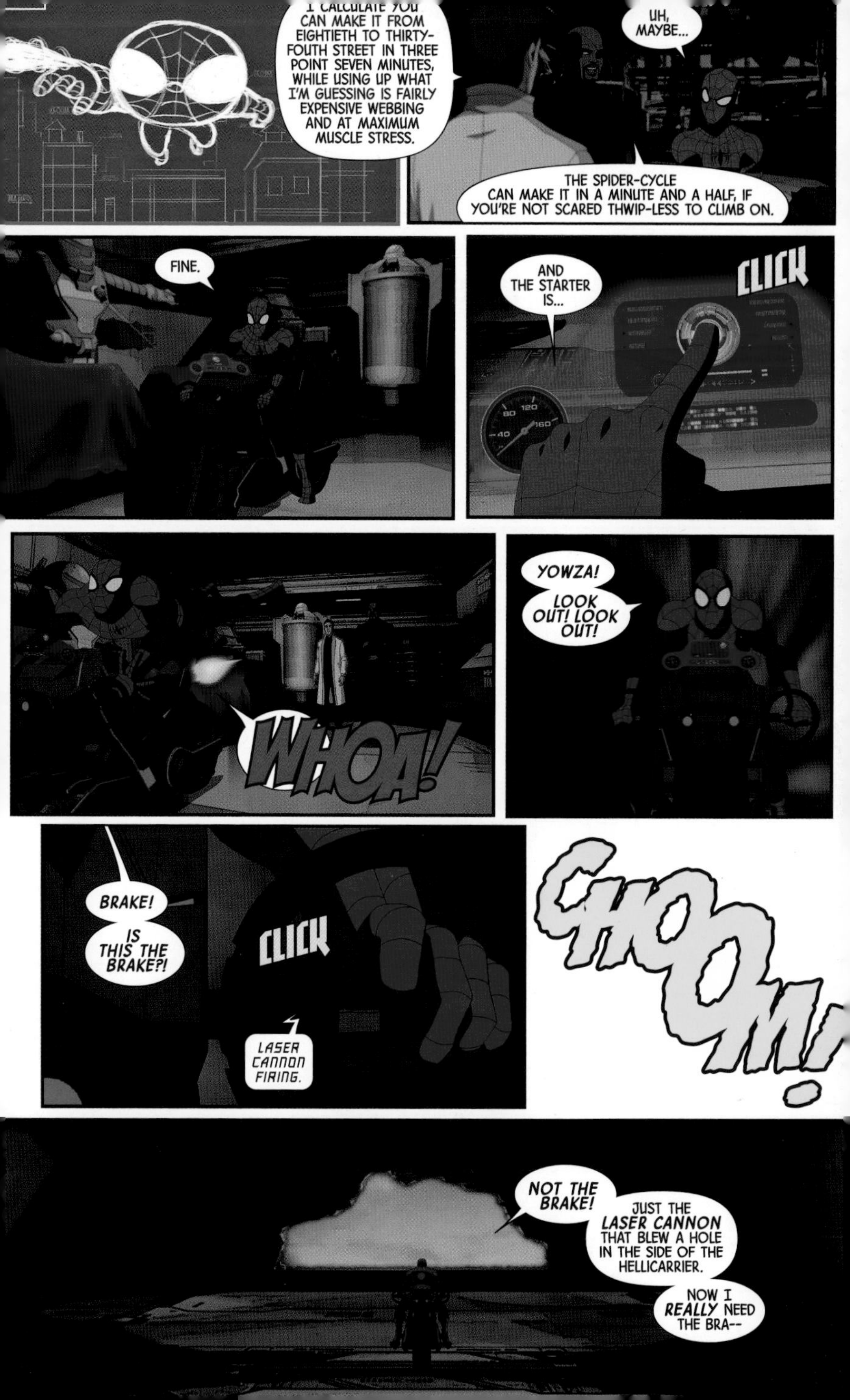
I CALCULATE YOU CAN MAKE IT FROM EIGHTIETH TO THIRTY-FOUTH STREET IN THREE POINT SEVEN MINUTES, WHILE USING UP WHAT I'M GUESSING IS FAIRLY EXPENSIVE WEBBING AND AT MAXIMUM MUSCLE STRESS.
UH, MAYBE...
THE SPIDER-CYCLE CAN MAKE IT IN A MINUTE AND A HALF, IF YOU'RE NOT SCARED THWIP-LESS TO CLIMB ON.
FINE.
AND THE STARTER IS...
CLICK
WHOA!
YOWZA!
LOOK OUT! LOOK OUT!
BRAKE!
IS THIS THE BRAKE?!
CLICK
LASER CANNON FIRING.
CHOOM!
NOT THE BRAKE!
JUST THE LASER CANNON THAT BLEW A HOLE IN THE SIDE OF THE HELLICARRIER.
NOW I REALLY NEED THE BRA--

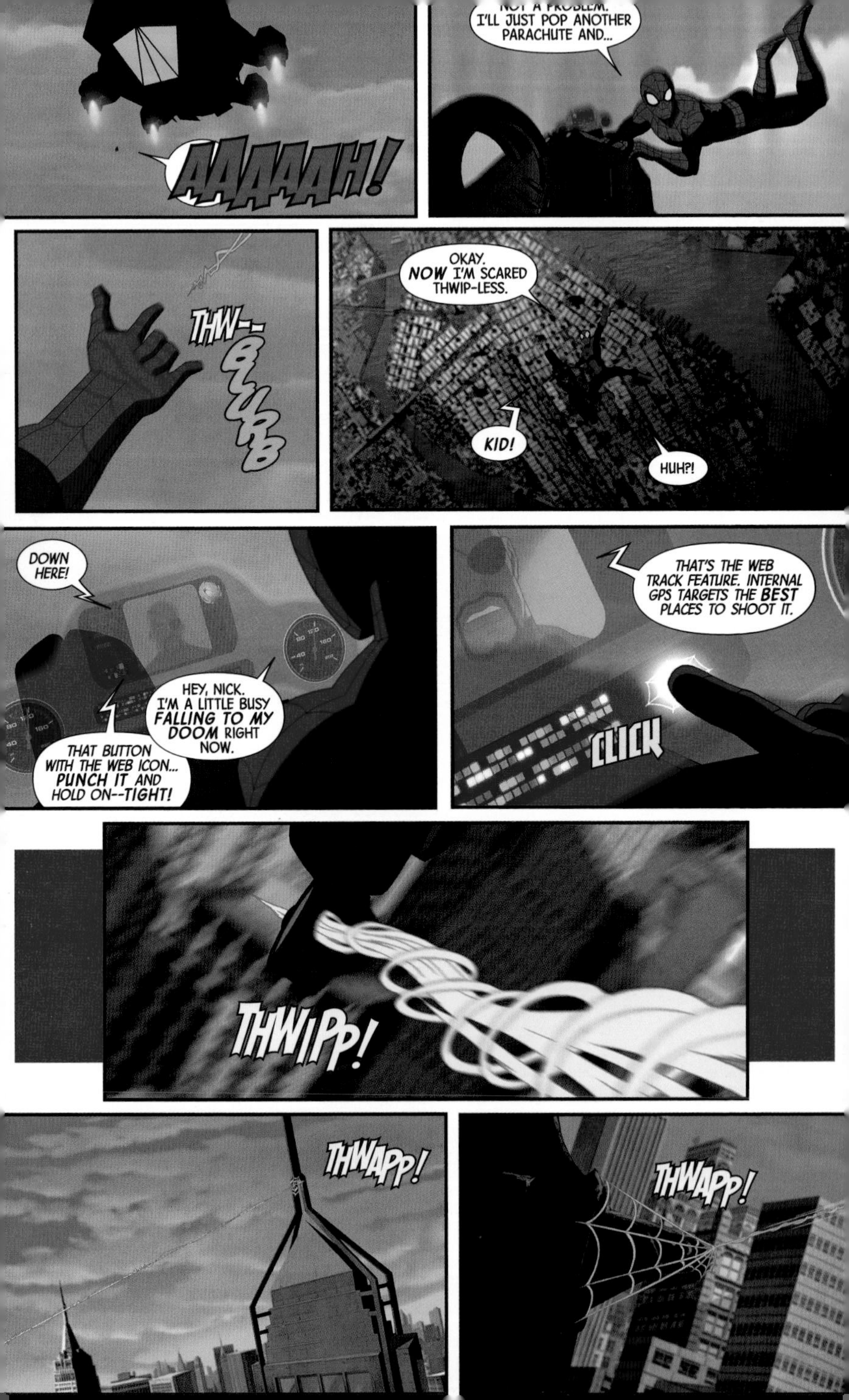
AAAAAH!
I'LL JUST POP ANOTHER PARACHUTE AND...
THW--
OKAY. NOW I'M SCARED THWIP-LESS.
KID!
HUH?!
DOWN HERE!
HEY, NICK. I'M A LITTLE BUSY FALLING TO MY DOOM RIGHT NOW.
THAT BUTTON WITH THE WEB ICON... PUNCH IT AND HOLD ON--TIGHT!
THAT'S THE WEB TRACK FEATURE. INTERNAL GPS TARGETS THE BEST PLACES TO SHOOT IT.
CLICK
THWIPP!
THWAPP!
THWAPP!

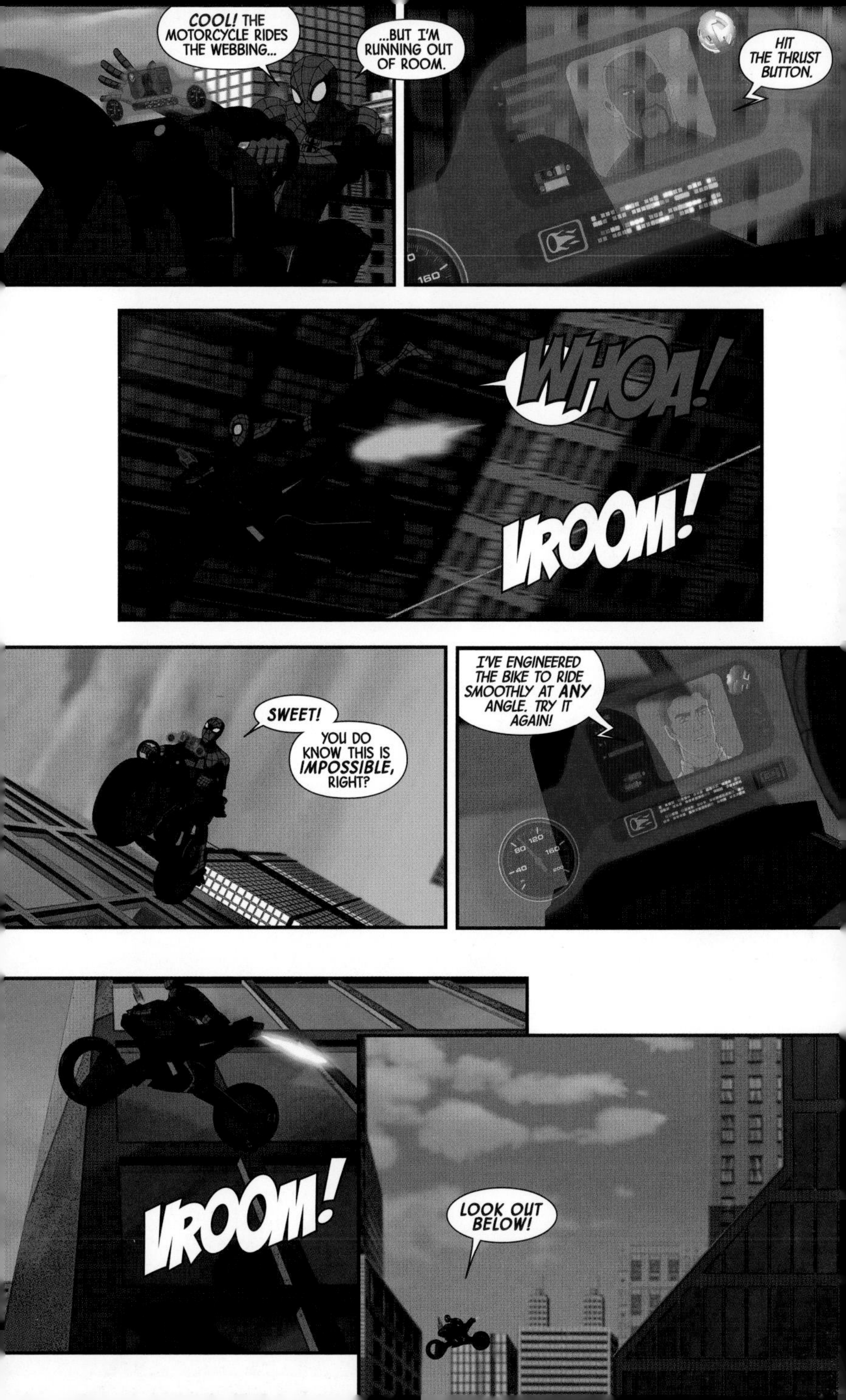
COOL! THE MOTORCYCLE RIDES THE WEBBING...
...BUT I'M RUNNING OUT OF ROOM.
HIT THE THRUST BUTTON.
WHOA!
VROOM!
SWEET!
YOU DO KNOW THIS IS IMPOSSIBLE, RIGHT?
I'VE ENGINEERED THE BIKE TO RIDE SMOOTHLY AT ANY ANGLE. TRY IT AGAIN!
VROOM!
LOOK OUT BELOW!

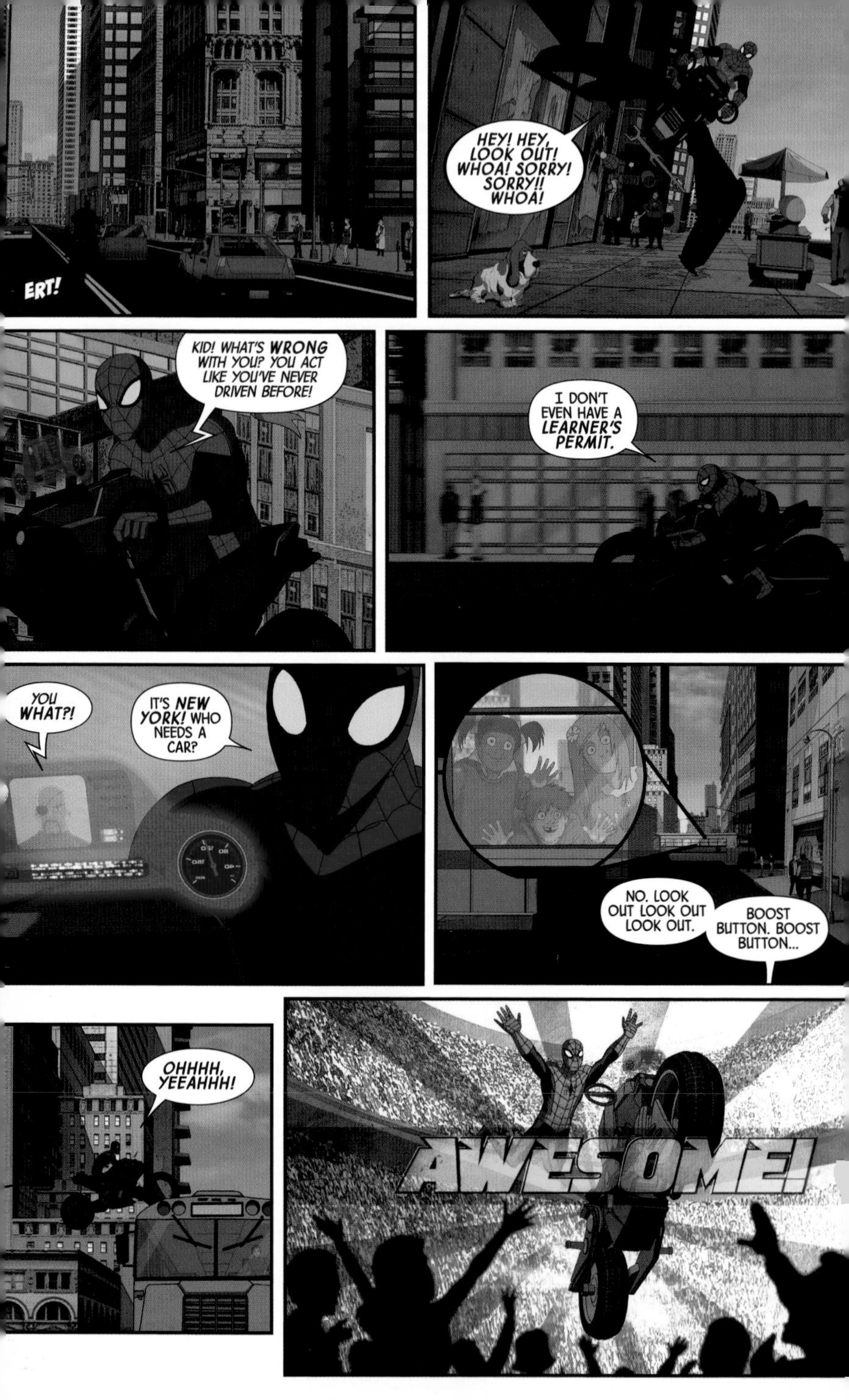
ERT!
HEY! HEY, LOOK OUT! WHOA! SORRY! SORRY!! WHOA!
KID! WHAT'S WRONG WITH YOU? YOU ACT LIKE YOU'VE NEVER DRIVEN BEFORE!
I DON'T EVEN HAVE A LEARNER'S PERMIT.
YOU WHAT?!
IT'S NEW YORK! WHO NEEDS A CAR?
NO. LOOK OUT LOOK OUT LOOK OUT.
BOOST BUTTON. BOOST BUTTON...
OHHHH, YEEAHHH!
AWESOME!

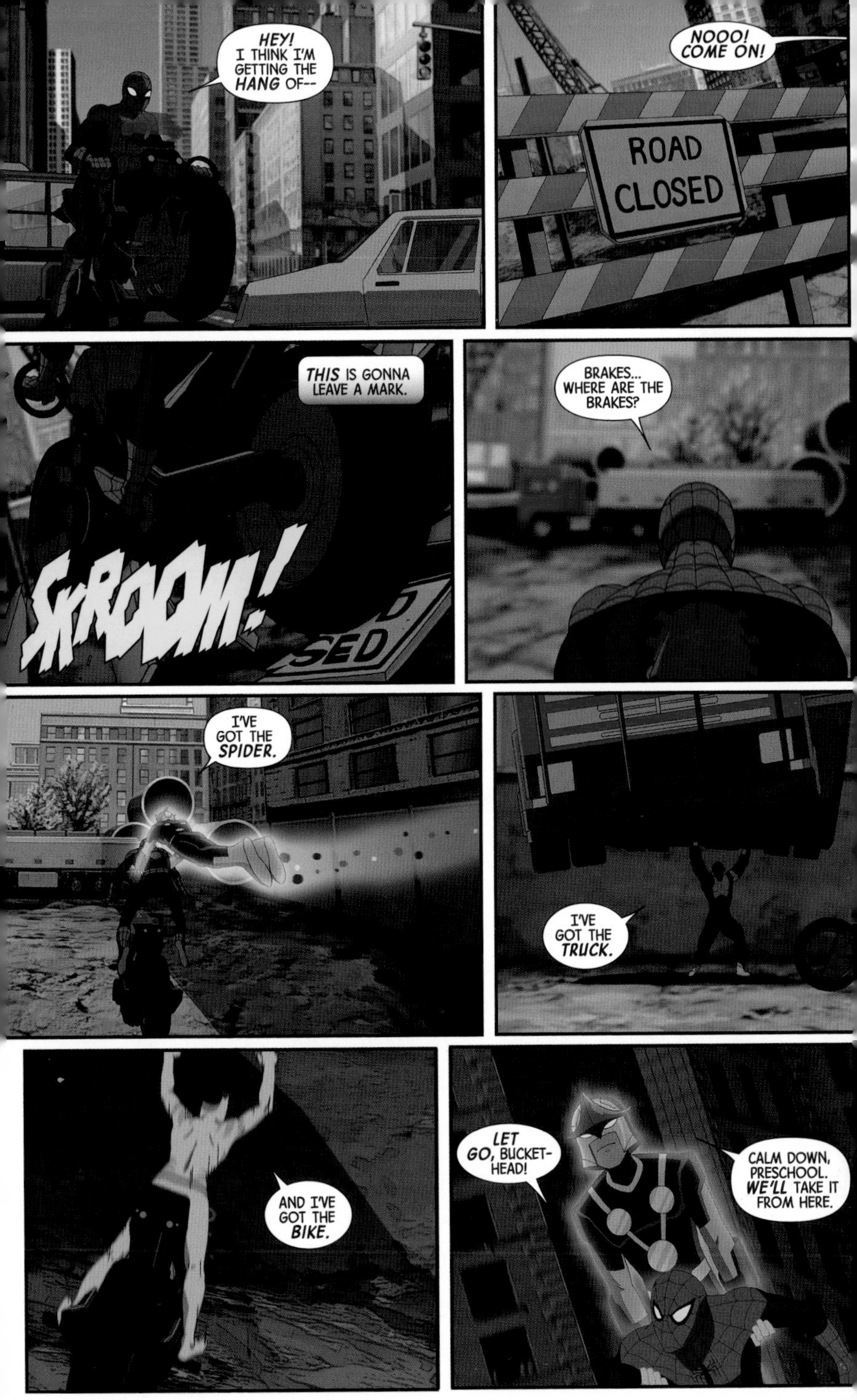
HEY! I THINK I'M GETTING THE HANG OF--
NOOO! COME ON!
ROAD CLOSED
THIS IS GONNA LEAVE A MARK.
SKROOM!
BRAKES... WHERE ARE THE BRAKES?
I'VE GOT THE SPIDER.
I'VE GOT THE TRUCK.
AND I'VE GOT THE BIKE.
LET GO, BUCKET-HEAD!
CALM DOWN, PRESCHOOL. WE'LL TAKE IT FROM HERE.

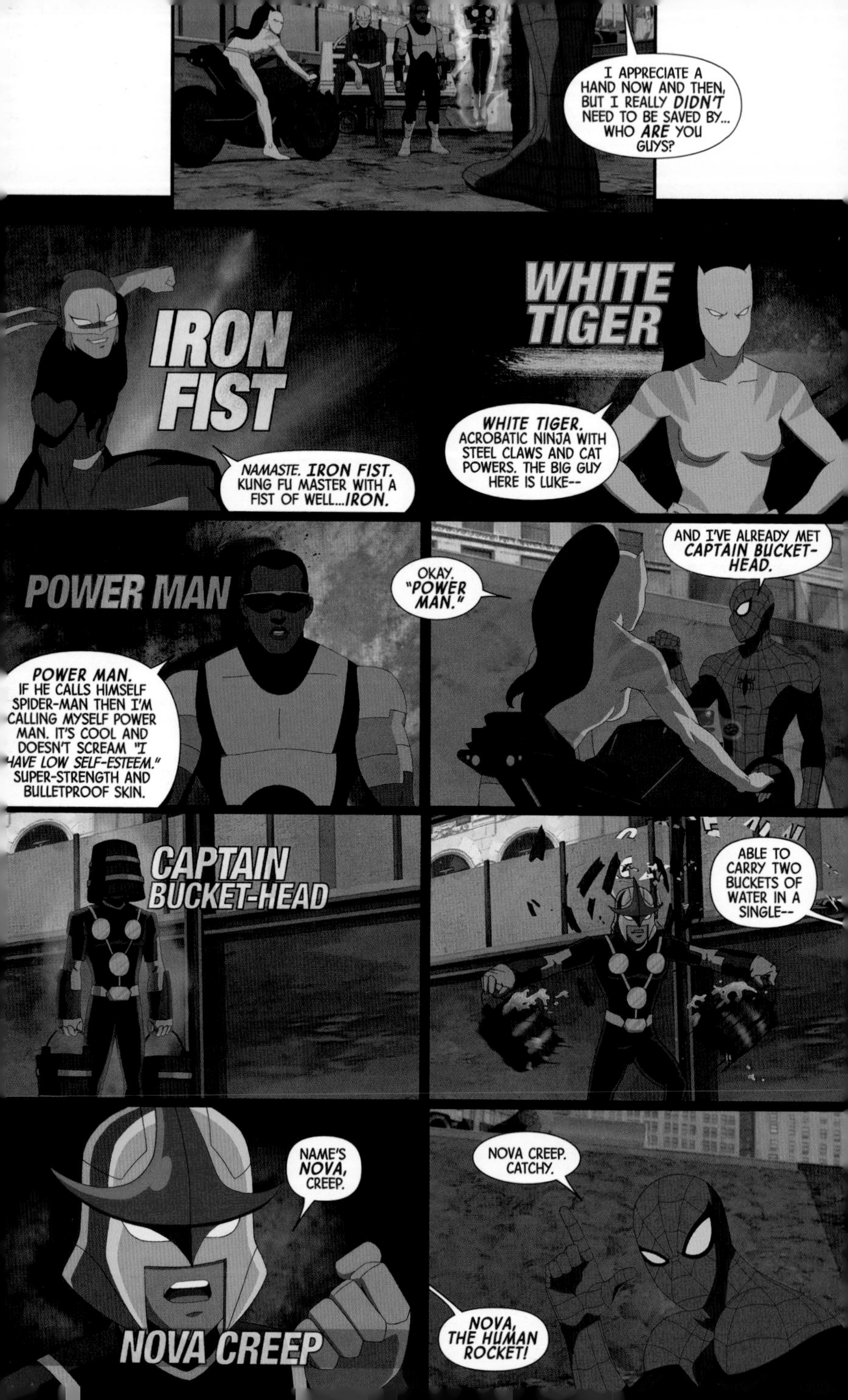
I APPRECIATE A HAND NOW AND THEN, BUT I REALLY DIDN'T NEED TO BE SAVED BY... WHO ARE YOU GUYS?
IRON FIST
NAMASTE. IRON FIST. KUNG FU MASTER WITH A FIST OF WELL...IRON.
WHITE TIGER
WHITE TIGER. ACROBATIC NINJA WITH STEEL CLAWS AND CAT POWERS. THE BIG GUY HERE IS LUKE--
POWER MAN
POWER MAN. IF HE CALLS HIMSELF SPIDER-MAN THEN I'M CALLING MYSELF POWER MAN. IT'S COOL AND DOESN'T SCREAM "I HAVE LOW SELF-ESTEEM." SUPER-STRENGTH AND BULLETPROOF SKIN.
OKAY. "POWER MAN."
AND I'VE ALREADY MET CAPTAIN BUCKET-HEAD.
CAPTAIN BUCKET-HEAD
ABLE TO CARRY TWO BUCKETS OF WATER IN A SINGLE--
NAME'S NOVA, CREEP.
NOVA CREEP
NOVA CREEP. CATCHY.
NOVA, THE HUMAN ROCKET!

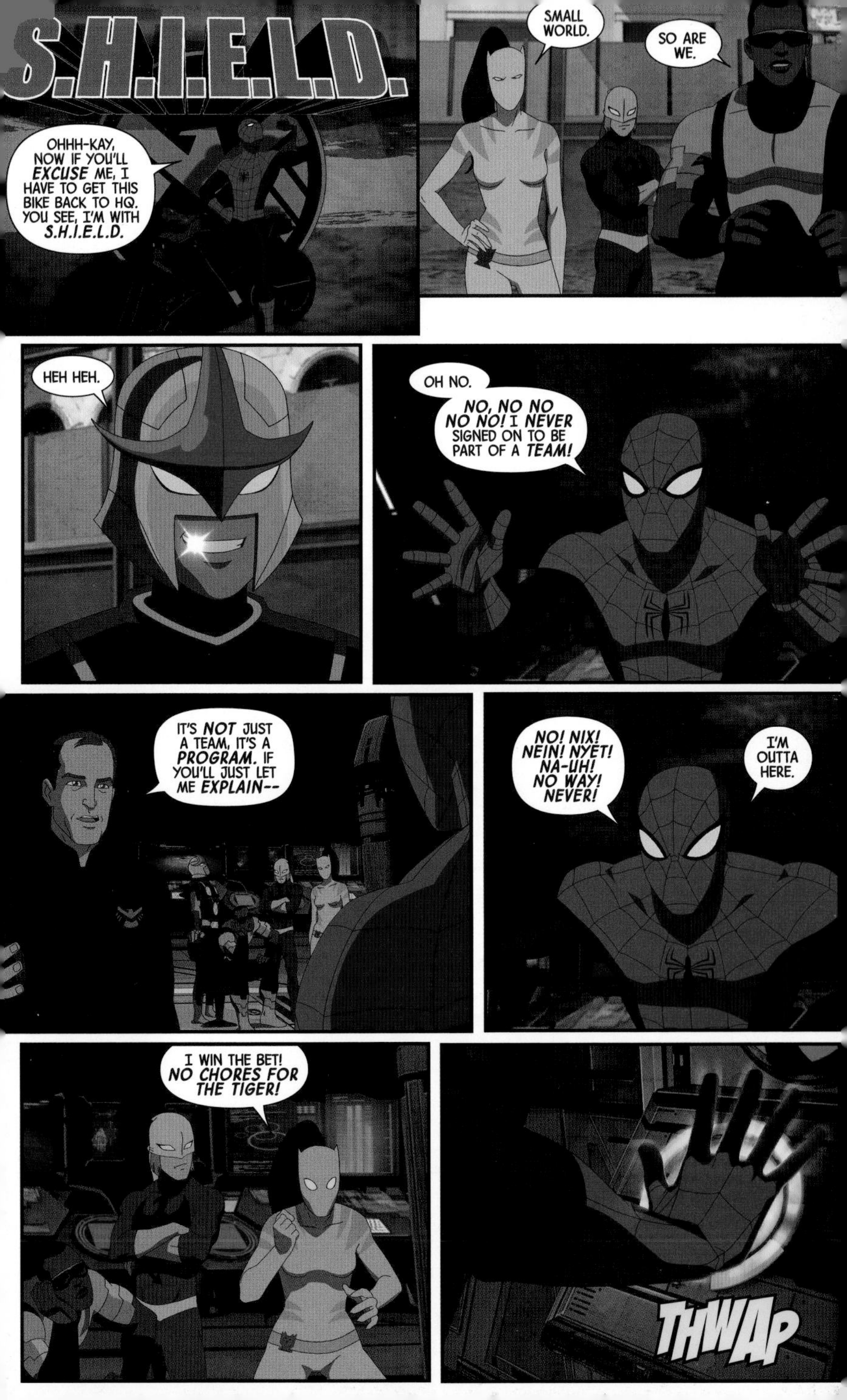
S.H.I.E.L.D.
OHHH-KAY, NOW IF YOU'LL EXCUSE ME, I HAVE TO GET THIS BIKE BACK TO HQ. YOU SEE, I'M WITH S.H.I.E.L.D.
SMALL WORLD.
SO ARE WE.
HEH HEH.
OH NO.
NO, NO NO NO NO! I NEVER SIGNED ON TO BE PART OF A TEAM!
IT'S NOT JUST A TEAM, IT'S A PROGRAM. IF YOU'LL JUST LET ME EXPLAIN--
NO! NIX! NEIN! NYET! NA-UH! NO WAY! NEVER!
I'M OUTTA HERE.
I WIN THE BET! NO CHORES FOR THE TIGER!
THWAP

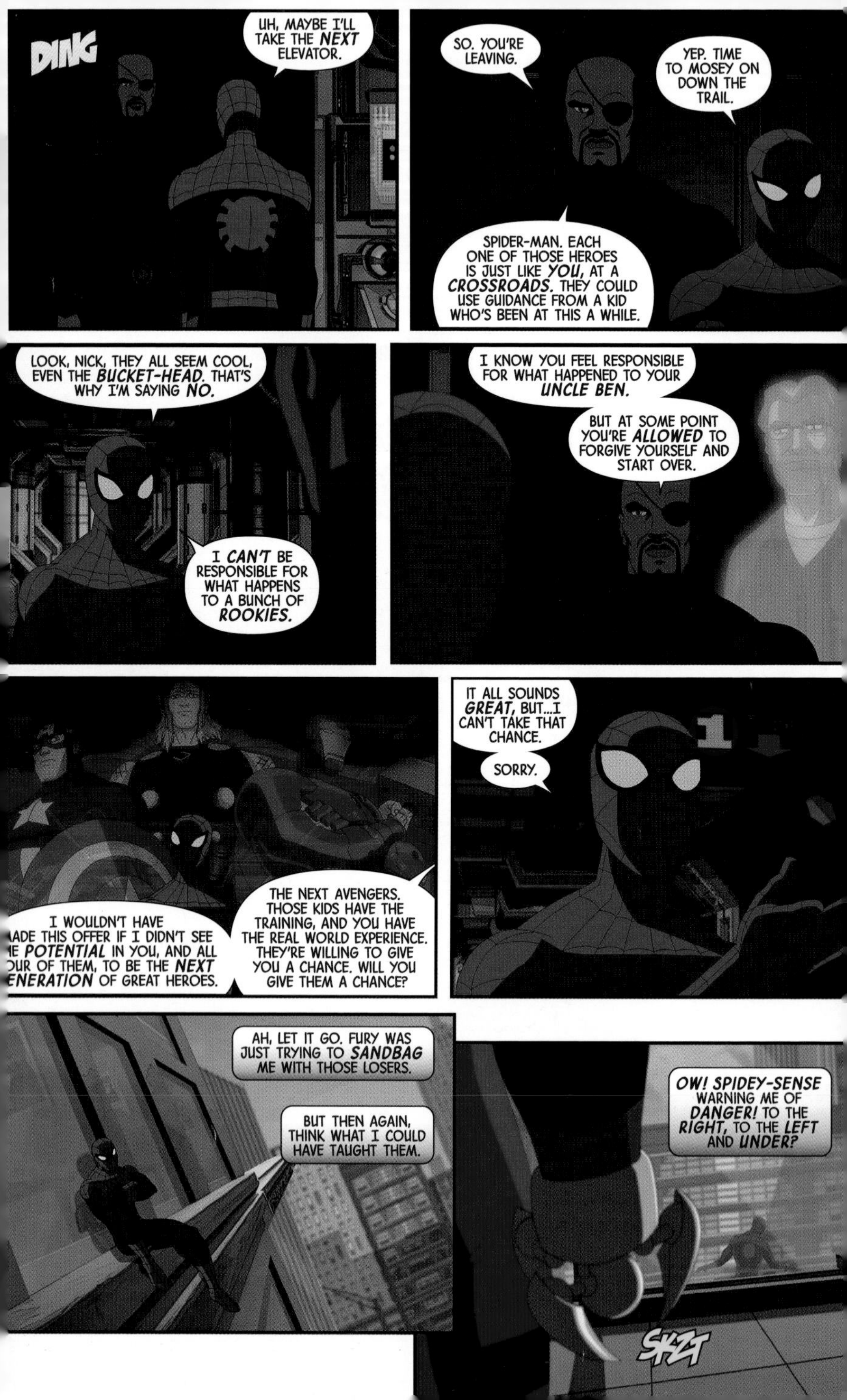
DING
UH, MAYBE I'LL TAKE THE NEXT ELEVATOR.
SO. YOU'RE LEAVING.
YEP. TIME TO MOSEY ON DOWN THE TRAIL.
SPIDER-MAN. EACH ONE OF THOSE HEROES IS JUST LIKE YOU, AT A CROSSROADS. THEY COULD USE GUIDANCE FROM A KID WHO'S BEEN AT THIS A WHILE.
LOOK, NICK, THEY ALL SEEM COOL, EVEN THE BUCKET-HEAD. THAT'S WHY I'M SAYING NO.
I CAN'T BE RESPONSIBLE FOR WHAT HAPPENS TO A BUNCH OF ROOKIES.
I KNOW YOU FEEL RESPONSIBLE FOR WHAT HAPPENED TO YOUR UNCLE BEN.
BUT AT SOME POINT YOU'RE ALLOWED TO FORGIVE YOURSELF AND START OVER.
I WOULDN'T HAVE ADE THIS OFFER IF I DIDN'T SEE E POTENTIAL IN YOU, AND ALL UR OF THEM, TO BE THE NEXT ENERATION OF GREAT HEROES.
THE NEXT AVENGERS. THOSE KIDS HAVE THE TRAINING, AND YOU HAVE THE REAL WORLD EXPERIENCE. THEY'RE WILLING TO GIVE YOU A CHANCE. WILL YOU GIVE THEM A CHANCE?
IT ALL SOUNDS GREAT, BUT...I CAN'T TAKE THAT CHANCE.
SORRY.
AH, LET IT GO. FURY WAS JUST TRYING TO SANDBAG ME WITH THOSE LOSERS.
BUT THEN AGAIN, THINK WHAT I COULD HAVE TAUGHT THEM.
OW! SPIDEY-SENSE WARNING ME OF DANGER! TO THE RIGHT, TO THE LEFT AND UNDER?
SKZT

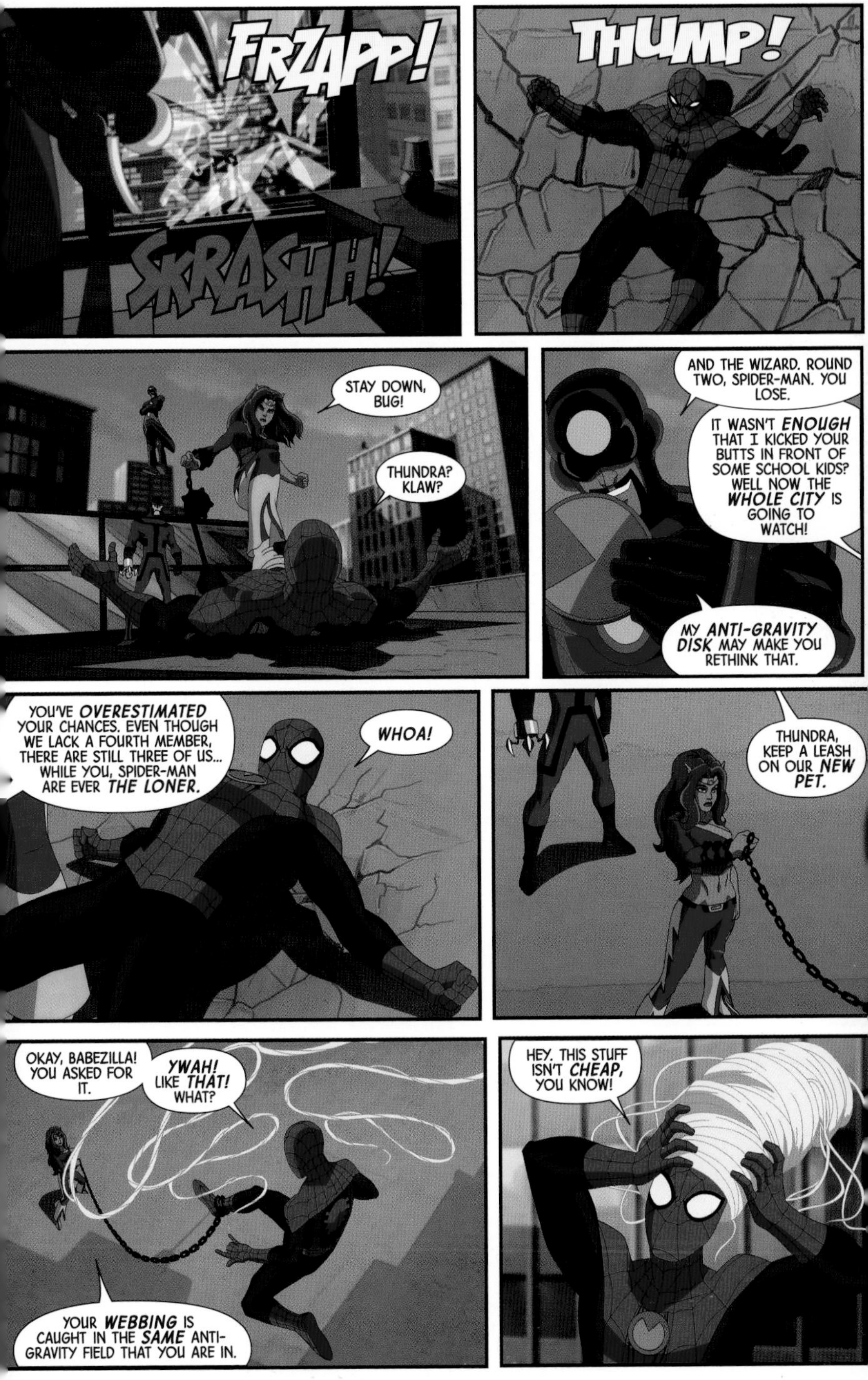
FRZAPP!
SKRASHH!
THUMP!
STAY DOWN, BUG!
THUNDRA? KLAW?
AND THE WIZARD. ROUND TWO, SPIDER-MAN. YOU LOSE.
IT WASN'T ENOUGH THAT I KICKED YOUR BUTTS IN FRONT OF SOME SCHOOL KIDS? WELL NOW THE WHOLE CITY IS GOING TO WATCH!
MY ANTI-GRAVITY DISK MAY MAKE YOU RETHINK THAT.
YOU'VE OVERESTIMATED YOUR CHANCES. EVEN THOUGH WE LACK A FOURTH MEMBER, THERE ARE STILL THREE OF US... WHILE YOU, SPIDER-MAN ARE EVER THE LONER.
WHOA!
THUNDRA, KEEP A LEASH ON OUR NEW PET.
OKAY, BABEZILLA! YOU ASKED FOR IT.
YWAH! LIKE THAT! WHAT?
YOUR WEBBING IS CAUGHT IN THE SAME ANTI-GRAVITY FIELD THAT YOU ARE IN.
HEY. THIS STUFF ISN'T CHEAP, YOU KNOW!

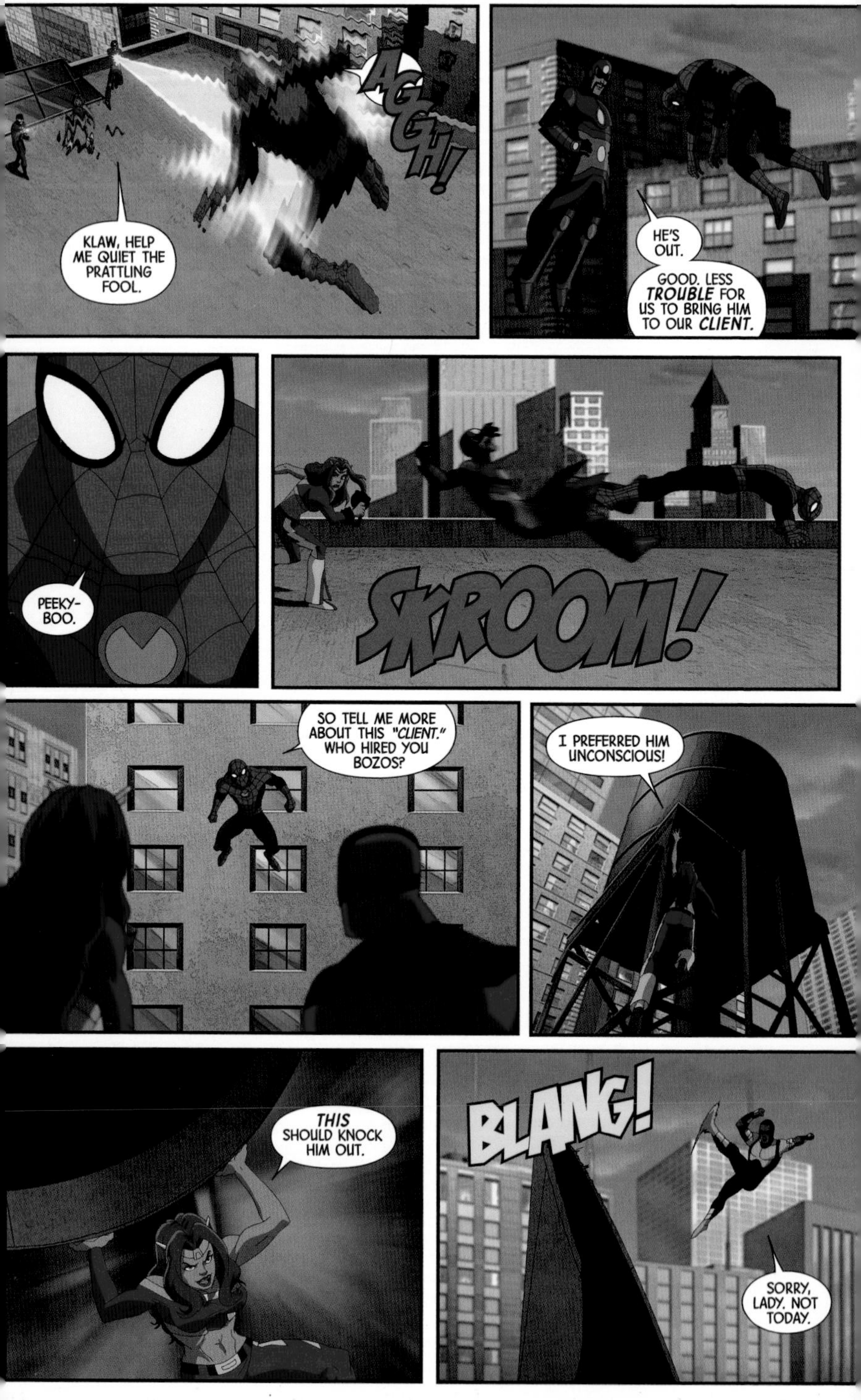
AGGH!
KLAW, HELP ME QUIET THE PRATTLING FOOL.
HE'S OUT.
GOOD. LESS TROUBLE FOR US TO BRING HIM TO OUR CLIENT.
PEEKY-BOO.
SKROOM!
SO TELL ME MORE ABOUT THIS "CLIENT." WHO HIRED YOU BOZOS?
I PREFERRED HIM UNCONSCIOUS!
THIS SHOULD KNOCK HIM OUT.
BLANG!
SORRY, LADY. NOT TODAY.

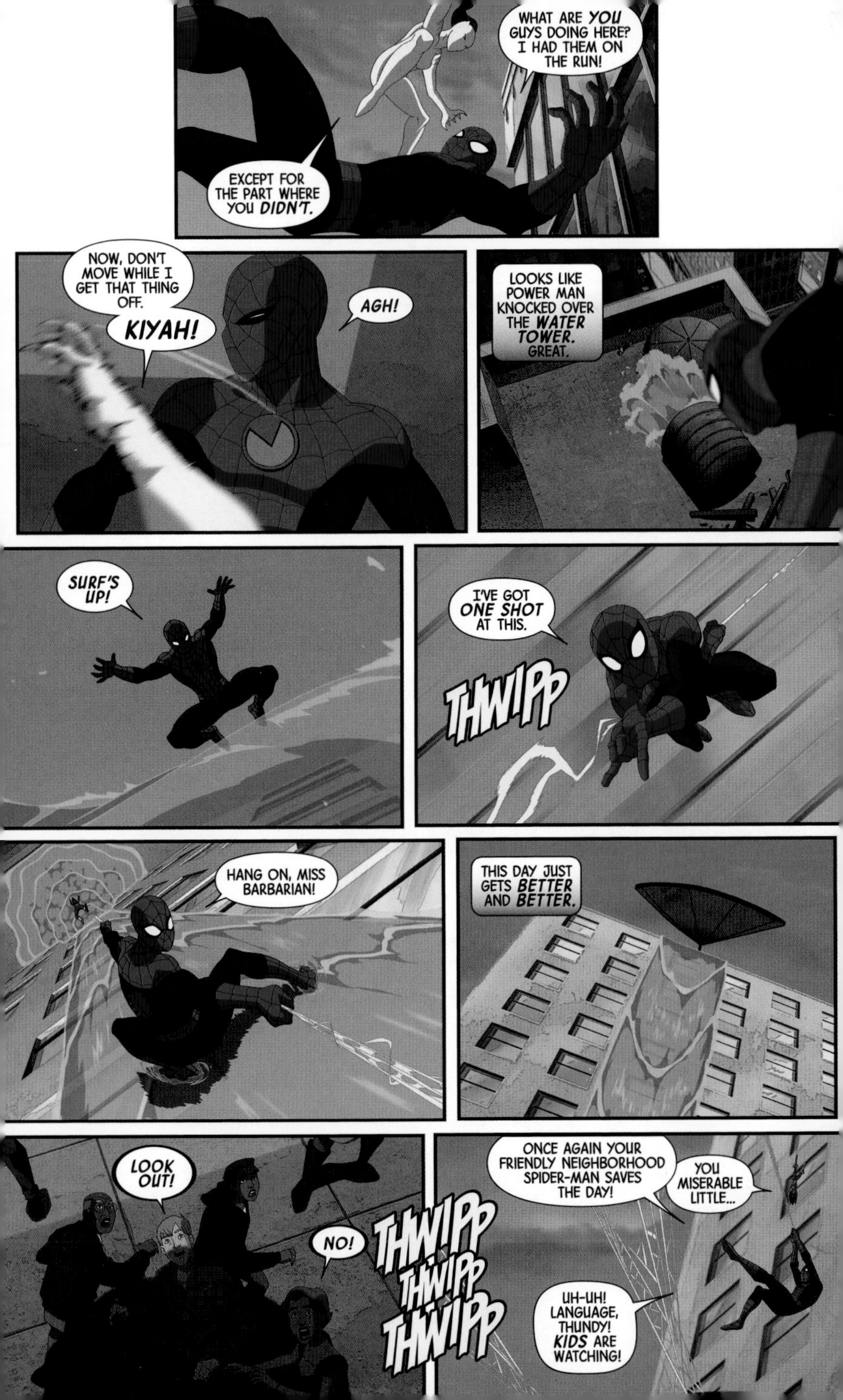
WHAT ARE YOU GUYS DOING HERE? I HAD THEM ON THE RUN!
EXCEPT FOR THE PART WHERE YOU DIDN'T.
NOW, DON'T MOVE WHILE I GET THAT THING OFF.
KIYAH!
AGH!
LOOKS LIKE POWER MAN KNOCKED OVER THE WATER TOWER. GREAT.
SURF'S UP!
I'VE GOT ONE SHOT AT THIS.
THWIPP
HANG ON, MISS BARBARIAN!
THIS DAY JUST GETS BETTER AND BETTER.
LOOK OUT!
NO!
THWIPP
THWIPP
THWIPP
ONCE AGAIN YOUR FRIENDLY NEIGHBORHOOD SPIDER-MAN SAVES THE DAY!
YOU MISERABLE LITTLE...
UH-UH! LANGUAGE, THUNDY! KIDS ARE WATCHING!

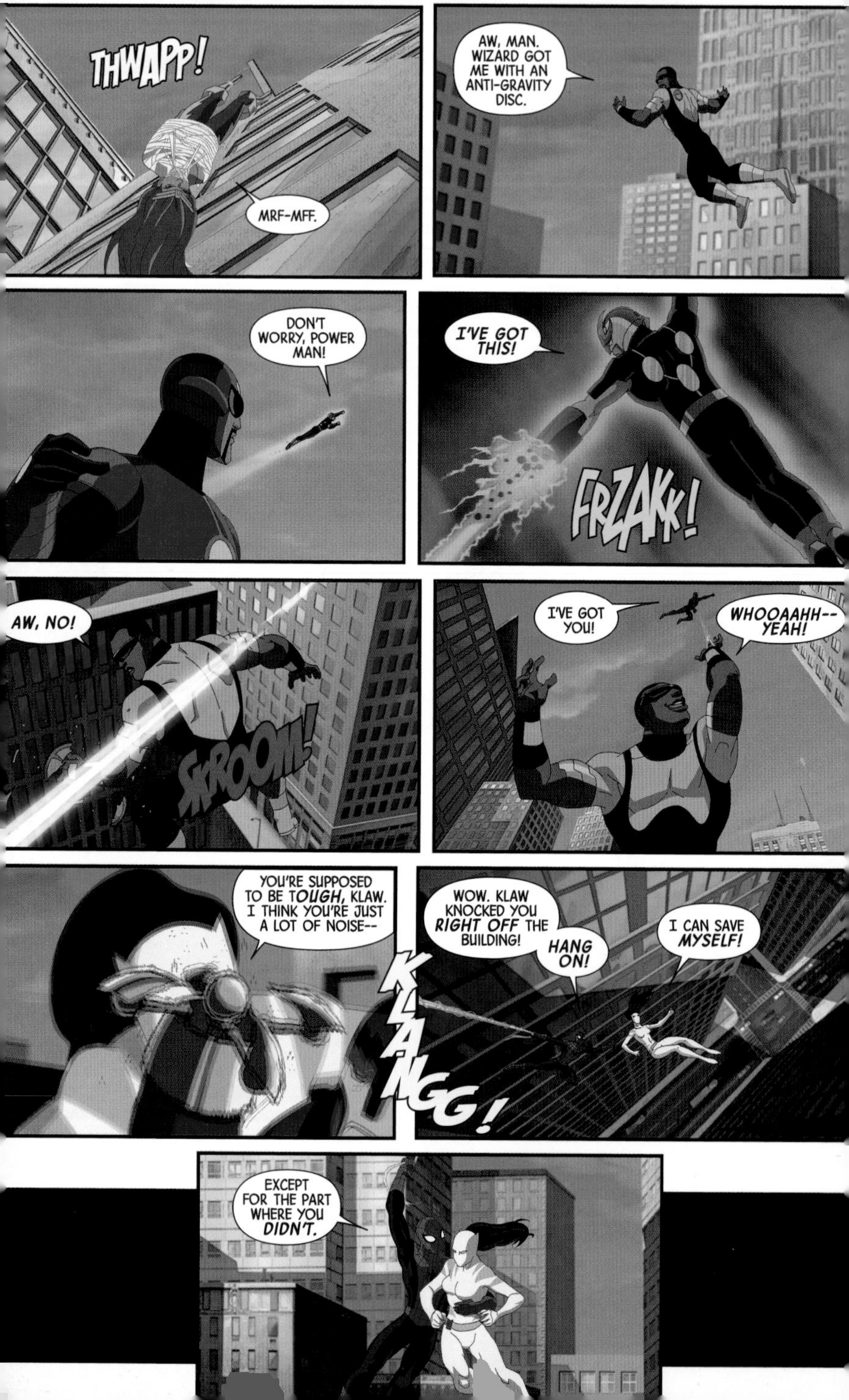
THWAPP!
MRF-MFF.
AW, MAN. WIZARD GOT ME WITH AN ANTI-GRAVITY DISC.
DON'T WORRY, POWER MAN!
I'VE GOT THIS!
FRZAKK!
AW, NO!
SKROOM!
I'VE GOT YOU!
WHOOAAHH-- YEAH!
YOU'RE SUPPOSED TO BE TOUGH, KLAW. I THINK YOU'RE JUST A LOT OF NOISE--
KLANGG!
WOW. KLAW KNOCKED YOU RIGHT OFF THE BUILDING!
HANG ON!
I CAN SAVE MYSELF!
EXCEPT FOR THE PART WHERE YOU DIDN'T.

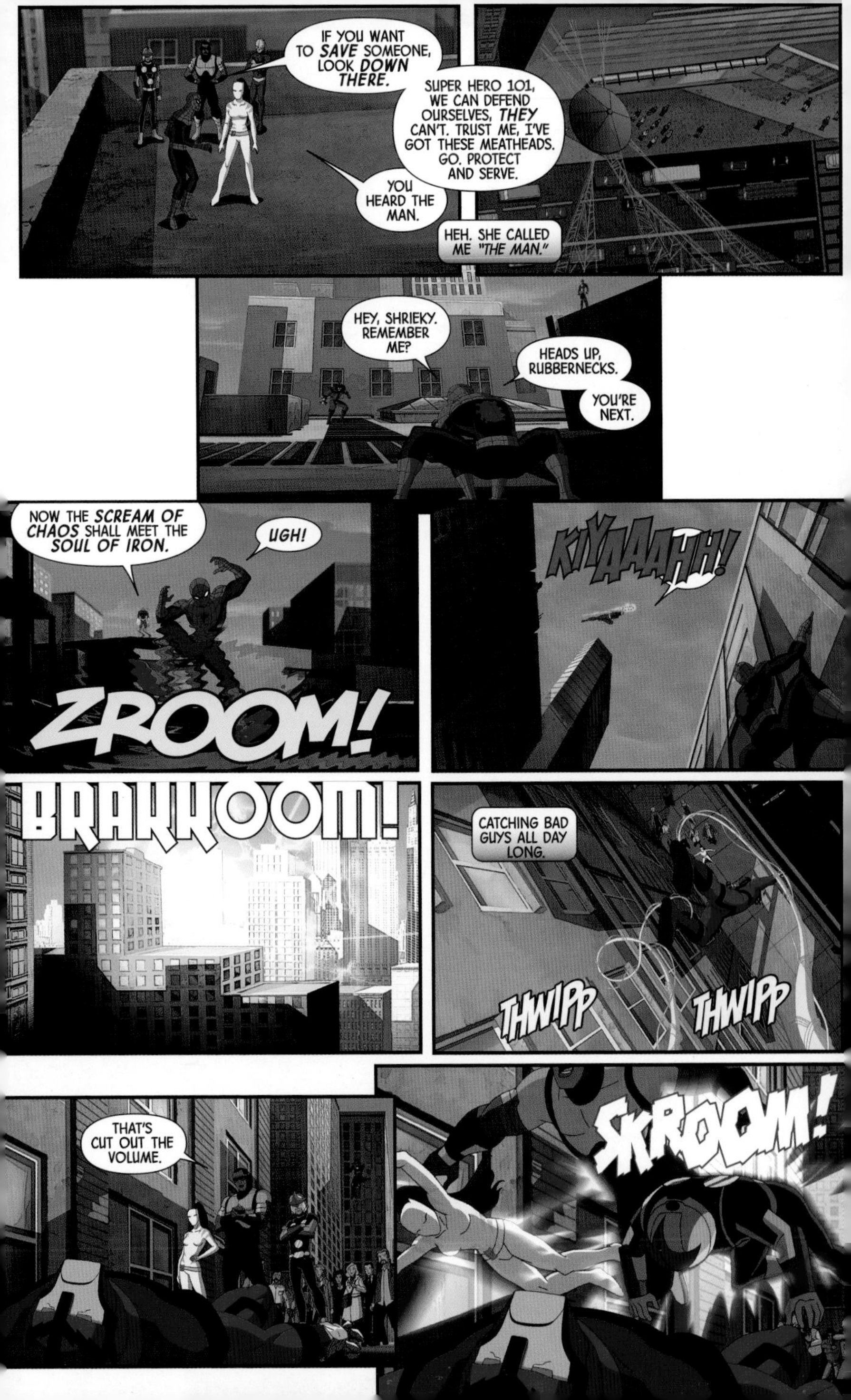
IF YOU WANT TO SAVE SOMEONE, LOOK DOWN THERE.
SUPER HERO 101, WE CAN DEFEND OURSELVES, THEY CAN'T. TRUST ME, I'VE GOT THESE MEATHEADS. GO. PROTECT AND SERVE.
YOU HEARD THE MAN.
HEH. SHE CALLED ME "THE MAN."
HEY, SHRIEKY. REMEMBER ME?
HEADS UP, RUBBERNECKS.
YOU'RE NEXT.
NOW THE SCREAM OF CHAOS SHALL MEET THE SOUL OF IRON.
UGH!
ZROOM!
KIYAAAHH!
BRAKKOOM!
CATCHING BAD GUYS ALL DAY LONG.
THWIPP
THWIPP
THAT'S CUT OUT THE VOLUME.
SKROOM!

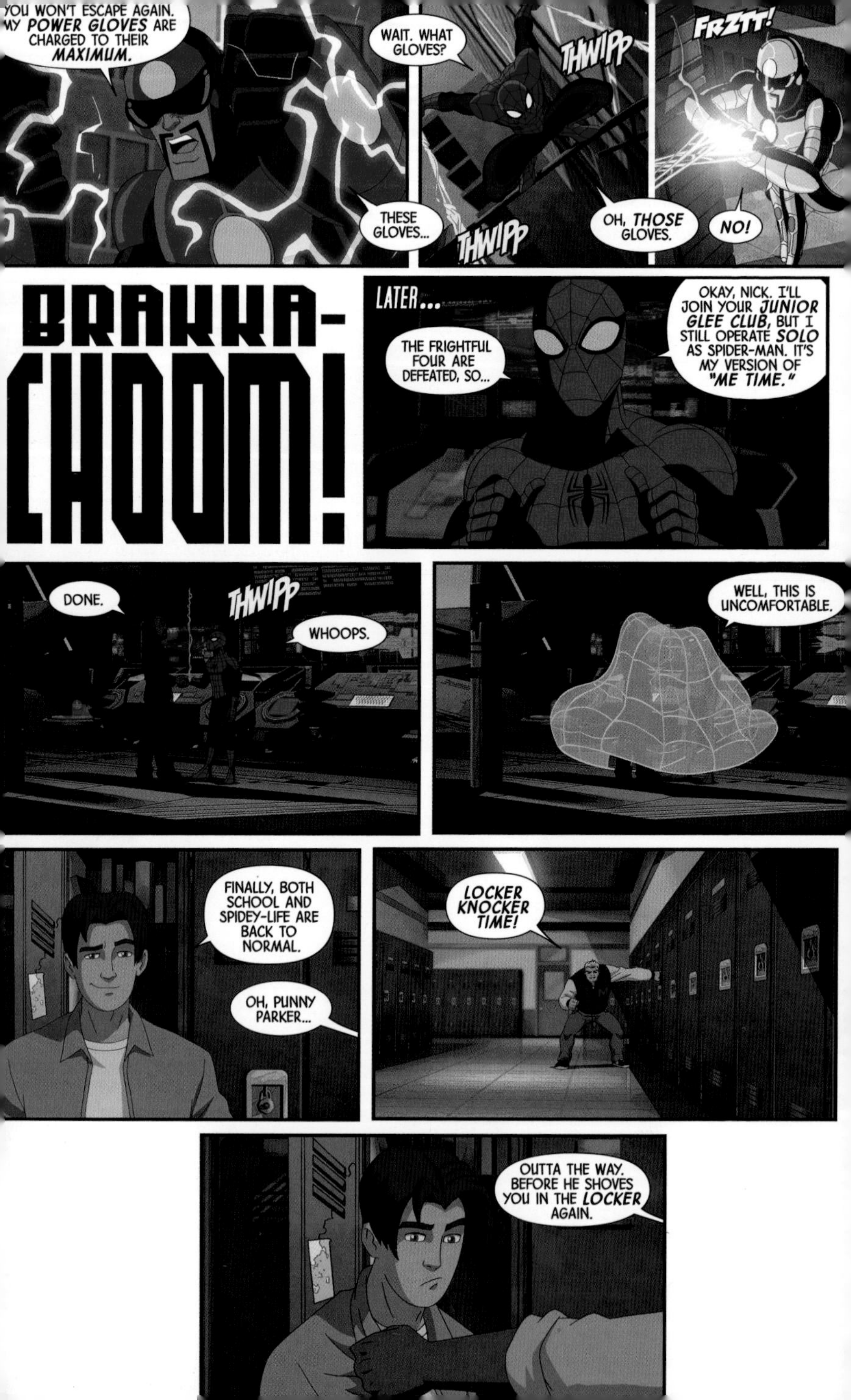
YOU WON'T ESCAPE AGAIN. MY POWER GLOVES ARE CHARGED TO THEIR MAXIMUM.
WAIT. WHAT GLOVES?
THWIPP
THESE GLOVES...
THWIPP
FRZTT!
OH, THOSE GLOVES.
NO!
BRAKKA-CHOOM!
LATER...
THE FRIGHTFUL FOUR ARE DEFEATED, SO...
OKAY, NICK. I'LL JOIN YOUR JUNIOR GLEE CLUB, BUT I STILL OPERATE SOLO AS SPIDER-MAN. IT'S MY VERSION OF "ME TIME."
DONE.
THWIPP
WHOOPS.
WELL, THIS IS UNCOMFORTABLE.
FINALLY, BOTH SCHOOL AND SPIDEY-LIFE ARE BACK TO NORMAL.
OH, PUNNY PARKER...
LOCKER KNOCKER TIME!
OUTTA THE WAY. BEFORE HE SHOVES YOU IN THE LOCKER AGAIN.

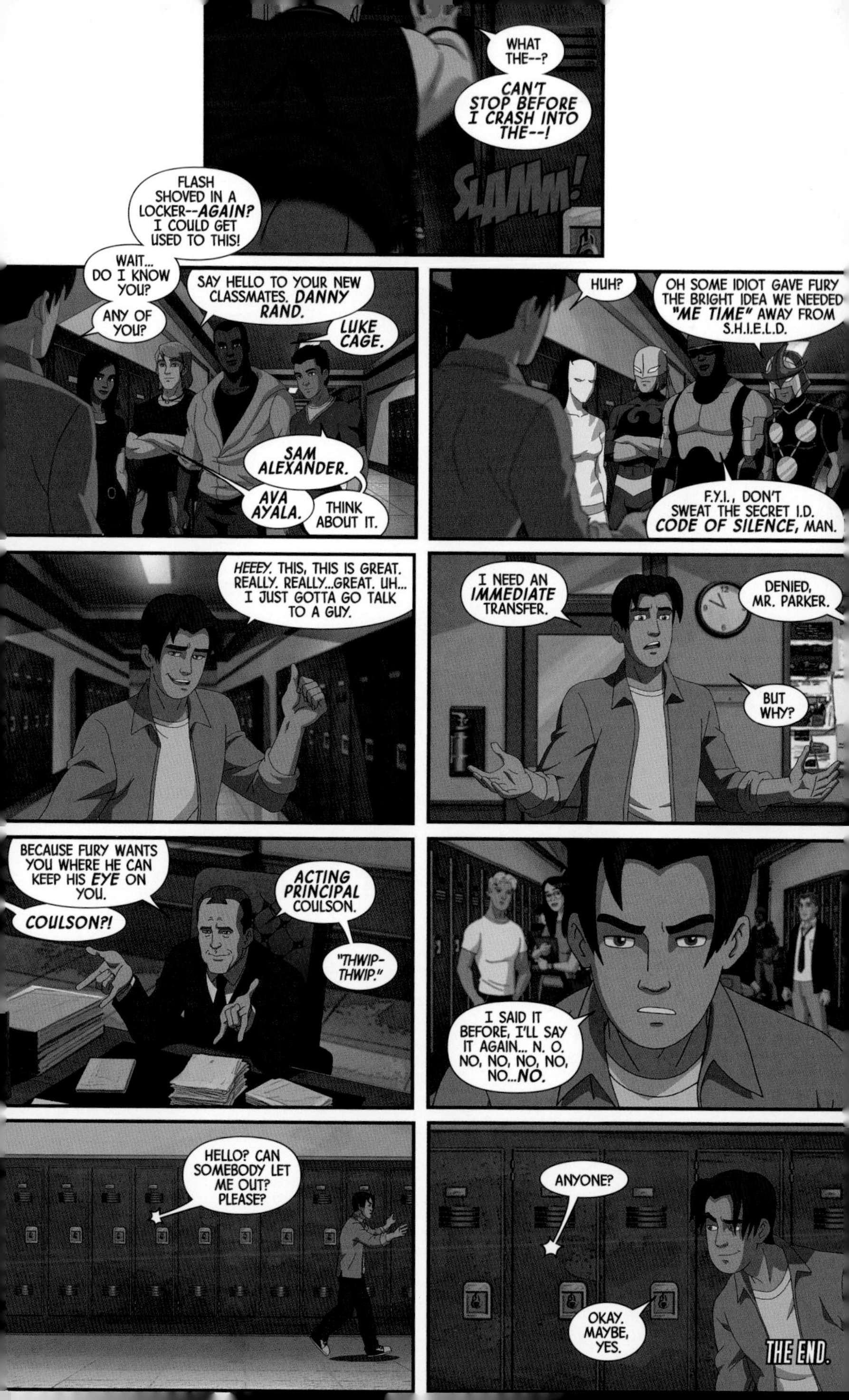
WHAT THE--?
CAN'T STOP BEFORE I CRASH INTO THE--!
SLAMM!
FLASH SHOVED IN A LOCKER--AGAIN? I COULD GET USED TO THIS!
WAIT... DO I KNOW YOU?
ANY OF YOU?
SAY HELLO TO YOUR NEW CLASSMATES. DANNY RAND.
LUKE CAGE.
SAM ALEXANDER.
AVA AYALA.
THINK ABOUT IT.
HUH?
OH SOME IDIOT GAVE FURY THE BRIGHT IDEA WE NEEDED "ME TIME" AWAY FROM S.H.I.E.L.D.
F.Y.I., DON'T SWEAT THE SECRET I.D. CODE OF SILENCE, MAN.
HEEEY. THIS, THIS IS GREAT. REALLY. REALLY...GREAT. UH... I JUST GOTTA GO TALK TO A GUY.
I NEED AN IMMEDIATE TRANSFER.
DENIED, MR. PARKER.
BUT WHY?
BECAUSE FURY WANTS YOU WHERE HE CAN KEEP HIS EYE ON YOU.
COULSON?!
ACTING PRINCIPAL COULSON.
"THWIP-THWIP."
I SAID IT BEFORE, I'LL SAY IT AGAIN... N. O. NO, NO, NO, NO, NO...NO.
HELLO? CAN SOMEBODY LET ME OUT? PLEASE?
ANYONE?
OKAY. MAYBE, YES.
THE END.

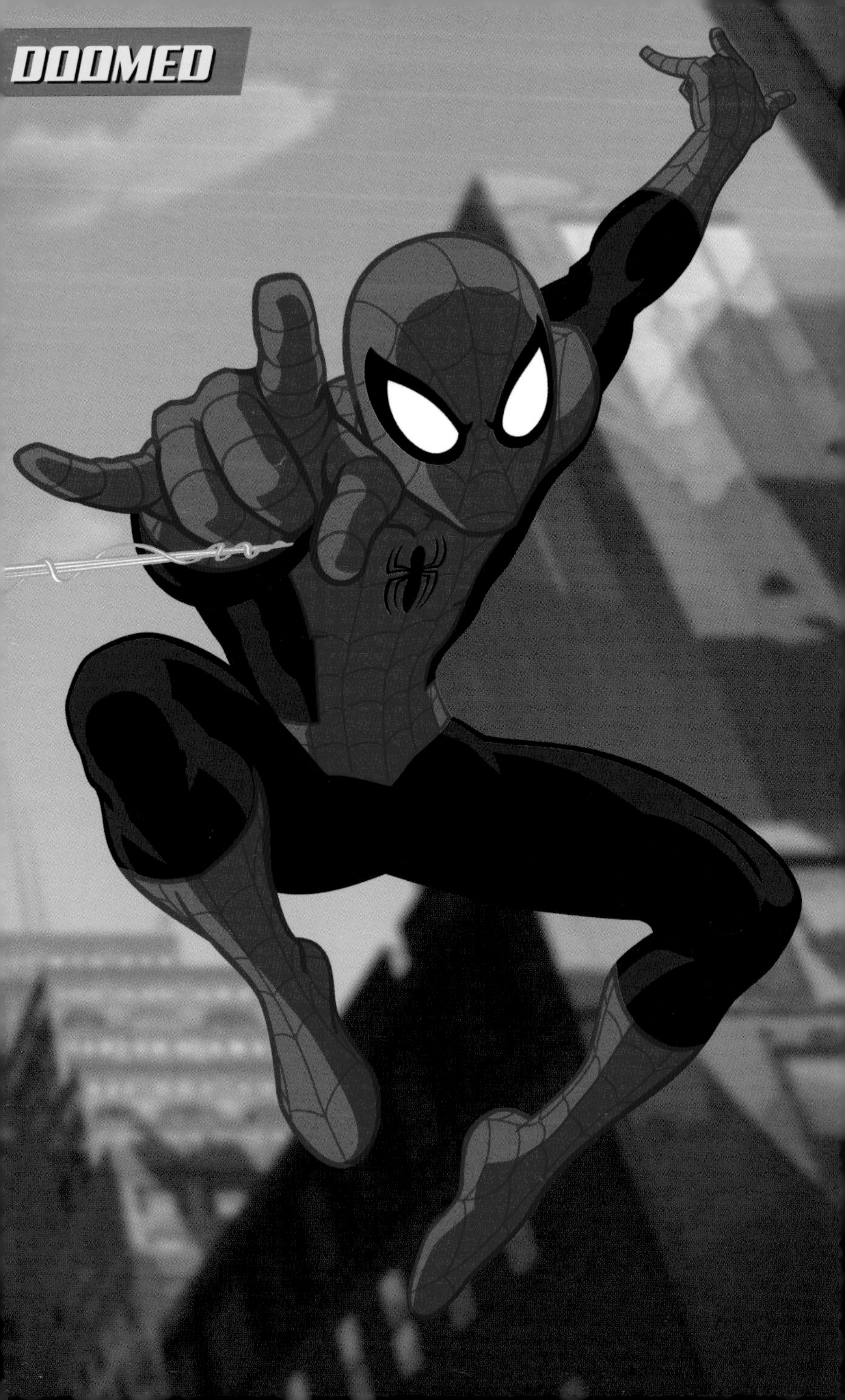

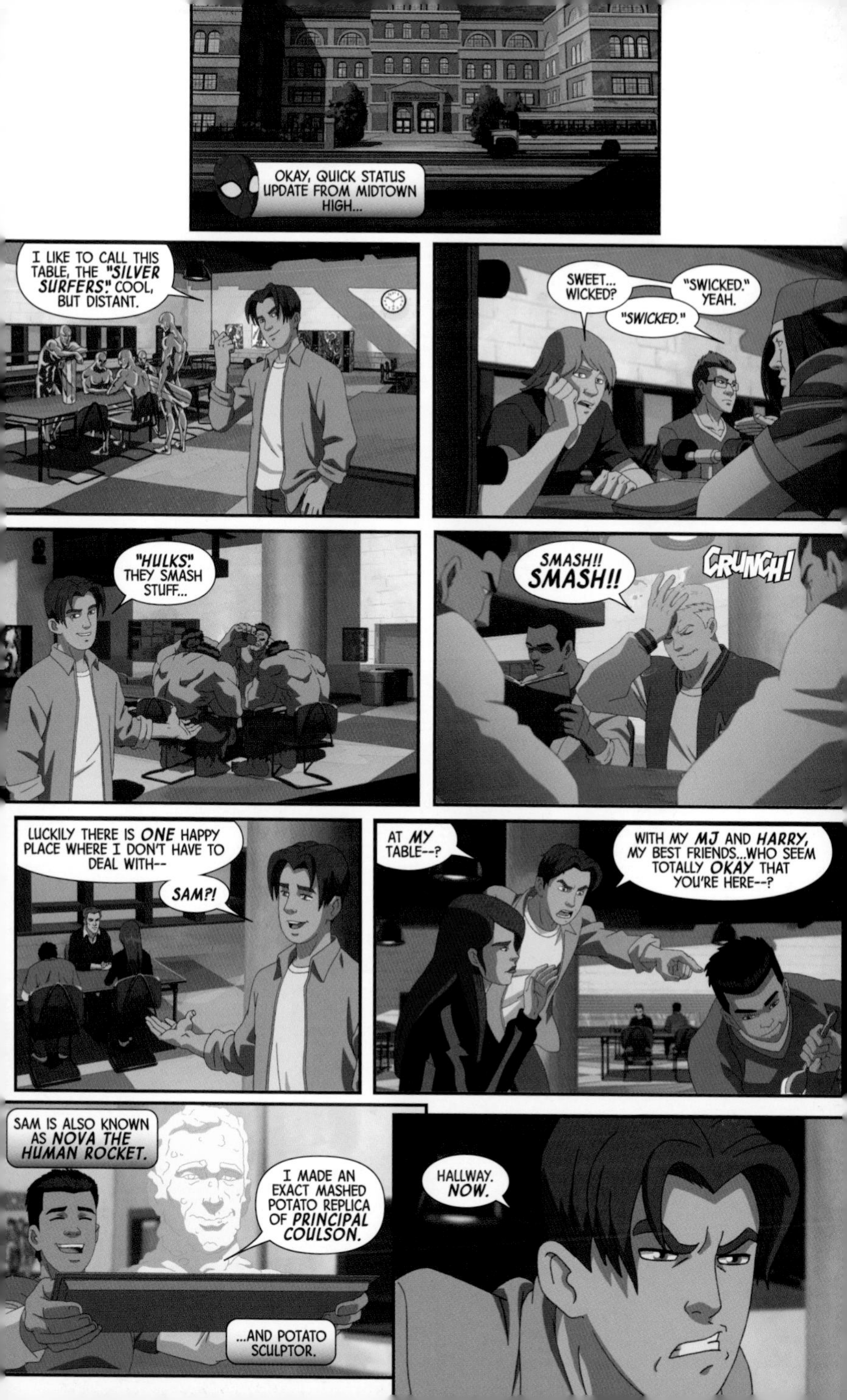
OKAY, QUICK STATUS UPDATE FROM MIDTOWN HIGH...
I LIKE TO CALL THIS TABLE, THE "SILVER SURFERS." COOL, BUT DISTANT.
SWEET... WICKED?
"SWICKED."
"SWICKED." YEAH.
"HULKS." THEY SMASH STUFF...
SMASH!! SMASH!!
CRUNCH!
LUCKILY THERE IS ONE HAPPY PLACE WHERE I DON'T HAVE TO DEAL WITH--
SAM?!
AT MY TABLE--?
WITH MY MJ AND HARRY, MY BEST FRIENDS...WHO SEEM TOTALLY OKAY THAT YOU'RE HERE--?
SAM IS ALSO KNOWN AS NOVA THE HUMAN ROCKET.
I MADE AN EXACT MASHED POTATO REPLICA OF PRINCIPAL COULSON.
...AND POTATO SCULPTOR.
HALLWAY. NOW.

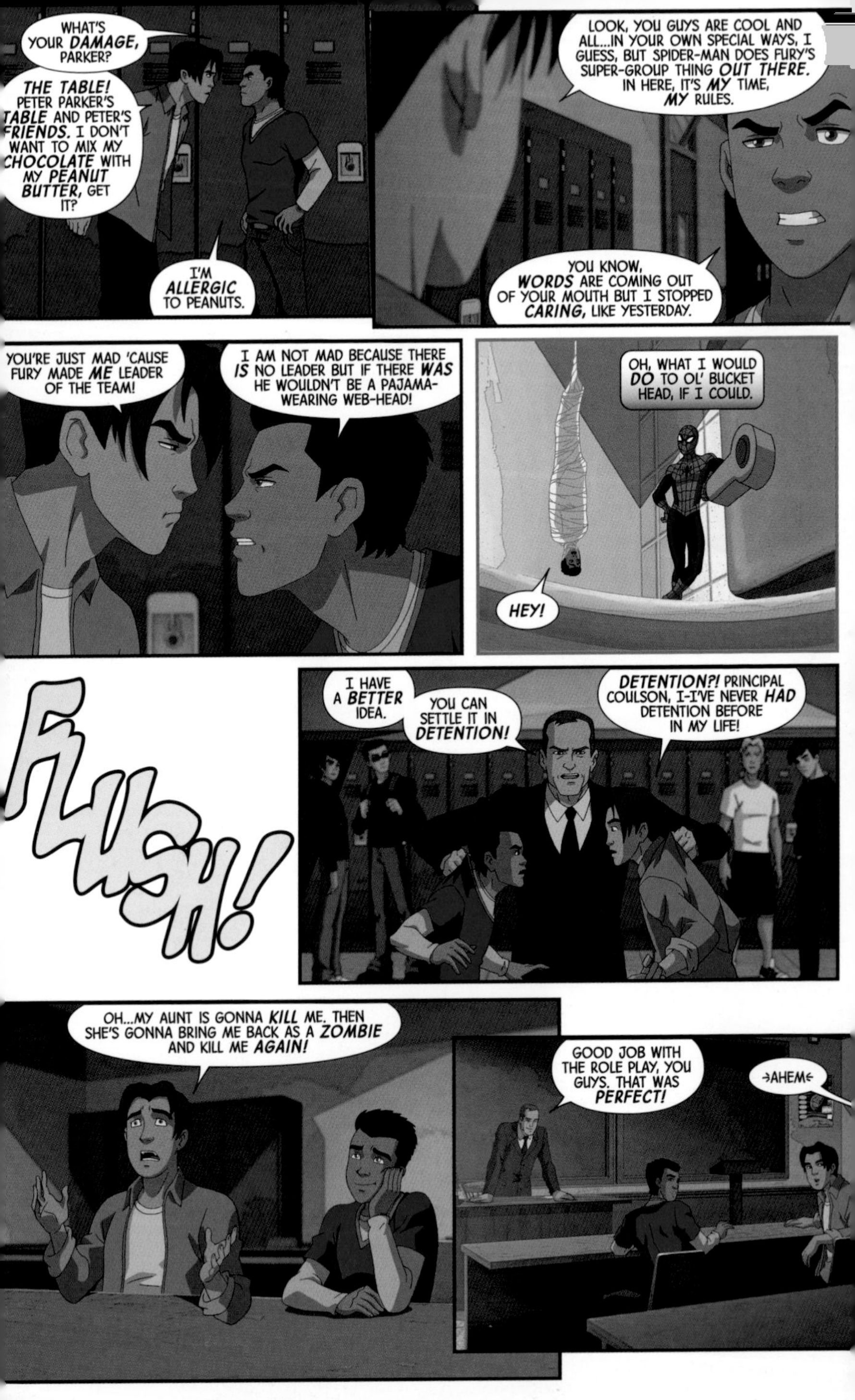

WHAT'S YOUR DAMAGE, PARKER?
THE TABLE! PETER PARKER'S TABLE AND PETER'S FRIENDS. I DON'T WANT TO MIX MY CHOCOLATE WITH MY PEANUT BUTTER, GET IT?
I'M ALLERGIC TO PEANUTS.
LOOK, YOU GUYS ARE COOL AND ALL...IN YOUR OWN SPECIAL WAYS, I GUESS, BUT SPIDER-MAN DOES FURY'S SUPER-GROUP THING OUT THERE. IN HERE, IT'S MY TIME, MY RULES.
YOU KNOW, WORDS ARE COMING OUT OF YOUR MOUTH BUT I STOPPED CARING, LIKE YESTERDAY.
YOU'RE JUST MAD 'CAUSE FURY MADE ME LEADER OF THE TEAM!
I AM NOT MAD BECAUSE THERE IS NO LEADER BUT IF THERE WAS HE WOULDN'T BE A PAJAMA-WEARING WEB-HEAD!
OH, WHAT I WOULD DO TO OL' BUCKET HEAD, IF I COULD.
HEY!
FLUSH!
I HAVE A BETTER IDEA.
YOU CAN SETTLE IT IN DETENTION!
DETENTION?! PRINCIPAL COULSON, I-I'VE NEVER HAD DETENTION BEFORE IN MY LIFE!
OH...MY AUNT IS GONNA KILL ME. THEN SHE'S GONNA BRING ME BACK AS A ZOMBIE AND KILL ME AGAIN!
GOOD JOB WITH THE ROLE PLAY, YOU GUYS. THAT WAS PERFECT!
AHEM

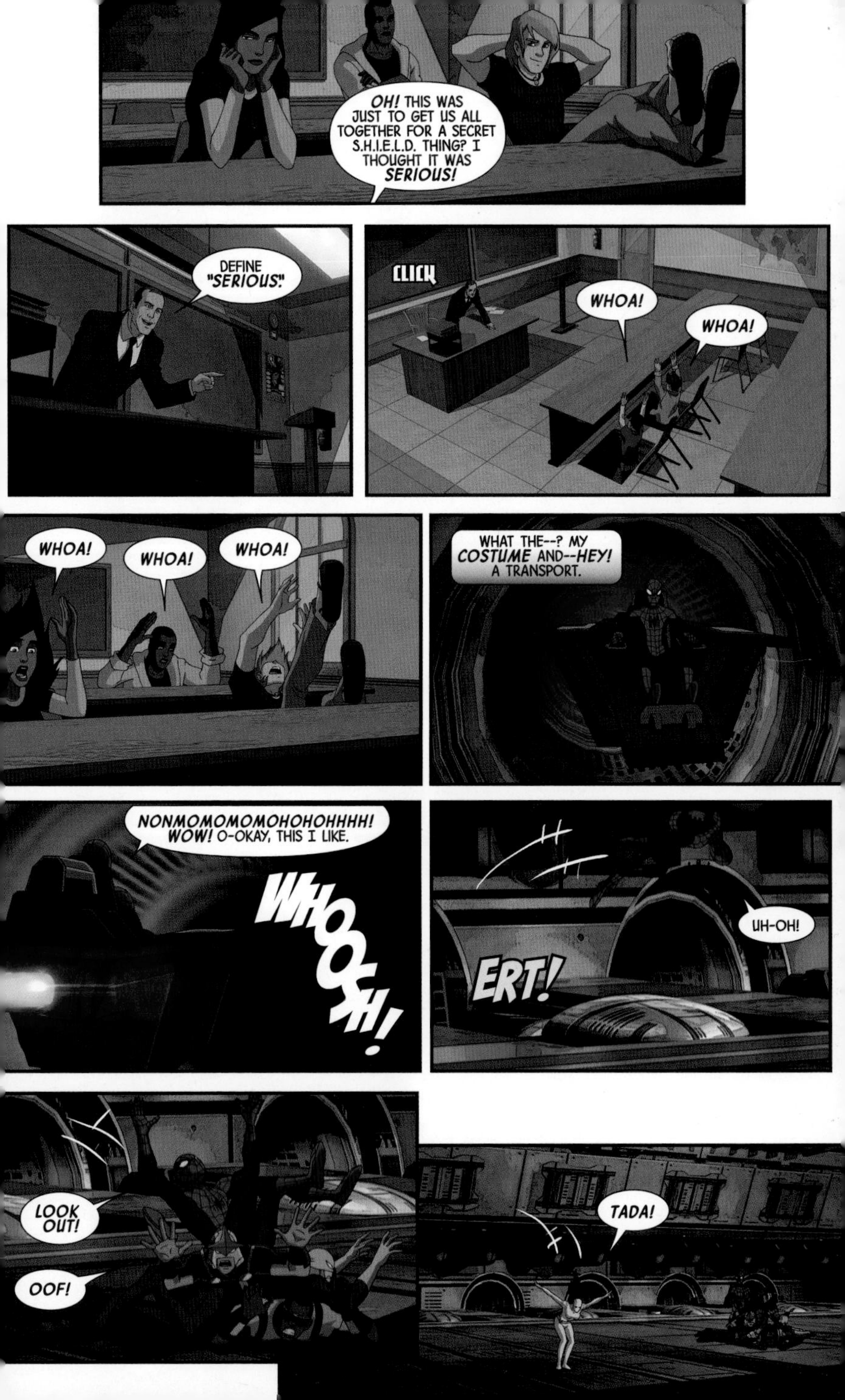
OH! THIS WAS JUST TO GET US ALL TOGETHER FOR A SECRET S.H.I.E.L.D. THING? I THOUGHT IT WAS SERIOUS!
DEFINE "SERIOUS."
CLICK
WHOA!
WHOA!
WHOA!
WHOA!
WHOA!
WHAT THE--? MY COSTUME AND--HEY! A TRANSPORT.
NONMOMOMOMOHOHOHHHH! WOW! O-OKAY, THIS I LIKE.
WHOOSH!
UH-OH!
ERT!
LOOK OUT!
OOF!
TADA!

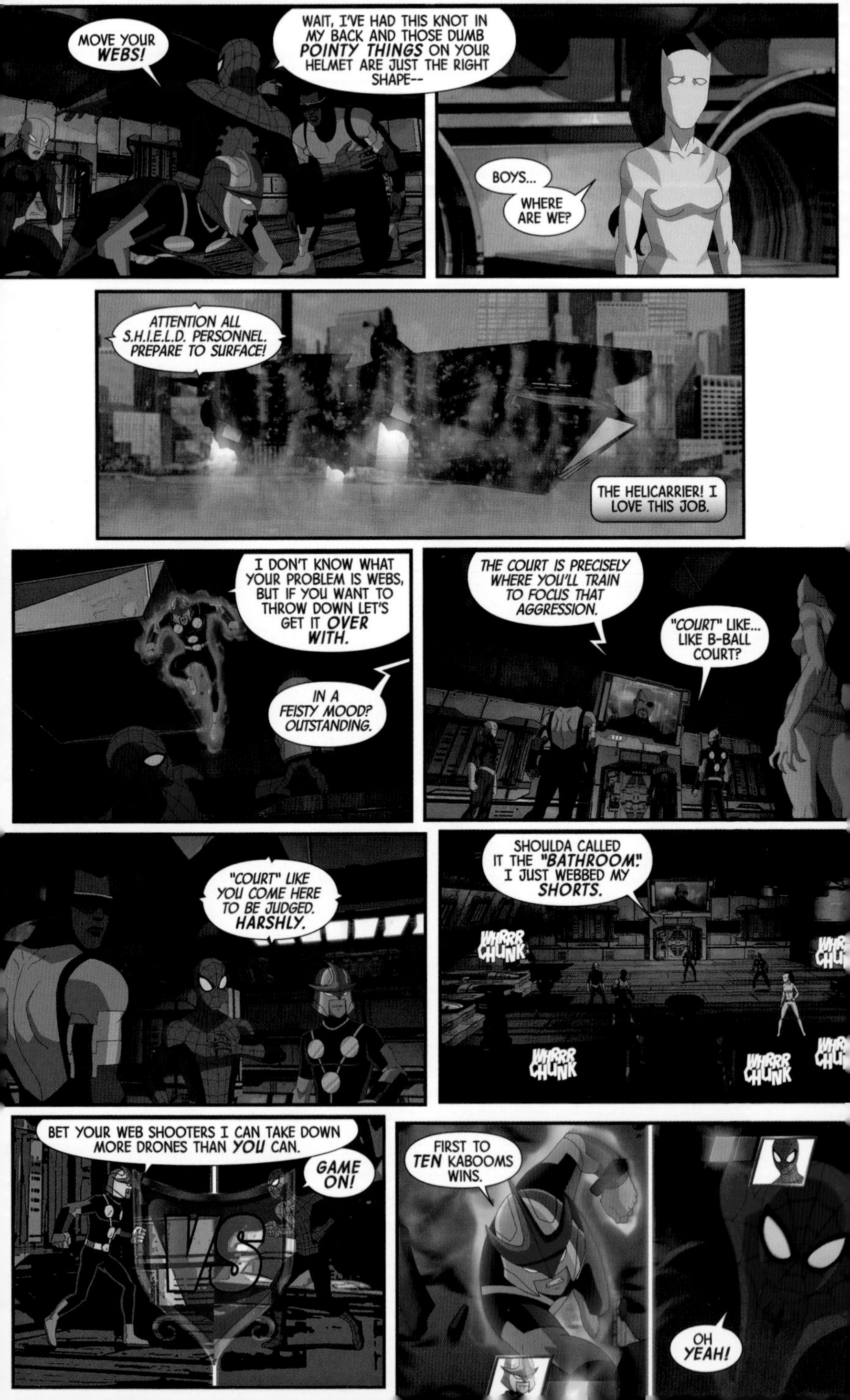
MOVE YOUR WEBS!
WAIT, I'VE HAD THIS KNOT IN MY BACK AND THOSE DUMB POINTY THINGS ON YOUR HELMET ARE JUST THE RIGHT SHAPE--
BOYS... WHERE ARE WE?
ATTENTION ALL S.H.I.E.L.D. PERSONNEL. PREPARE TO SURFACE!
THE HELICARRIER! I LOVE THIS JOB.
I DON'T KNOW WHAT YOUR PROBLEM IS WEBS, BUT IF YOU WANT TO THROW DOWN LET'S GET IT OVER WITH.
IN A FEISTY MOOD? OUTSTANDING.
THE COURT IS PRECISELY WHERE YOU'LL TRAIN TO FOCUS THAT AGGRESSION.
"COURT" LIKE... LIKE B-BALL COURT?
"COURT" LIKE YOU COME HERE TO BE JUDGED. HARSHLY.
SHOULDA CALLED IT THE "BATHROOM." I JUST WEBBED MY SHORTS.
WHRRR CHUNK
WHRRR CHUNK
WHRRR CHUNK
BET YOUR WEB SHOOTERS I CAN TAKE DOWN MORE DRONES THAN YOU CAN.
GAME ON!
VS
FIRST TO TEN KABOOMS WINS.
OH YEAH!

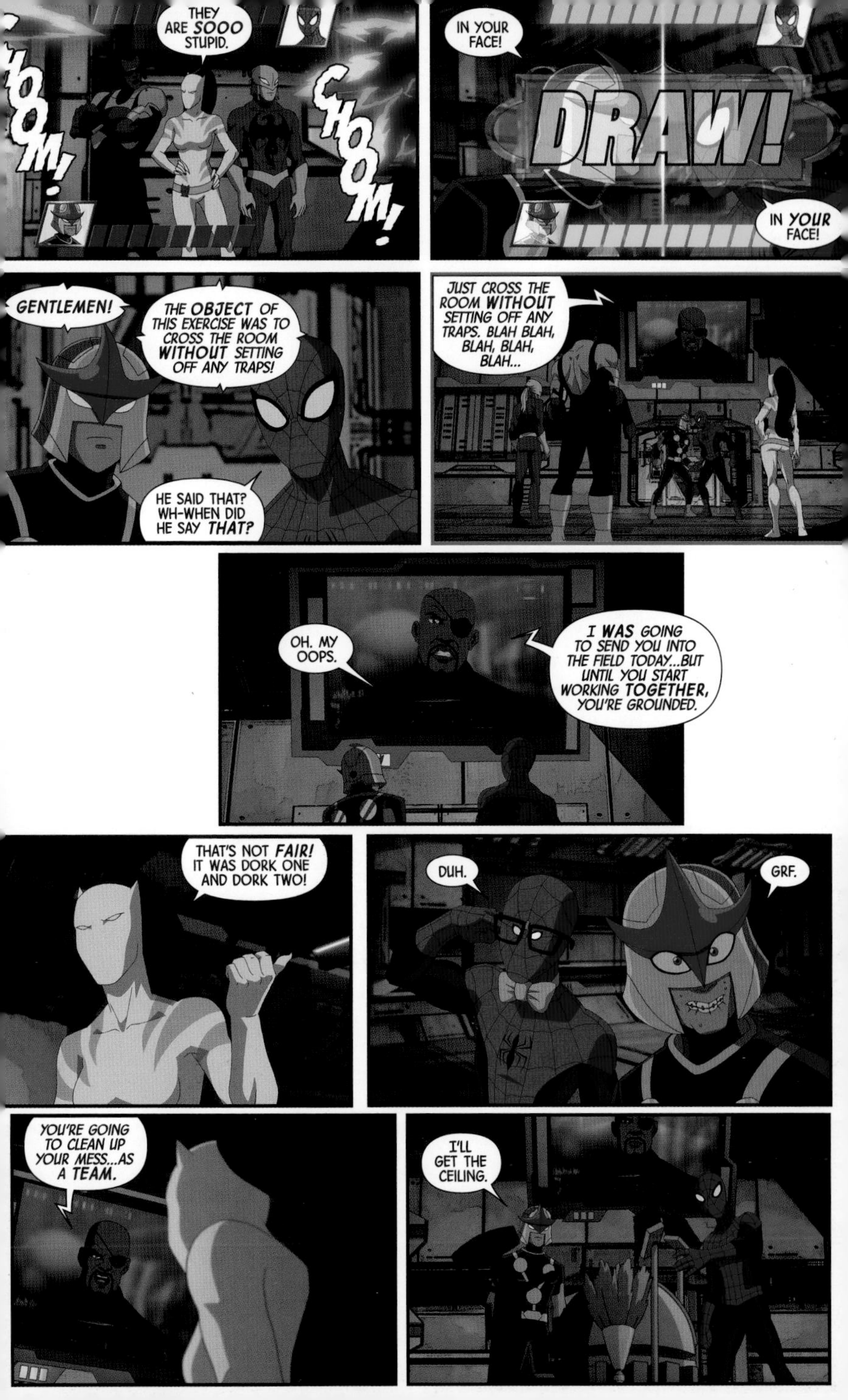
THEY ARE SOOO STUPID.
CHOOM!
CHOOM!
IN YOUR FACE!
DRAW!
IN YOUR FACE!
GENTLEMEN!
THE OBJECT OF THIS EXERCISE WAS TO CROSS THE ROOM WITHOUT SETTING OFF ANY TRAPS!
HE SAID THAT? WH-WHEN DID HE SAY THAT?
JUST CROSS THE ROOM WITHOUT SETTING OFF ANY TRAPS. BLAH BLAH, BLAH, BLAH, BLAH...
OH. MY OOPS.
I WAS GOING TO SEND YOU INTO THE FIELD TODAY...BUT UNTIL YOU START WORKING TOGETHER, YOU'RE GROUNDED.
THAT'S NOT FAIR! IT WAS DORK ONE AND DORK TWO!
DUH.
GRF.
YOU'RE GOING TO CLEAN UP YOUR MESS...AS A TEAM.
I'LL GET THE CEILING.

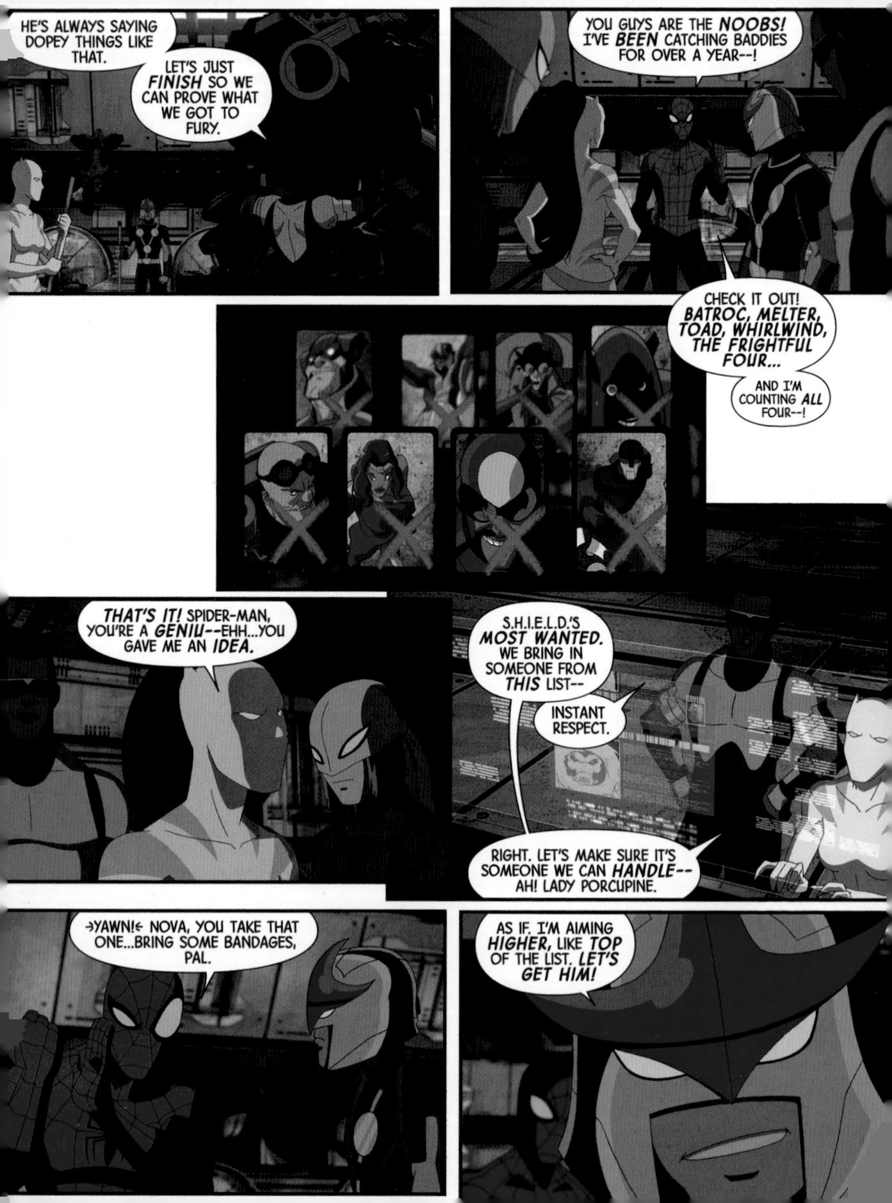
HE'S ALWAYS SAYING DOPEY THINGS LIKE THAT.
LET'S JUST FINISH SO WE CAN PROVE WHAT WE GOT TO FURY.
YOU GUYS ARE THE NOOBS! I'VE BEEN CATCHING BADDIES FOR OVER A YEAR--!
CHECK IT OUT! BATROC, MELTER, TOAD, WHIRLWIND, THE FRIGHTFUL FOUR...
AND I'M COUNTING ALL FOUR--!
THAT'S IT! SPIDER-MAN, YOU'RE A GENIU--EHH...YOU GAVE ME AN IDEA.
S.H.I.E.L.D.'S MOST WANTED. WE BRING IN SOMEONE FROM THIS LIST--
INSTANT RESPECT.
RIGHT. LET'S MAKE SURE IT'S SOMEONE WE CAN HANDLE--AH! LADY PORCUPINE.
›YAWN!‹ NOVA, YOU TAKE THAT ONE...BRING SOME BANDAGES, PAL.
AS IF. I'M AIMING HIGHER, LIKE TOP OF THE LIST. LET'S GET HIM!

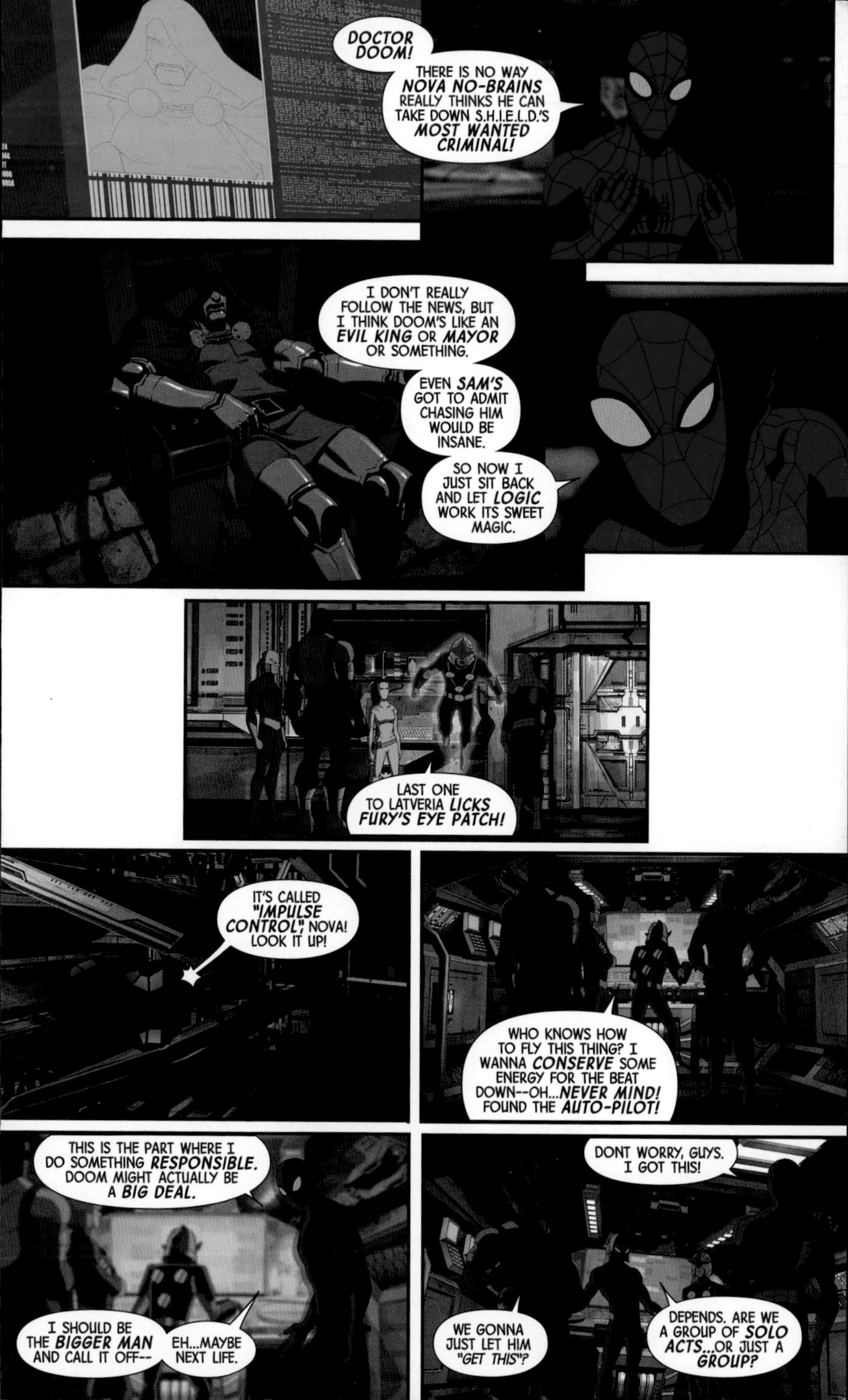
DOCTOR DOOM!
THERE IS NO WAY NOVA NO-BRAINS REALLY THINKS HE CAN TAKE DOWN S.H.I.E.L.D.'S MOST WANTED CRIMINAL!
I DON'T REALLY FOLLOW THE NEWS, BUT I THINK DOOM'S LIKE AN EVIL KING OR MAYOR OR SOMETHING.
EVEN SAM'S GOT TO ADMIT CHASING HIM WOULD BE INSANE.
SO NOW I JUST SIT BACK AND LET LOGIC WORK ITS SWEET MAGIC.
LAST ONE TO LATVERIA LICKS FURY'S EYE PATCH!
IT'S CALLED "IMPULSE CONTROL," NOVA! LOOK IT UP!
WHO KNOWS HOW TO FLY THIS THING? I WANNA CONSERVE SOME ENERGY FOR THE BEAT DOWN--OH...NEVER MIND! FOUND THE AUTO-PILOT!
THIS IS THE PART WHERE I DO SOMETHING RESPONSIBLE. DOOM MIGHT ACTUALLY BE A BIG DEAL.
I SHOULD BE THE BIGGER MAN AND CALL IT OFF--
EH...MAYBE NEXT LIFE.
DONT WORRY, GUYS. I GOT THIS!
WE GONNA JUST LET HIM "GET THIS"?
DEPENDS. ARE WE A GROUP OF SOLO ACTS...OR JUST A GROUP?

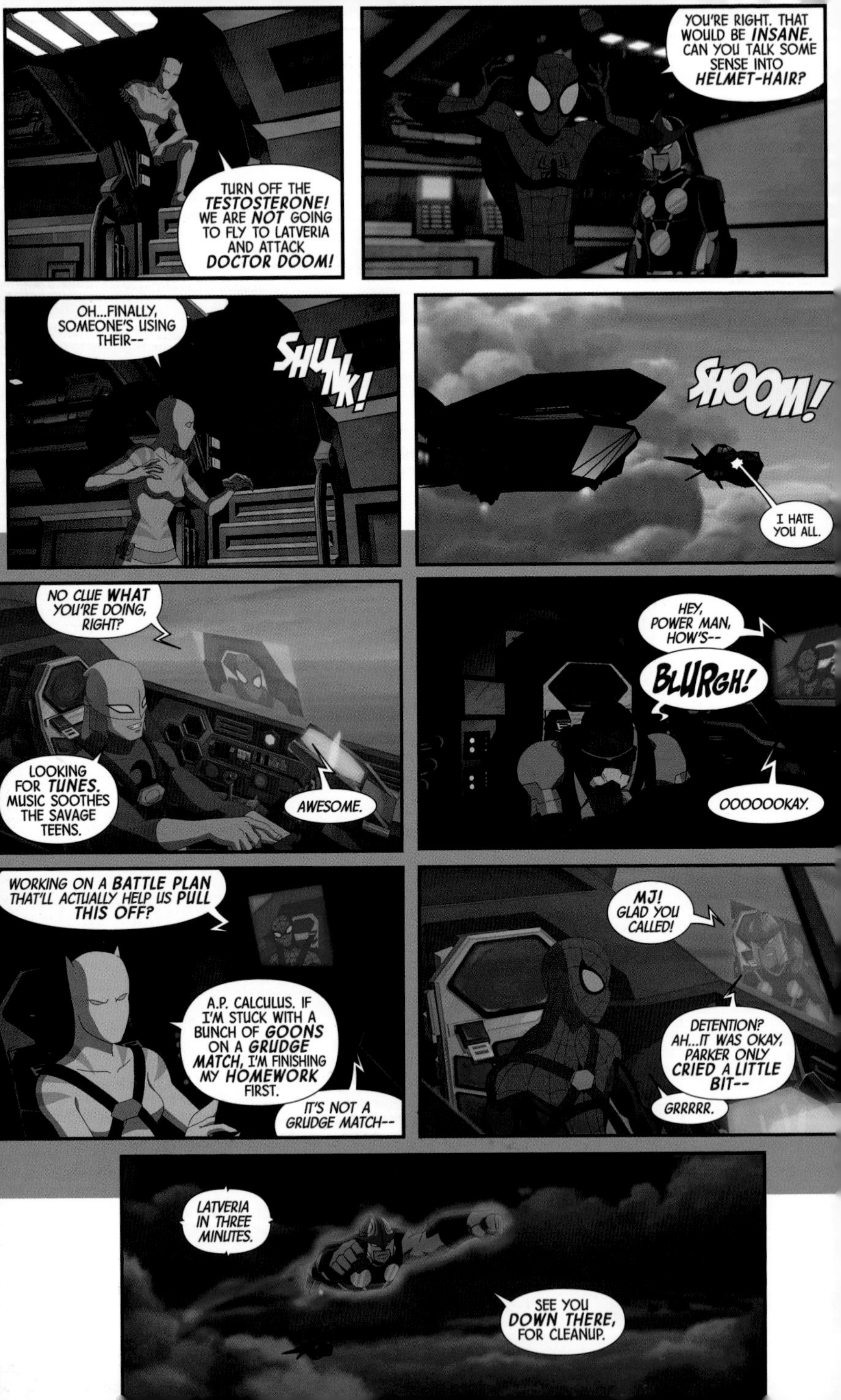
TURN OFF THE TESTOSTERONE! WE ARE NOT GOING TO FLY TO LATVERIA AND ATTACK DOCTOR DOOM!
YOU'RE RIGHT. THAT WOULD BE INSANE. CAN YOU TALK SOME SENSE INTO HELMET-HAIR?
OH...FINALLY, SOMEONE'S USING THEIR--
SHUNK!
SHOOM!
I HATE YOU ALL.
NO CLUE WHAT YOU'RE DOING, RIGHT?
LOOKING FOR TUNES. MUSIC SOOTHES THE SAVAGE TEENS.
AWESOME.
HEY, POWER MAN, HOW'S--
BLURGH!
OOOOOOKAY.
WORKING ON A BATTLE PLAN THAT'LL ACTUALLY HELP US PULL THIS OFF?
A.P. CALCULUS. IF I'M STUCK WITH A BUNCH OF GOONS ON A GRUDGE MATCH, I'M FINISHING MY HOMEWORK FIRST.
IT'S NOT A GRUDGE MATCH--
MJ! GLAD YOU CALLED!
DETENTION? AH...IT WAS OKAY, PARKER ONLY CRIED A LITTLE BIT--
GRRRRR.
LATVERIA IN THREE MINUTES.
SEE YOU DOWN THERE, FOR CLEANUP.

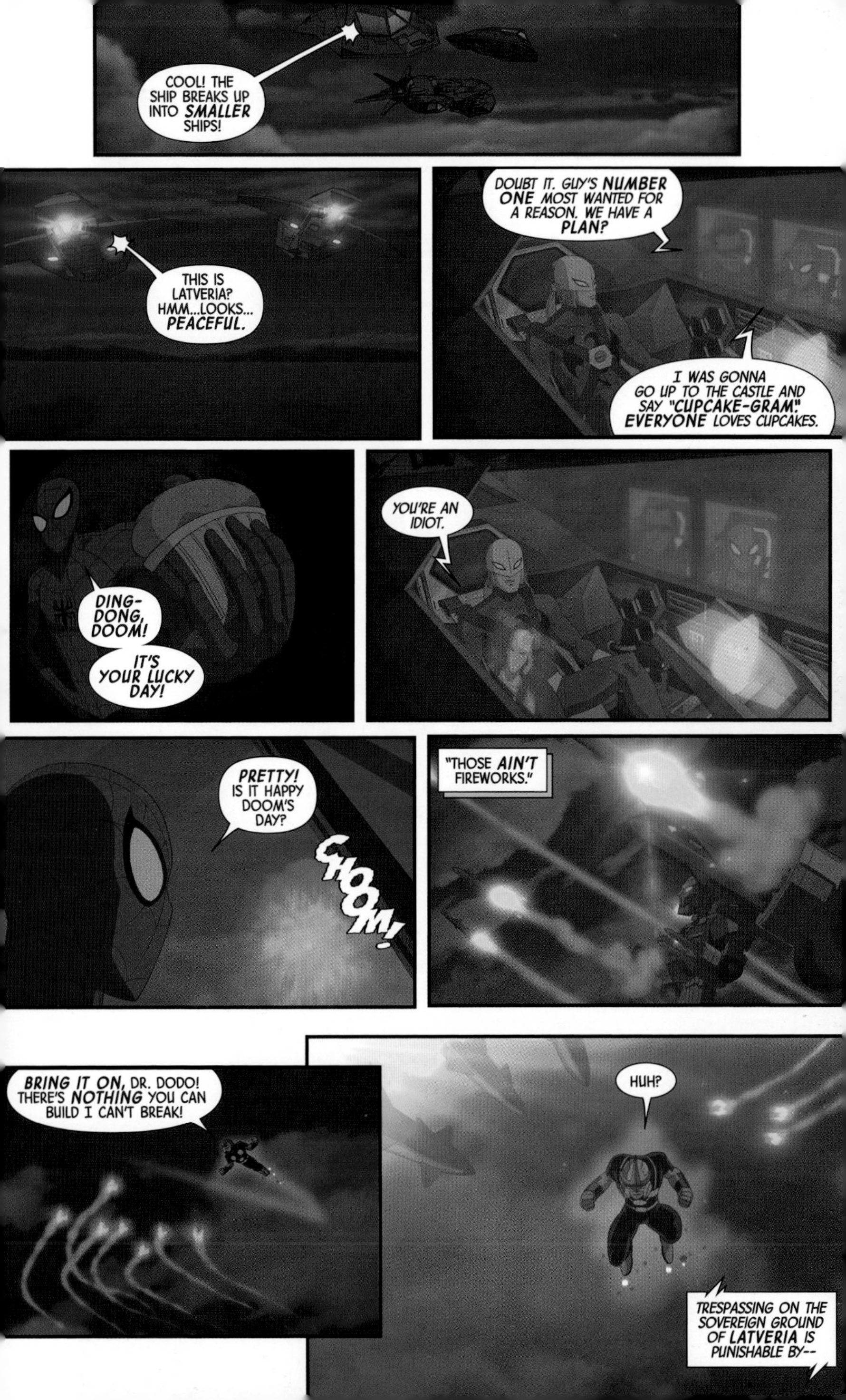
COOL! THE SHIP BREAKS UP INTO SMALLER SHIPS!
THIS IS LATVERIA? HMM...LOOKS... PEACEFUL.
DOUBT IT. GUY'S NUMBER ONE MOST WANTED FOR A REASON. WE HAVE A PLAN?
I WAS GONNA GO UP TO THE CASTLE AND SAY "CUPCAKE-GRAM." EVERYONE LOVES CUPCAKES.
DING-DONG, DOOM!
IT'S YOUR LUCKY DAY!
YOU'RE AN IDIOT.
PRETTY! IS IT HAPPY DOOM'S DAY?
CHOOM!
"THOSE AIN'T FIREWORKS."
BRING IT ON, DR. DODO! THERE'S NOTHING YOU CAN BUILD I CAN'T BREAK!
HUH?
TRESPASSING ON THE SOVEREIGN GROUND OF LATVERIA IS PUNISHABLE BY--

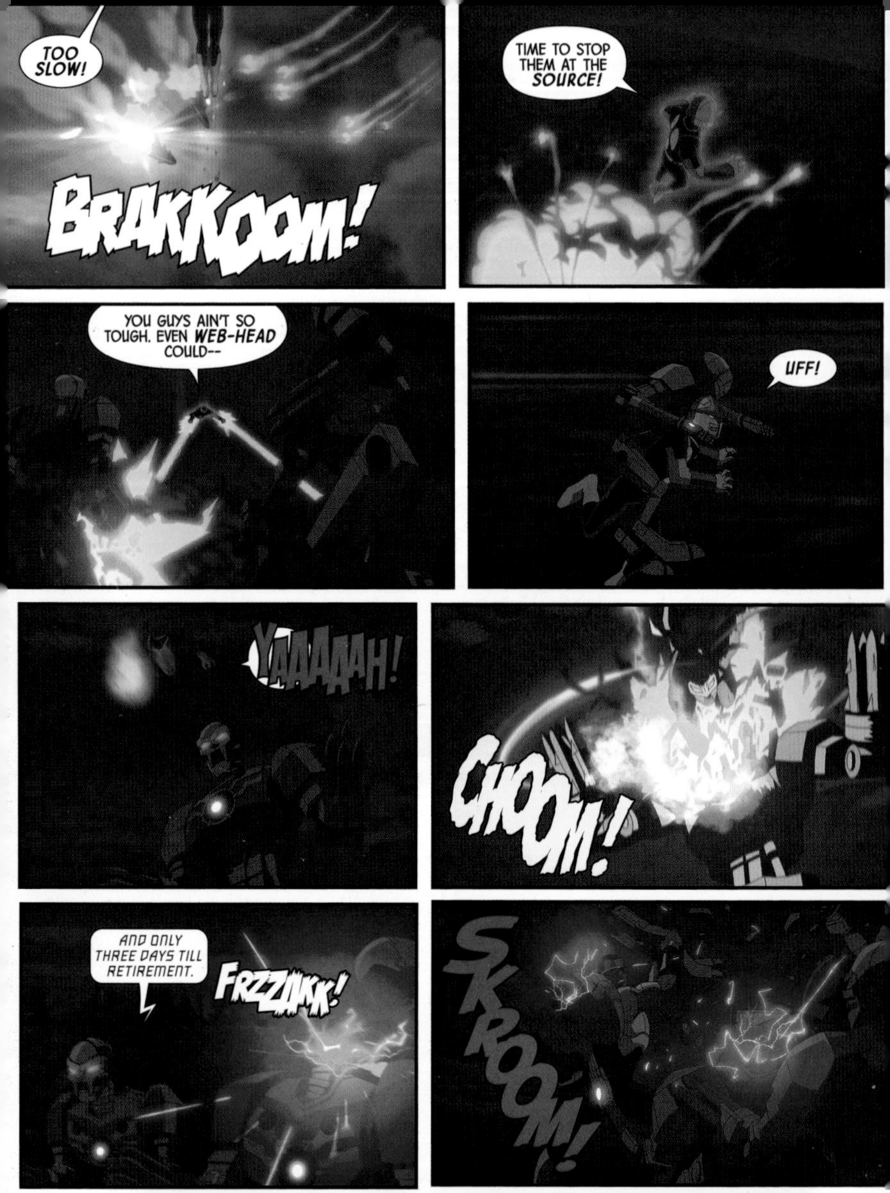
TOO SLOW!
BRAKKOOM!
TIME TO STOP THEM AT THE SOURCE!
YOU GUYS AIN'T SO TOUGH. EVEN WEB-HEAD COULD--
UFF!
YAAAAAH!
CHOOM!
AND ONLY THREE DAYS TILL RETIREMENT.
FRZZAKK!
SKROOM!

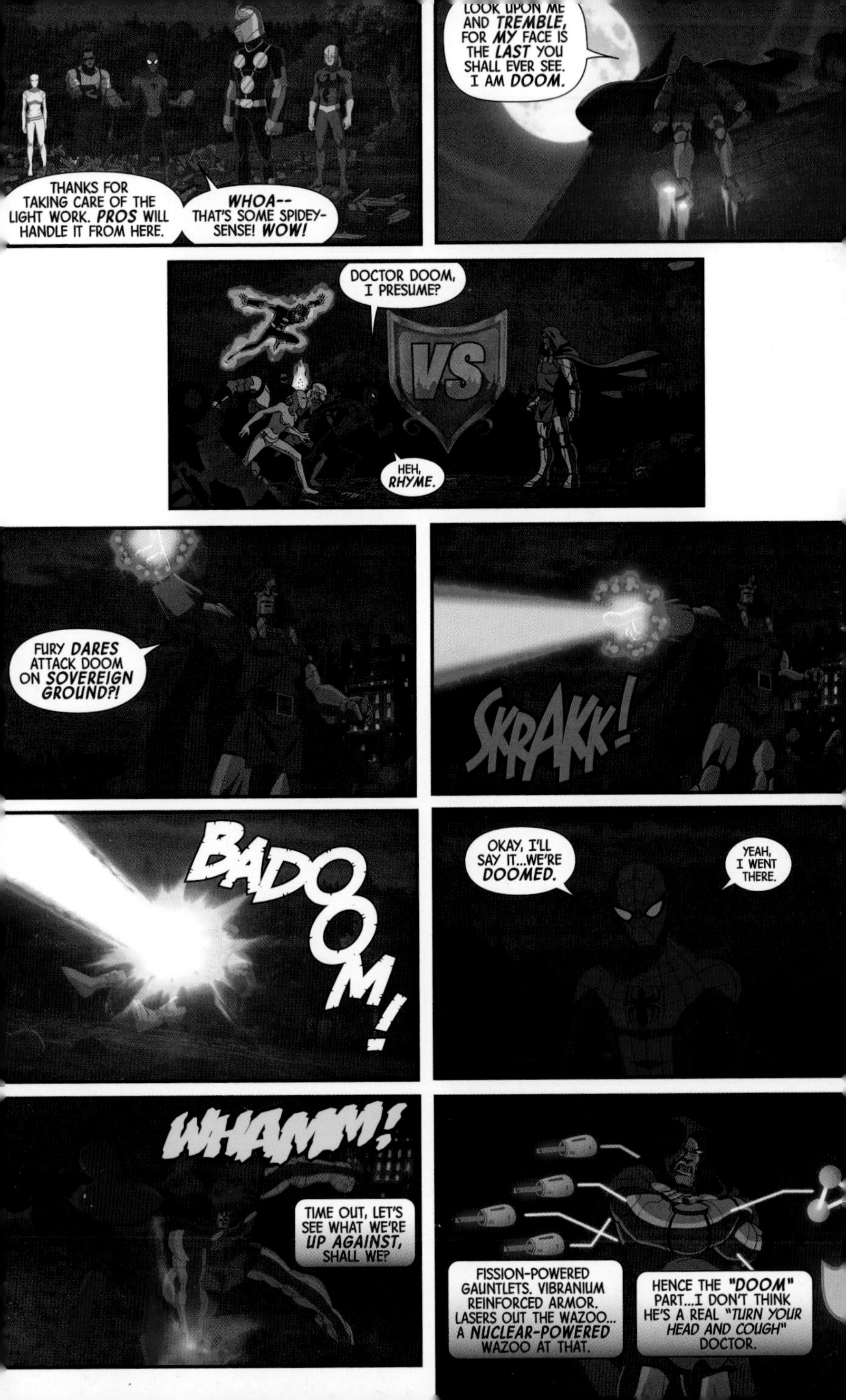
THANKS FOR TAKING CARE OF THE LIGHT WORK. PROS WILL HANDLE IT FROM HERE.
WHOA-- THAT'S SOME SPIDEY-SENSE! WOW!
LOOK UPON ME AND TREMBLE, FOR MY FACE IS THE LAST YOU SHALL EVER SEE. I AM DOOM.
DOCTOR DOOM, I PRESUME?
VS
HEH, RHYME.
FURY DARES ATTACK DOOM ON SOVEREIGN GROUND?!
SKRAKK!
BADOOOM!
OKAY, I'LL SAY IT...WE'RE DOOMED.
YEAH, I WENT THERE.
WHAMM!
TIME OUT, LET'S SEE WHAT WE'RE UP AGAINST, SHALL WE?
FISSION-POWERED GAUNTLETS. VIBRANIUM REINFORCED ARMOR. LASERS OUT THE WAZOO... A NUCLEAR-POWERED WAZOO AT THAT.
HENCE THE "DOOM" PART...I DON'T THINK HE'S A REAL "TURN YOUR HEAD AND COUGH" DOCTOR.

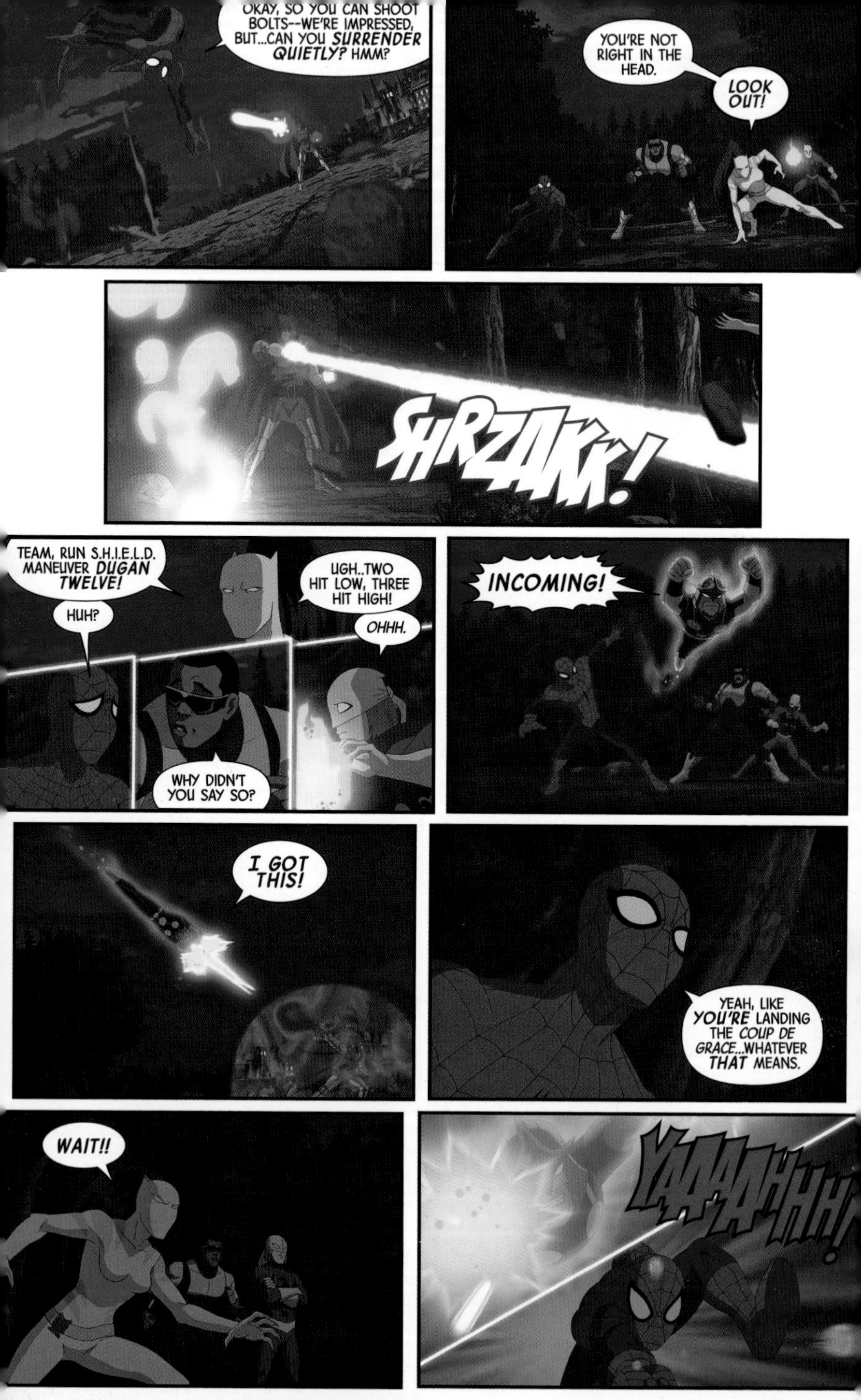
OKAY, SO YOU CAN SHOOT BOLTS--WE'RE IMPRESSED, BUT...CAN YOU SURRENDER QUIETLY? HMM?
YOU'RE NOT RIGHT IN THE HEAD.
LOOK OUT!
SHRZAKK!
TEAM, RUN S.H.I.E.L.D. MANEUVER DUGAN TWELVE!
HUH?
UGH..TWO HIT LOW, THREE HIT HIGH!
OHHH.
WHY DIDN'T YOU SAY SO?
INCOMING!
I GOT THIS!
YEAH, LIKE YOU'RE LANDING THE COUP DE GRACE...WHATEVER THAT MEANS.
WAIT!!
YAAAHHH!

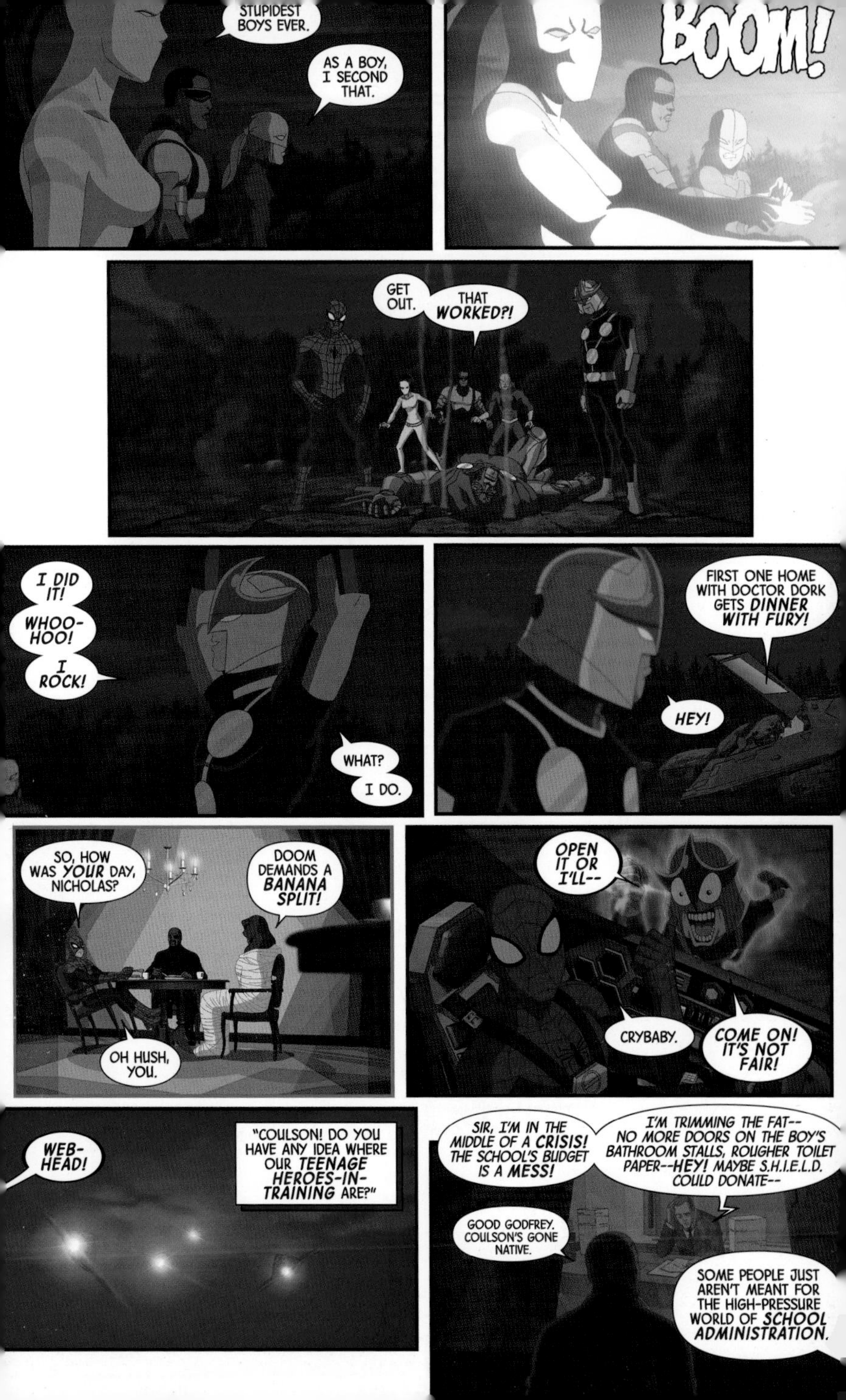
STUPIDEST BOYS EVER.
AS A BOY, I SECOND THAT.
BOOM!
GET OUT.
THAT WORKED?!
I DID IT!
WHOO-HOO!
I ROCK!
WHAT?
I DO.
FIRST ONE HOME WITH DOCTOR DORK GETS DINNER WITH FURY!
HEY!
SO, HOW WAS YOUR DAY, NICHOLAS?
DOOM DEMANDS A BANANA SPLIT!
OH HUSH, YOU.
OPEN IT OR I'LL--
CRYBABY.
COME ON! IT'S NOT FAIR!
WEB-HEAD!
"COULSON! DO YOU HAVE ANY IDEA WHERE OUR TEENAGE HEROES-IN-TRAINING ARE?"
SIR, I'M IN THE MIDDLE OF A CRISIS! THE SCHOOL'S BUDGET IS A MESS!
I'M TRIMMING THE FAT-- NO MORE DOORS ON THE BOY'S BATHROOM STALLS, ROUGHER TOILET PAPER--HEY! MAYBE S.H.I.E.L.D. COULD DONATE--
GOOD GODFREY. COULSON'S GONE NATIVE.
SOME PEOPLE JUST AREN'T MEANT FOR THE HIGH-PRESSURE WORLD OF SCHOOL ADMINISTRATION.

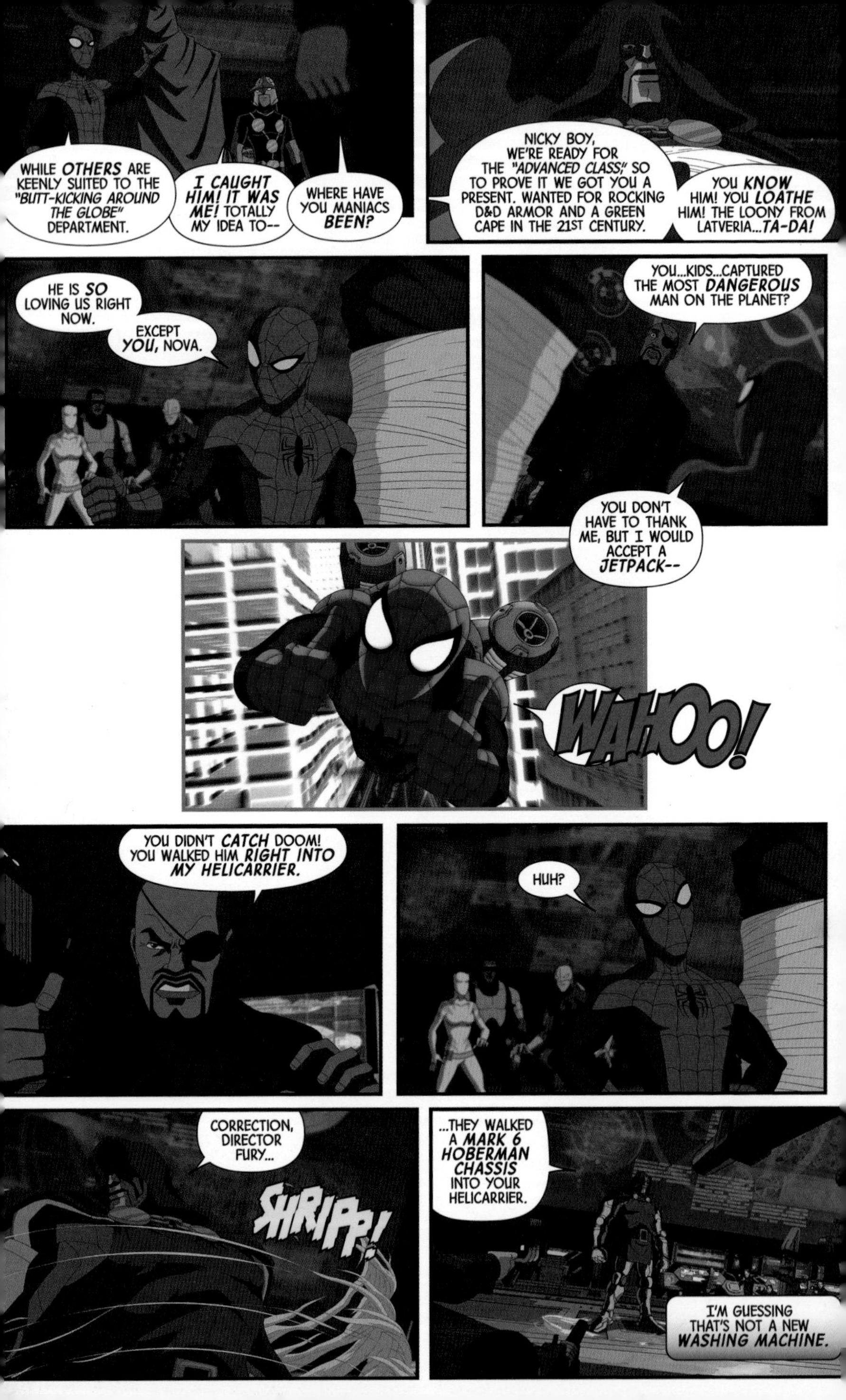

WHILE OTHERS ARE KEENLY SUITED TO THE "BUTT-KICKING AROUND THE GLOBE" DEPARTMENT.
I CAUGHT HIM! IT WAS ME! TOTALLY MY IDEA TO--
WHERE HAVE YOU MANIACS BEEN?
NICKY BOY, WE'RE READY FOR THE "ADVANCED CLASS," SO TO PROVE IT WE GOT YOU A PRESENT. WANTED FOR ROCKING D&D ARMOR AND A GREEN CAPE IN THE 21ST CENTURY.
YOU KNOW HIM! YOU LOATHE HIM! THE LOONY FROM LATVERIA...TA-DA!
HE IS SO LOVING US RIGHT NOW.
EXCEPT YOU, NOVA.
YOU...KIDS...CAPTURED THE MOST DANGEROUS MAN ON THE PLANET?
YOU DON'T HAVE TO THANK ME, BUT I WOULD ACCEPT A JETPACK--
WAHOO!
YOU DIDN'T CATCH DOOM! YOU WALKED HIM RIGHT INTO MY HELICARRIER.
HUH?
CORRECTION, DIRECTOR FURY...
SHRIPP!
...THEY WALKED A MARK 6 HOBERMAN CHASSIS INTO YOUR HELICARRIER.
I'M GUESSING THAT'S NOT A NEW WASHING MACHINE.

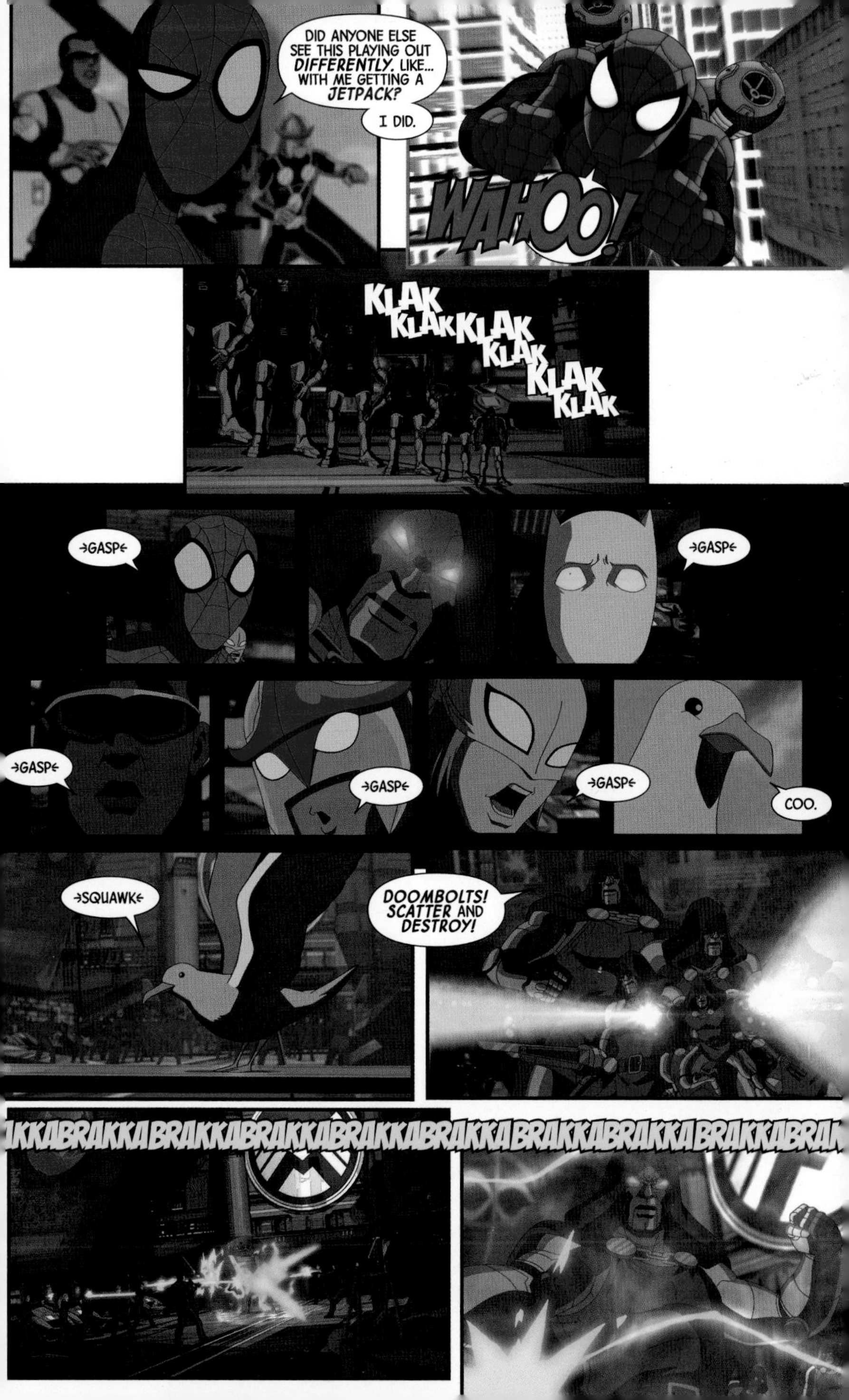

DID ANYONE ELSE SEE THIS PLAYING OUT DIFFERENTLY. LIKE... WITH ME GETTING A JETPACK?
I DID.
WAHOO!
KLAK KLAK KLAK KLAK KLAK KLAK
→GASP←
→GASP←
→GASP←
→GASP←
→GASP←
COO.
→SQUAWK←
DOOMBOLTS! SCATTER AND DESTROY!
BRAKKABRAKKABRAKKABRAKKABRAKKABRAKKABRAKKABRAKKABRAKKABRAKKA

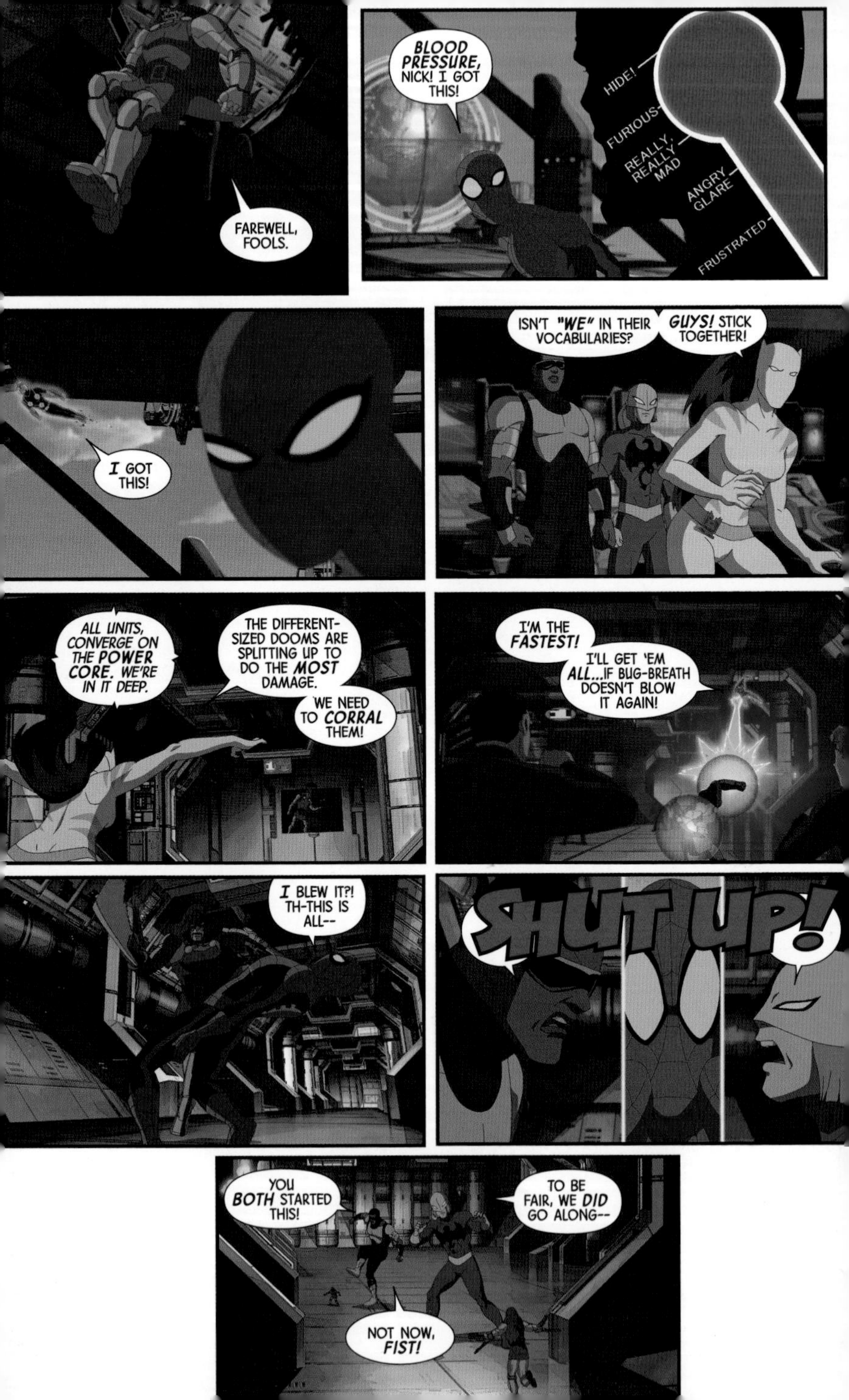

FAREWELL, FOOLS.
BLOOD PRESSURE, NICK! I GOT THIS!
HIDE!
FURIOUS
REALLY, REALLY MAD
ANGRY GLARE
FRUSTRATED
I GOT THIS!
ISN'T "WE" IN THEIR VOCABULARIES?
GUYS! STICK TOGETHER!
ALL UNITS, CONVERGE ON THE POWER CORE. WE'RE IN IT DEEP.
THE DIFFERENT-SIZED DOOMS ARE SPLITTING UP TO DO THE MOST DAMAGE.
WE NEED TO CORRAL THEM!
I'M THE FASTEST!
I'LL GET 'EM ALL...IF BUG-BREATH DOESN'T BLOW IT AGAIN!
I BLEW IT?! TH-THIS IS ALL--
SHUT UP!
YOU BOTH STARTED THIS!
TO BE FAIR, WE DID GO ALONG--
NOT NOW, FIST!

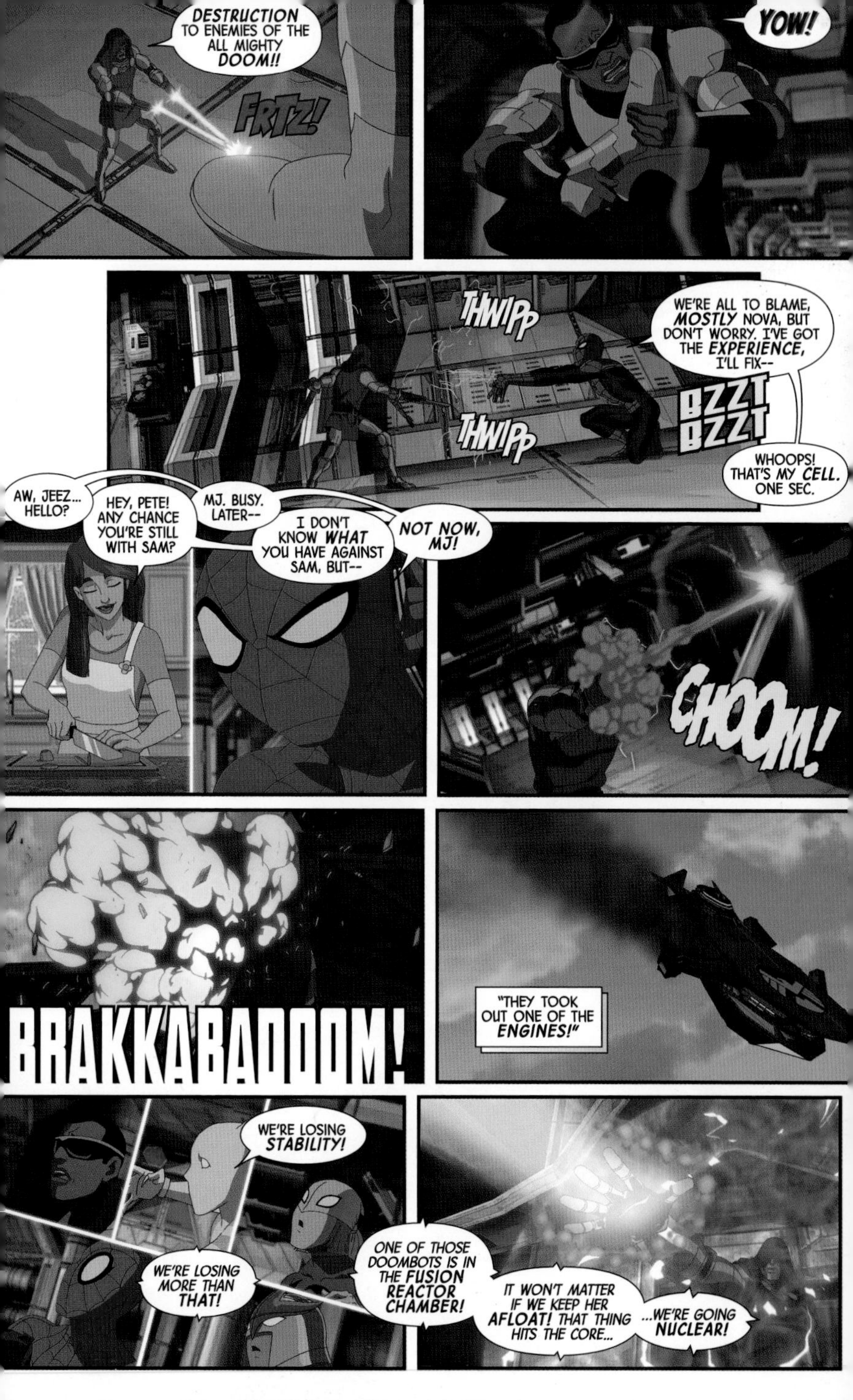
DESTRUCTION TO ENEMIES OF THE ALL MIGHTY DOOM!!
FRTZ!
YOW!
THWIPP
THWIPP
WE'RE ALL TO BLAME, MOSTLY NOVA, BUT DON'T WORRY. I'VE GOT THE EXPERIENCE, I'LL FIX--
BZZT BZZT
WHOOPS! THAT'S MY CELL. ONE SEC.
AW, JEEZ... HELLO?
HEY, PETE! ANY CHANCE YOU'RE STILL WITH SAM?
MJ. BUSY. LATER--
I DON'T KNOW WHAT YOU HAVE AGAINST SAM, BUT--
NOT NOW, MJ!
CHOOM!
BRAKKABADOOM!
"THEY TOOK OUT ONE OF THE ENGINES!"
WE'RE LOSING STABILITY!
WE'RE LOSING MORE THAN THAT!
ONE OF THOSE DOOMBOTS IS IN THE FUSION REACTOR CHAMBER!
IT WON'T MATTER IF WE KEEP HER AFLOAT! THAT THING HITS THE CORE...
...WE'RE GOING NUCLEAR!

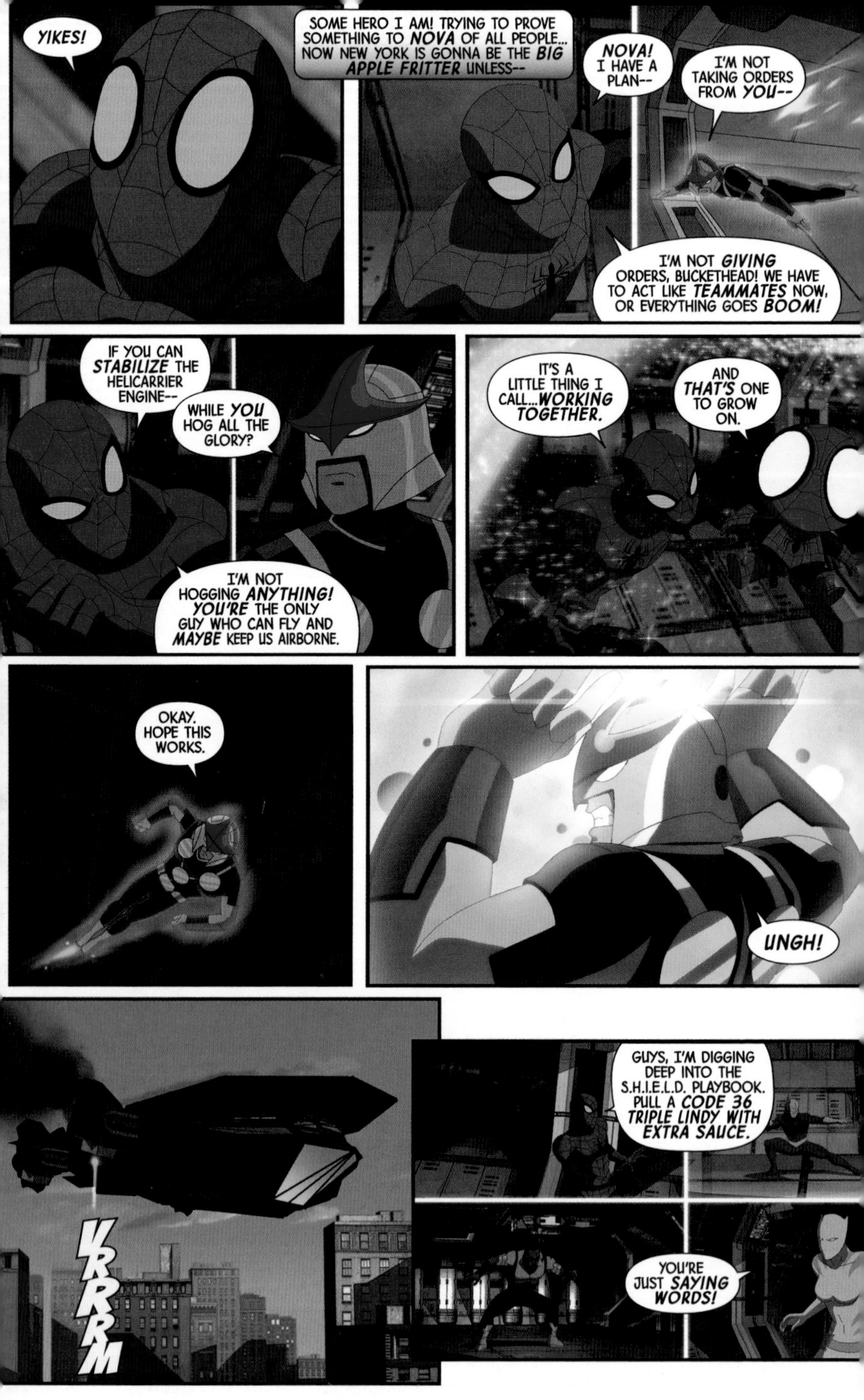
YIKES!
SOME HERO I AM! TRYING TO PROVE SOMETHING TO NOVA OF ALL PEOPLE... NOW NEW YORK IS GONNA BE THE BIG APPLE FRITTER UNLESS--
NOVA! I HAVE A PLAN--
I'M NOT TAKING ORDERS FROM YOU--
I'M NOT GIVING ORDERS, BUCKETHEAD! WE HAVE TO ACT LIKE TEAMMATES NOW, OR EVERYTHING GOES BOOM!
IF YOU CAN STABILIZE THE HELICARRIER ENGINE--
WHILE YOU HOG ALL THE GLORY?
I'M NOT HOGGING ANYTHING! YOU'RE THE ONLY GUY WHO CAN FLY AND MAYBE KEEP US AIRBORNE.
IT'S A LITTLE THING I CALL...WORKING TOGETHER.
AND THAT'S ONE TO GROW ON.
OKAY. HOPE THIS WORKS.
UNGH!
VRRRM
GUYS, I'M DIGGING DEEP INTO THE S.H.I.E.L.D. PLAYBOOK. PULL A CODE 36 TRIPLE LINDY WITH EXTRA SAUCE.
YOU'RE JUST SAYING WORDS!

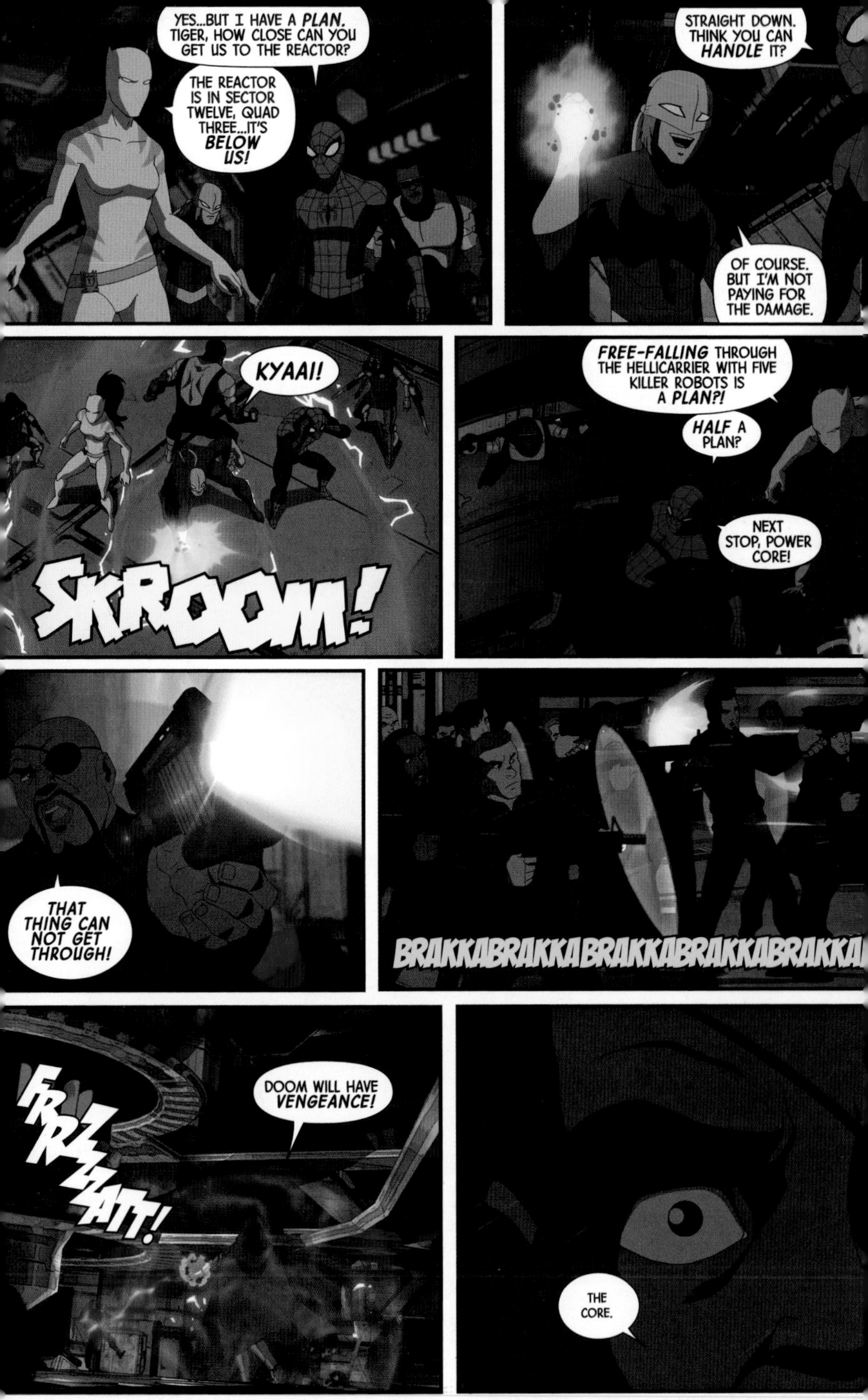
YES...BUT I HAVE A PLAN. TIGER, HOW CLOSE CAN YOU GET US TO THE REACTOR?
THE REACTOR IS IN SECTOR TWELVE, QUAD THREE...IT'S BELOW US!
STRAIGHT DOWN. THINK YOU CAN HANDLE IT?
OF COURSE. BUT I'M NOT PAYING FOR THE DAMAGE.
KYAAI!
SKROOM!
FREE-FALLING THROUGH THE HELLICARRIER WITH FIVE KILLER ROBOTS IS A PLAN?!
HALF A PLAN?
NEXT STOP, POWER CORE!
THAT THING CAN NOT GET THROUGH!
BRAKKABRAKKABRAKKABRAKKABRAKKA
FRZZATT!
DOOM WILL HAVE VENGEANCE!
THE CORE.

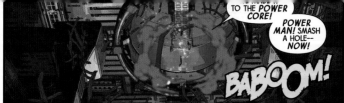

TO THE *POWER CORE!*

POWER *MAN!* SMASH A HOLE-- *NOW!*

BABOOM!

GRAB ON TO EACH OTHER AND I'LL SAVE US FROM *SPLATTING* ON THE GROUND, AND--

THWIPP

UGH! YOU GUYS WEIGH *A TON!*

WHAT HAVE YOU BEEN *EATING?*

→BURP←

HUH?

THAT ACTUALLY *WORKED.*

WE LANDED SAFELY.

ARE *DONE* PATTING YOURSELF ON THE BACK?

THE SHIP'S STABLE. NOVA'S *BACK* IN THE GAME, GUYS!

I'VE GOT HIM-- *ERGH!*

REGARDS FROM VICTOR VON DOOM.

KROOM!

NOVA!!

IN A FEW MOMENTS DOOM SHALL HAVE HIS *REVENGE!*

FINISH IT, WEBS!

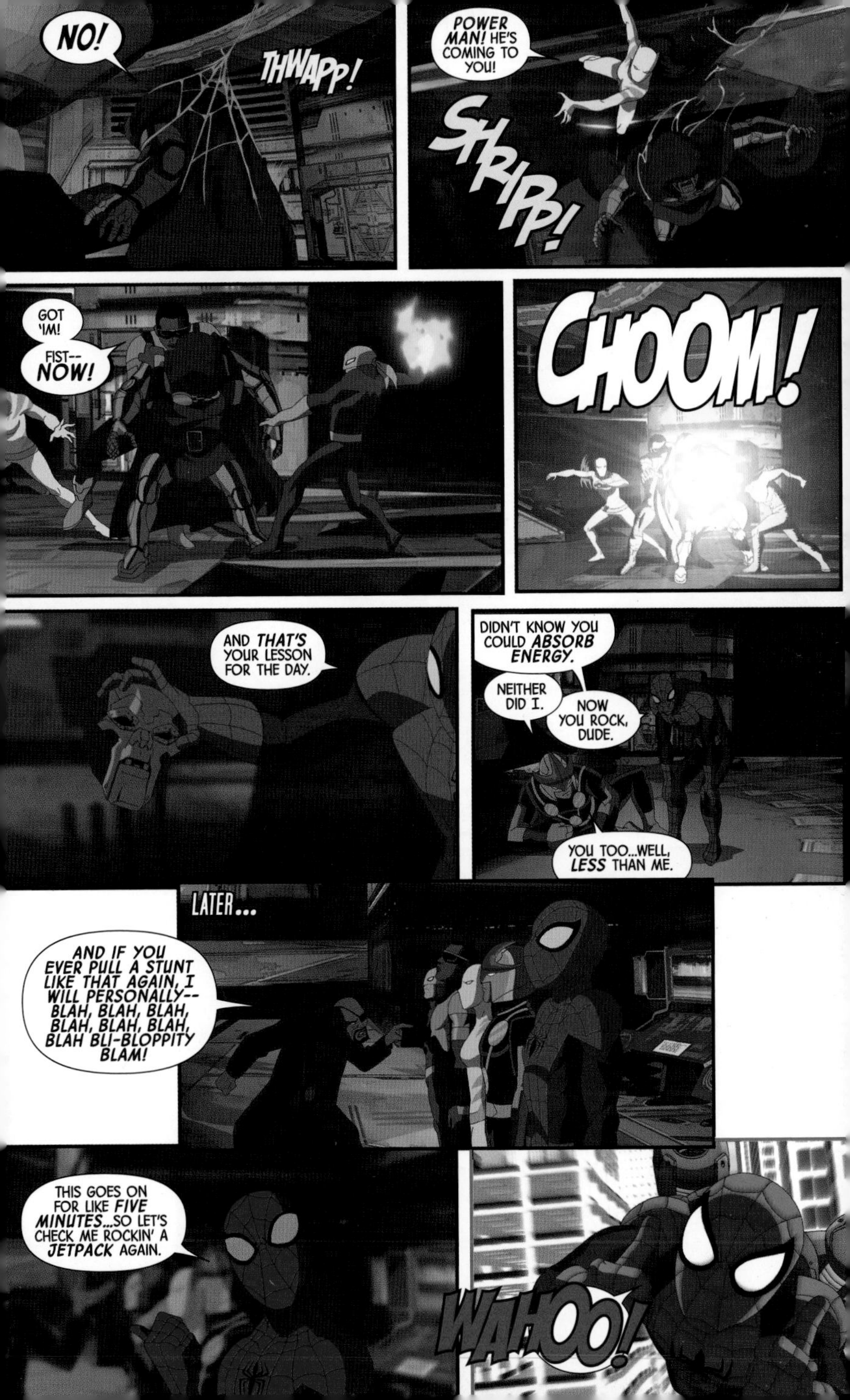
NO!
THWAPP!
POWER MAN! HE'S COMING TO YOU!
SHRIPP!
GOT 'IM!
FIST-- NOW!
CHOOM!
AND THAT'S YOUR LESSON FOR THE DAY.
DIDN'T KNOW YOU COULD ABSORB ENERGY.
NEITHER DID I.
NOW YOU ROCK, DUDE.
YOU TOO...WELL, LESS THAN ME.
LATER...
AND IF YOU EVER PULL A STUNT LIKE THAT AGAIN, I WILL PERSONALLY-- BLAH, BLAH, BLAH, BLAH, BLAH, BLAH, BLAH BLI-BLOPPITY BLAM!
THIS GOES ON FOR LIKE FIVE MINUTES...SO LET'S CHECK ME ROCKIN' A JETPACK AGAIN.
WAHOO!

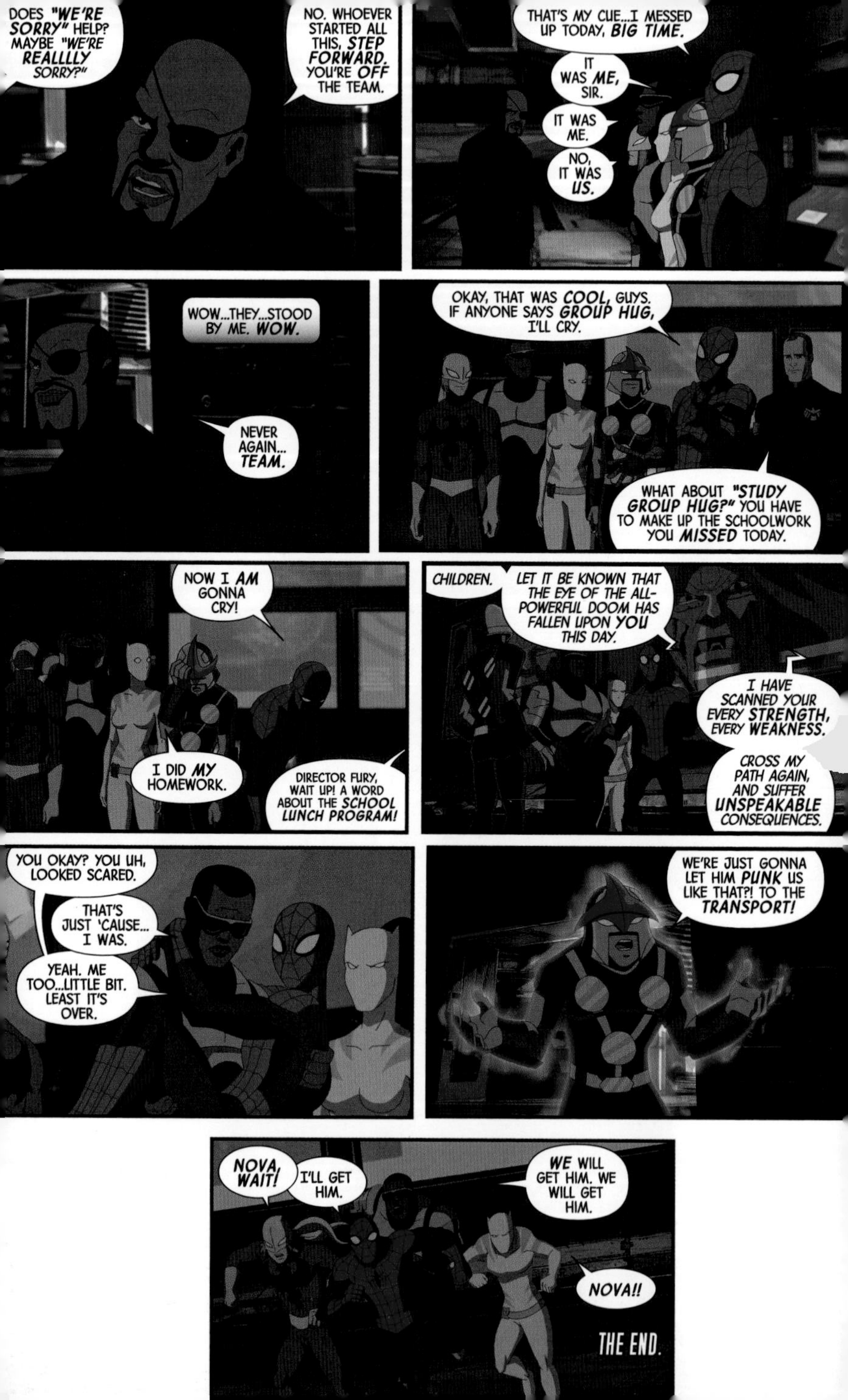
DOES "WE'RE SORRY" HELP? MAYBE "WE'RE REALLLLY SORRY?"
NO. WHOEVER STARTED ALL THIS, STEP FORWARD. YOU'RE OFF THE TEAM.
THAT'S MY CUE...I MESSED UP TODAY, BIG TIME.
IT WAS ME, SIR.
IT WAS ME.
NO, IT WAS US.
WOW...THEY...STOOD BY ME. WOW.
NEVER AGAIN... TEAM.
OKAY, THAT WAS COOL, GUYS. IF ANYONE SAYS GROUP HUG, I'LL CRY.
WHAT ABOUT "STUDY GROUP HUG?" YOU HAVE TO MAKE UP THE SCHOOLWORK YOU MISSED TODAY.
NOW I AM GONNA CRY!
I DID MY HOMEWORK.
DIRECTOR FURY, WAIT UP! A WORD ABOUT THE SCHOOL LUNCH PROGRAM!
CHILDREN.
LET IT BE KNOWN THAT THE EYE OF THE ALL-POWERFUL DOOM HAS FALLEN UPON YOU THIS DAY.
I HAVE SCANNED YOUR EVERY STRENGTH, EVERY WEAKNESS.
CROSS MY PATH AGAIN, AND SUFFER UNSPEAKABLE CONSEQUENCES.
YOU OKAY? YOU UH, LOOKED SCARED.
THAT'S JUST 'CAUSE... I WAS.
YEAH. ME TOO...LITTLE BIT. LEAST IT'S OVER.
WE'RE JUST GONNA LET HIM PUNK US LIKE THAT?! TO THE TRANSPORT!
NOVA, WAIT!
I'LL GET HIM.
WE WILL GET HIM. WE WILL GET HIM.
NOVA!!
THE END.

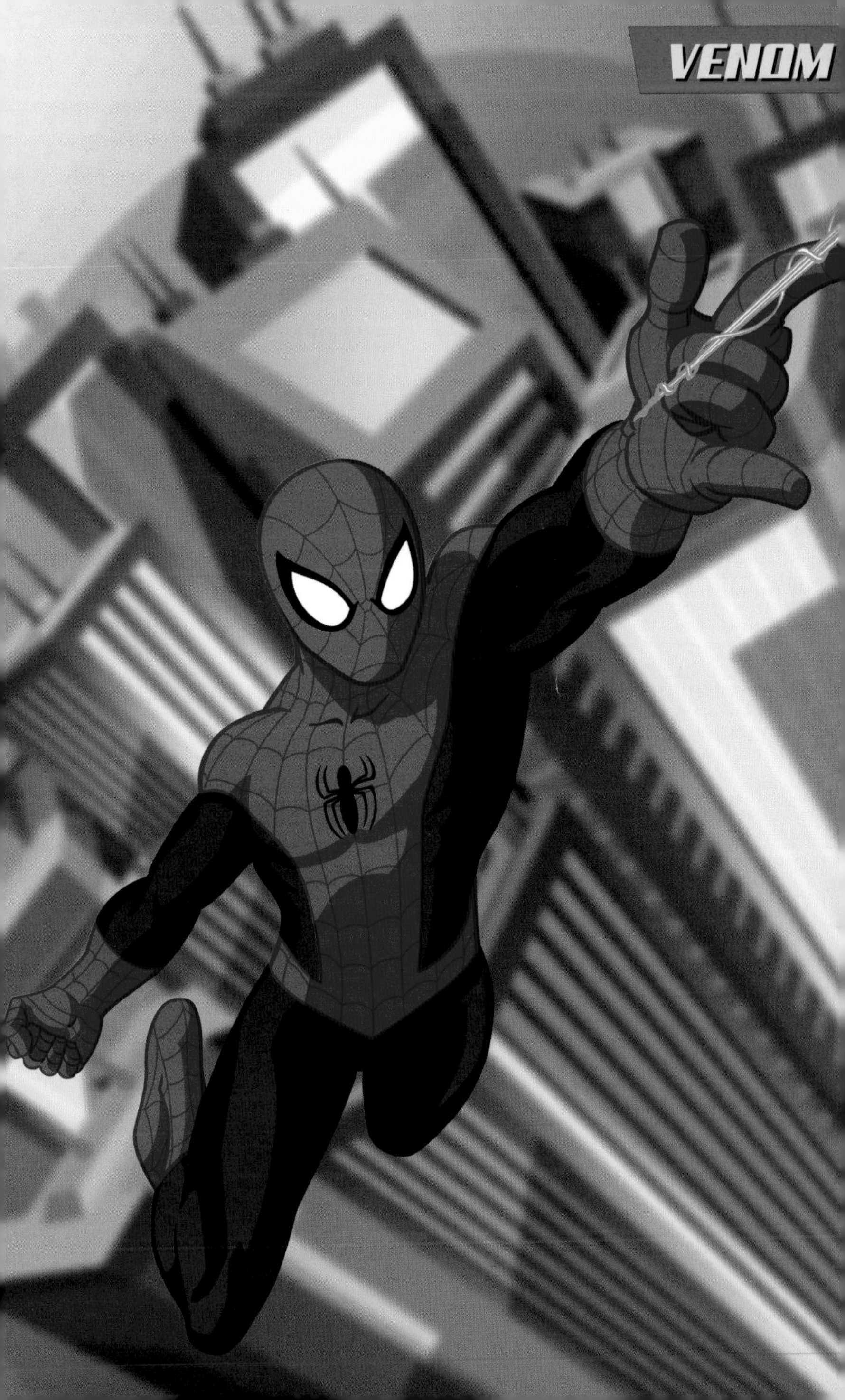

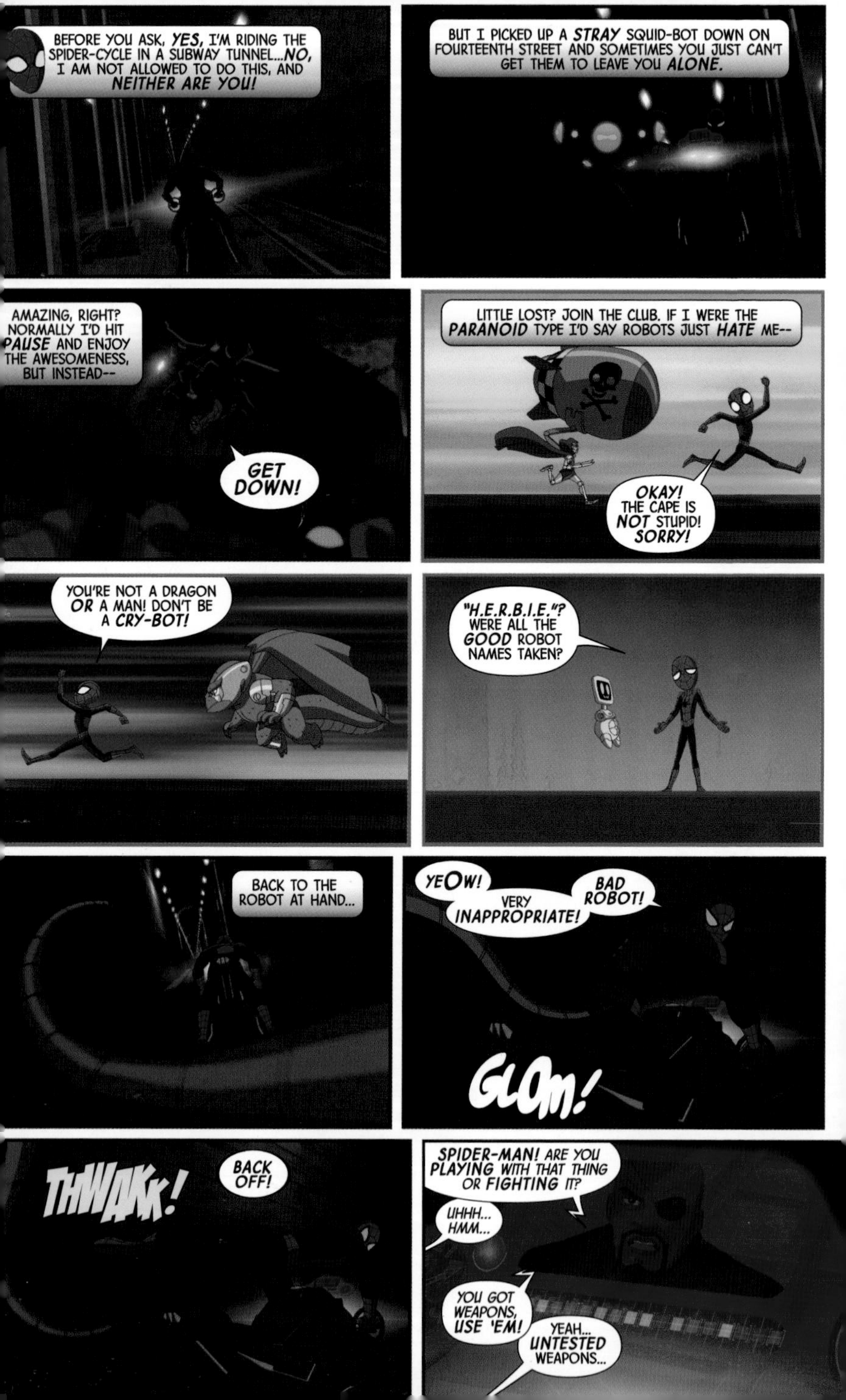
BEFORE YOU ASK, YES, I'M RIDING THE SPIDER-CYCLE IN A SUBWAY TUNNEL...NO, I AM NOT ALLOWED TO DO THIS, AND NEITHER ARE YOU!
BUT I PICKED UP A STRAY SQUID-BOT DOWN ON FOURTEENTH STREET AND SOMETIMES YOU JUST CAN'T GET THEM TO LEAVE YOU ALONE.
AMAZING, RIGHT? NORMALLY I'D HIT PAUSE AND ENJOY THE AWESOMENESS, BUT INSTEAD--
GET DOWN!
LITTLE LOST? JOIN THE CLUB. IF I WERE THE PARANOID TYPE I'D SAY ROBOTS JUST HATE ME--
OKAY! THE CAPE IS NOT STUPID! SORRY!
YOU'RE NOT A DRAGON OR A MAN! DON'T BE A CRY-BOT!
"H.E.R.B.I.E."? WERE ALL THE GOOD ROBOT NAMES TAKEN?
BACK TO THE ROBOT AT HAND...
YEOW!
VERY INAPPROPRIATE!
BAD ROBOT!
GLOM!
THWAKK!
BACK OFF!
SPIDER-MAN! ARE YOU PLAYING WITH THAT THING OR FIGHTING IT?
UHHH... HMM...
YOU GOT WEAPONS, USE 'EM!
YEAH... UNTESTED WEAPONS...

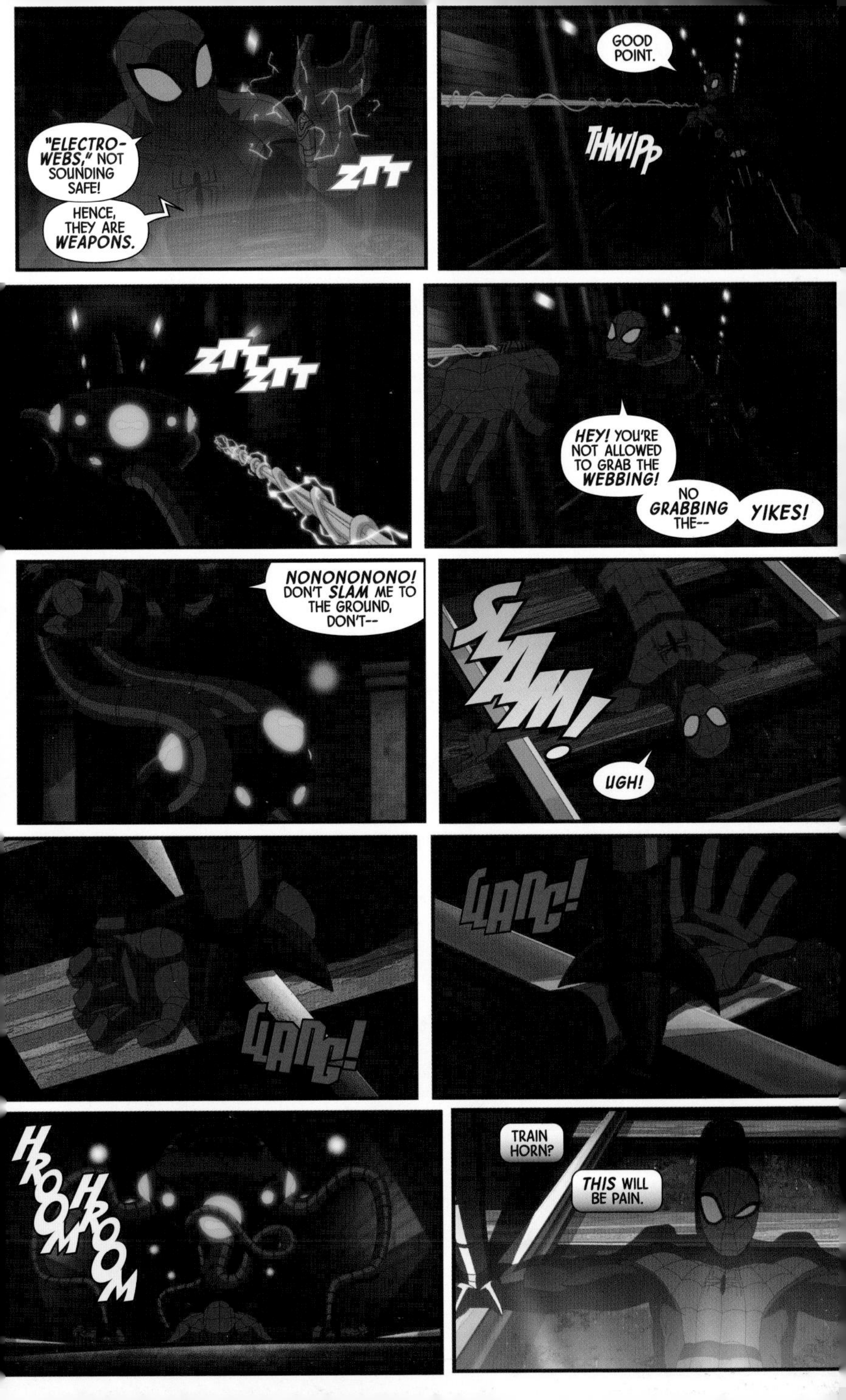

"ELECTRO-WEBS," NOT SOUNDING SAFE!
HENCE, THEY ARE WEAPONS.
ZTT
GOOD POINT.
THWIPP
ZTT ZTT
HEY! YOU'RE NOT ALLOWED TO GRAB THE WEBBING!
NO GRABBING THE--
YIKES!
NONONONONO! DON'T SLAM ME TO THE GROUND, DON'T--
SLAM!
UGH!
CLANG!
CLANG!
HROOM HROOM
TRAIN HORN?
THIS WILL BE PAIN.

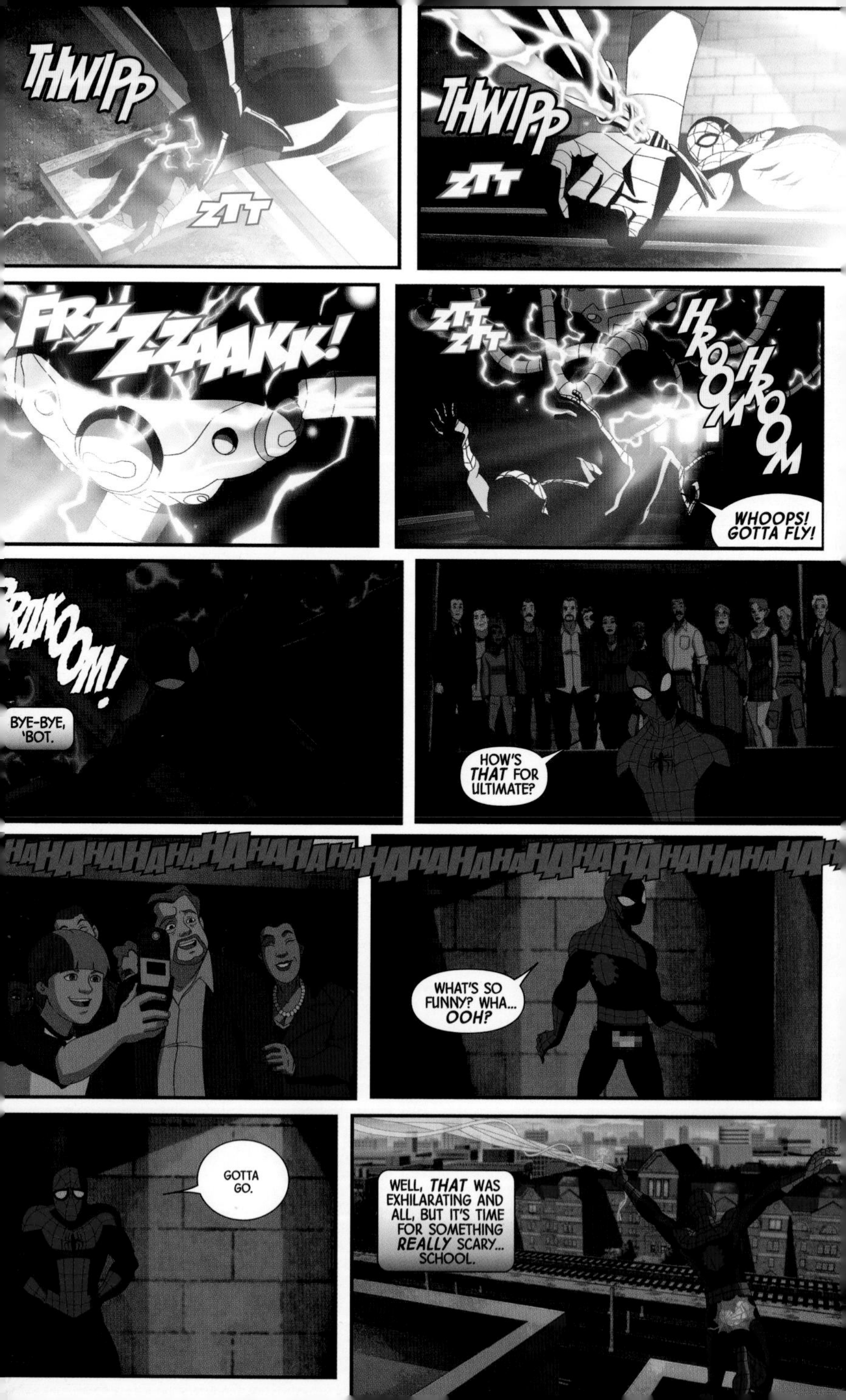
THWIPP
ZTT
THWIPP
ZTT
FRZZZAAKK!
ZTT ZTT
HROOMHROOM
WHOOPS! GOTTA FLY!
BRAKOOM!
BYE-BYE, 'BOT.
HOW'S THAT FOR ULTIMATE?
HAHAHAHAHAHAHAHAHAHAHAHAHAHAHAHAHAHAHAH
WHAT'S SO FUNNY? WHA... OOH?
GOTTA GO.
WELL, THAT WAS EXHILARATING AND ALL, BUT IT'S TIME FOR SOMETHING REALLY SCARY... SCHOOL.

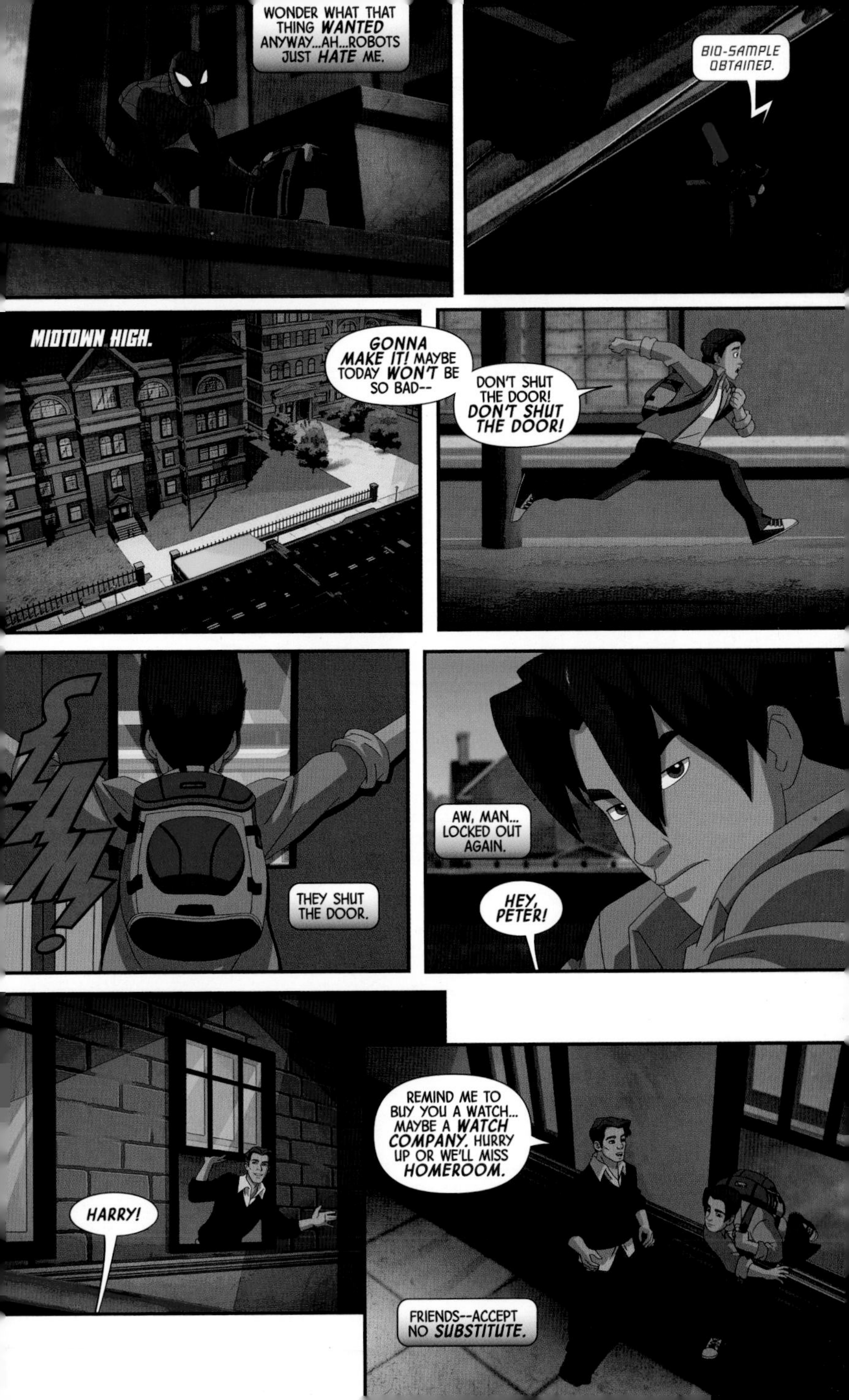
WONDER WHAT THAT THING WANTED ANYWAY...AH...ROBOTS JUST HATE ME.
BIO-SAMPLE OBTAINED.
MIDTOWN HIGH.
GONNA MAKE IT! MAYBE TODAY WON'T BE SO BAD--
DON'T SHUT THE DOOR! DON'T SHUT THE DOOR!
THEY SHUT THE DOOR.
AW, MAN... LOCKED OUT AGAIN.
HEY, PETER!
HARRY!
REMIND ME TO BUY YOU A WATCH... MAYBE A WATCH COMPANY. HURRY UP OR WE'LL MISS HOMEROOM.
FRIENDS--ACCEPT NO SUBSTITUTE.

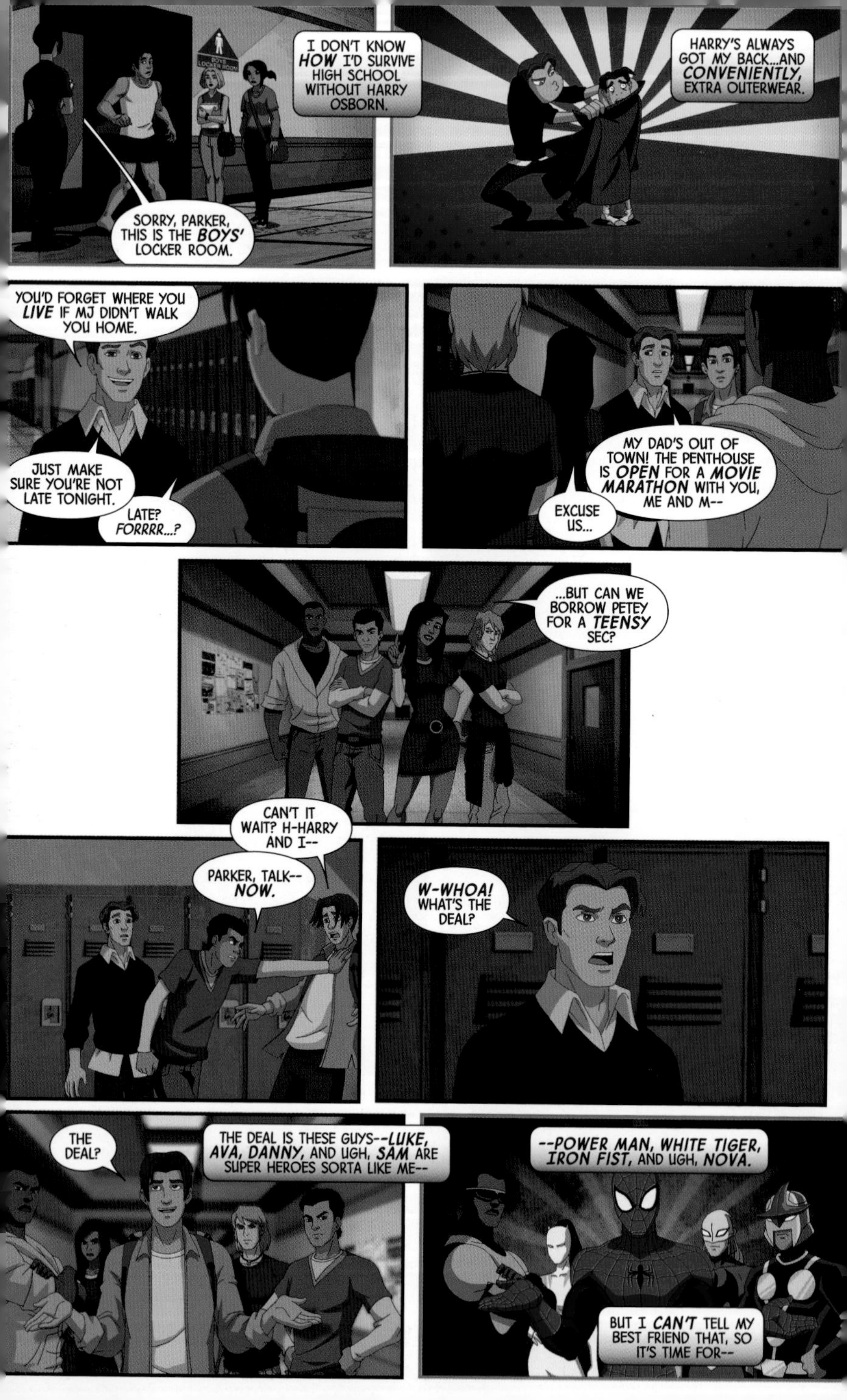

I DON'T KNOW HOW I'D SURVIVE HIGH SCHOOL WITHOUT HARRY OSBORN.
BOYS' LOCKER ROOM
SORRY, PARKER, THIS IS THE BOYS' LOCKER ROOM.
HARRY'S ALWAYS GOT MY BACK...AND CONVENIENTLY, EXTRA OUTERWEAR.
YOU'D FORGET WHERE YOU LIVE IF MJ DIDN'T WALK YOU HOME.
JUST MAKE SURE YOU'RE NOT LATE TONIGHT.
LATE? FORRRR...?
MY DAD'S OUT OF TOWN! THE PENTHOUSE IS OPEN FOR A MOVIE MARATHON WITH YOU, ME AND M--
EXCUSE US...
...BUT CAN WE BORROW PETEY FOR A TEENSY SEC?
CAN'T IT WAIT? H-HARRY AND I--
PARKER, TALK-- NOW.
W-WHOA! WHAT'S THE DEAL?
THE DEAL?
THE DEAL IS THESE GUYS--LUKE, AVA, DANNY, AND UGH, SAM ARE SUPER HEROES SORTA LIKE ME--
--POWER MAN, WHITE TIGER, IRON FIST, AND UGH, NOVA.
BUT I CAN'T TELL MY BEST FRIEND THAT, SO IT'S TIME FOR--

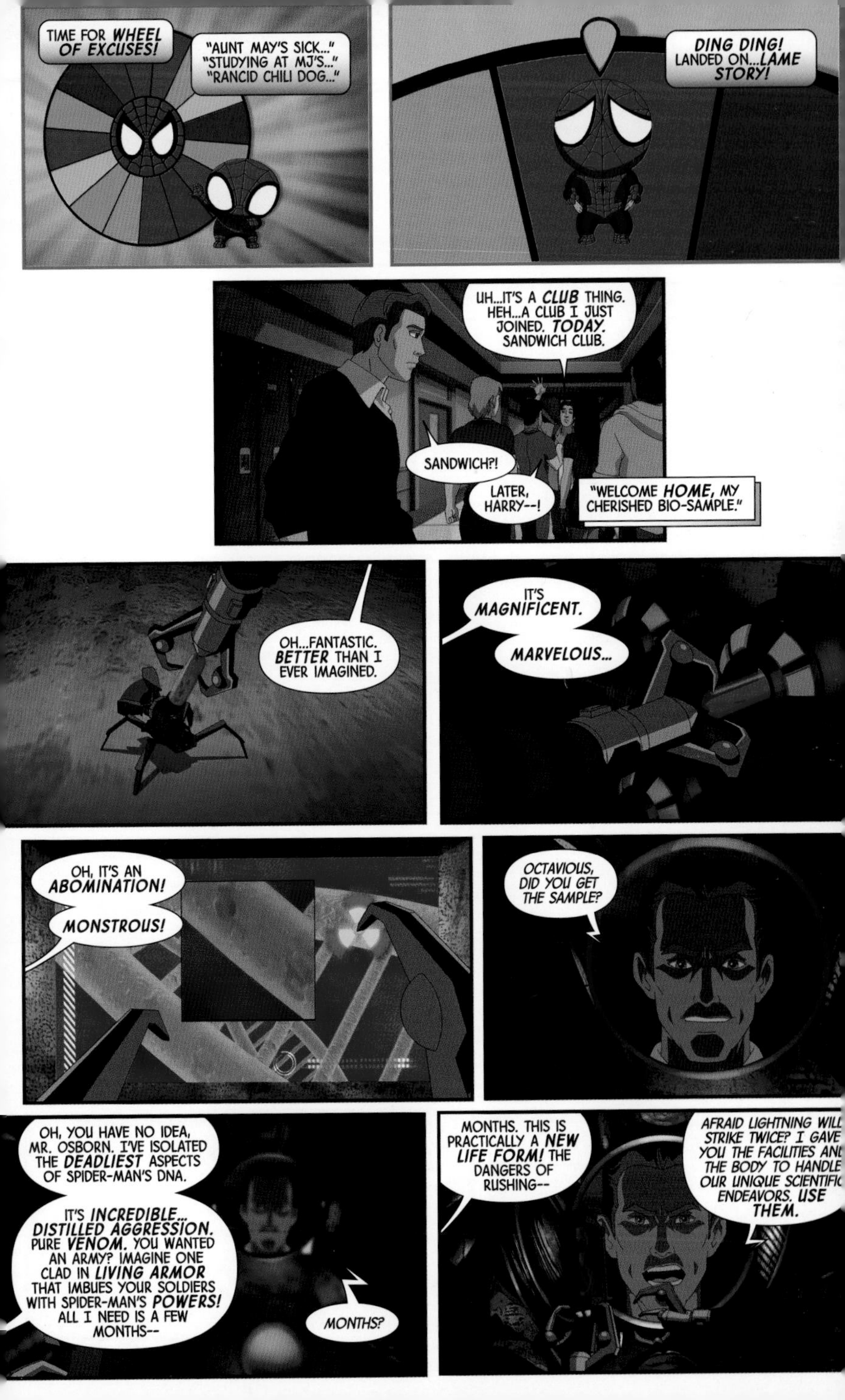
TIME FOR WHEEL OF EXCUSES!
"AUNT MAY'S SICK..." "STUDYING AT MJ'S..." "RANCID CHILI DOG..."
DING DING! LANDED ON...LAME STORY!
UH...IT'S A CLUB THING. HEH...A CLUB I JUST JOINED. TODAY. SANDWICH CLUB.
SANDWICH?!
LATER, HARRY--!
"WELCOME HOME, MY CHERISHED BIO-SAMPLE."
OH...FANTASTIC. BETTER THAN I EVER IMAGINED.
IT'S MAGNIFICENT.
MARVELOUS...
OH, IT'S AN ABOMINATION!
MONSTROUS!
OCTAVIOUS, DID YOU GET THE SAMPLE?
OH, YOU HAVE NO IDEA, MR. OSBORN. I'VE ISOLATED THE DEADLIEST ASPECTS OF SPIDER-MAN'S DNA.
IT'S INCREDIBLE... DISTILLED AGGRESSION. PURE VENOM. YOU WANTED AN ARMY? IMAGINE ONE CLAD IN LIVING ARMOR THAT IMBUES YOUR SOLDIERS WITH SPIDER-MAN'S POWERS! ALL I NEED IS A FEW MONTHS--
MONTHS?
MONTHS. THIS IS PRACTICALLY A NEW LIFE FORM! THE DANGERS OF RUSHING--
AFRAID LIGHTNING WILL STRIKE TWICE? I GAVE YOU THE FACILITIES AND THE BODY TO HANDLE OUR UNIQUE SCIENTIFIC ENDEAVORS. USE THEM.

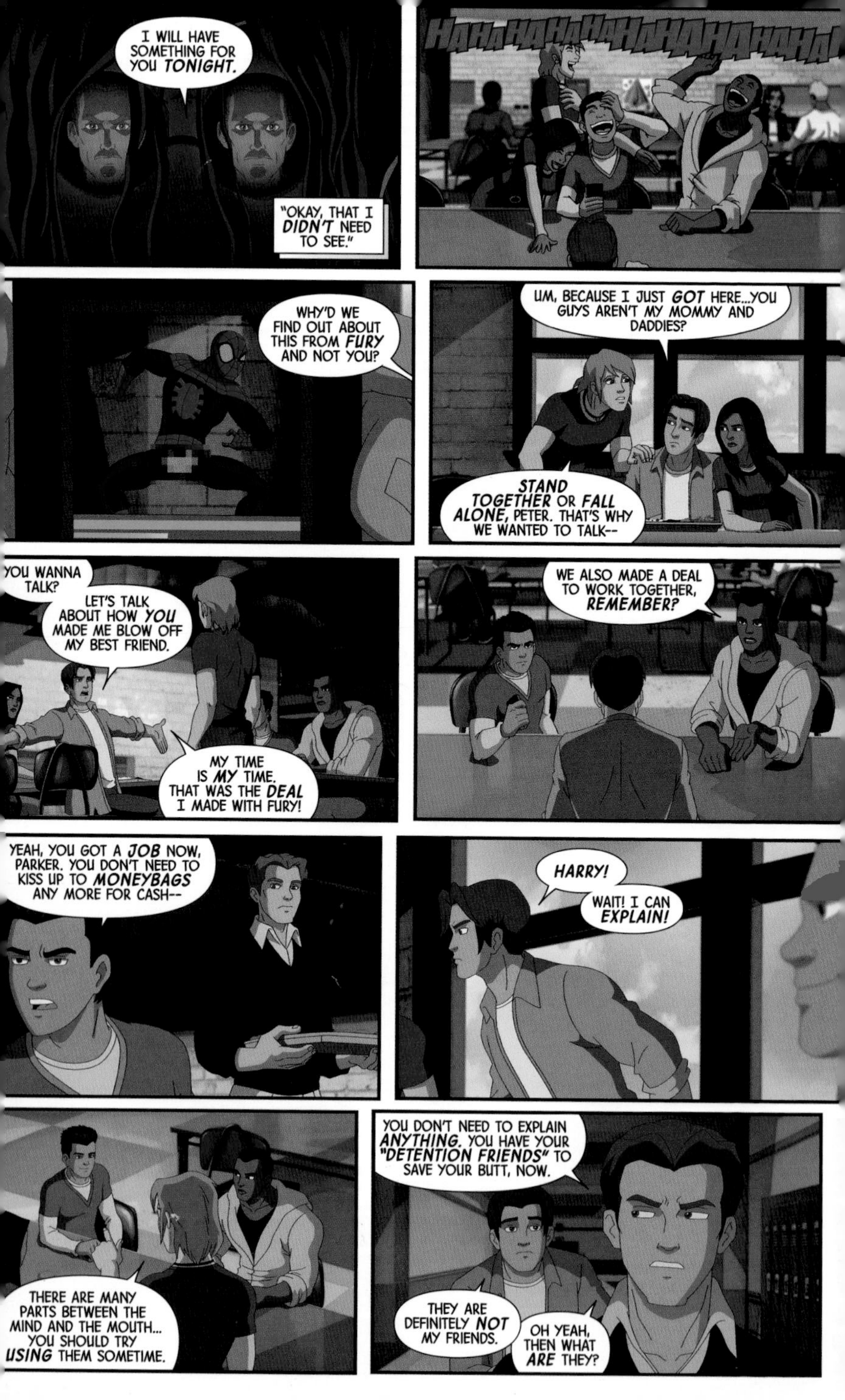
I WILL HAVE SOMETHING FOR YOU TONIGHT.
"OKAY, THAT I DIDN'T NEED TO SEE."
HAHAHAHAHAHAHAHAHAHAHAHA!
WHY'D WE FIND OUT ABOUT THIS FROM FURY AND NOT YOU?
UM, BECAUSE I JUST GOT HERE...YOU GUYS AREN'T MY MOMMY AND DADDIES?
STAND TOGETHER OR FALL ALONE, PETER. THAT'S WHY WE WANTED TO TALK--
YOU WANNA TALK?
LET'S TALK ABOUT HOW YOU MADE ME BLOW OFF MY BEST FRIEND.
MY TIME IS MY TIME. THAT WAS THE DEAL I MADE WITH FURY!
WE ALSO MADE A DEAL TO WORK TOGETHER, REMEMBER?
YEAH, YOU GOT A JOB NOW, PARKER. YOU DON'T NEED TO KISS UP TO MONEYBAGS ANY MORE FOR CASH--
HARRY!
WAIT! I CAN EXPLAIN!
THERE ARE MANY PARTS BETWEEN THE MIND AND THE MOUTH... YOU SHOULD TRY USING THEM SOMETIME.
YOU DON'T NEED TO EXPLAIN ANYTHING. YOU HAVE YOUR "DETENTION FRIENDS" TO SAVE YOUR BUTT, NOW.
THEY ARE DEFINITELY NOT MY FRIENDS.
OH YEAH, THEN WHAT ARE THEY?

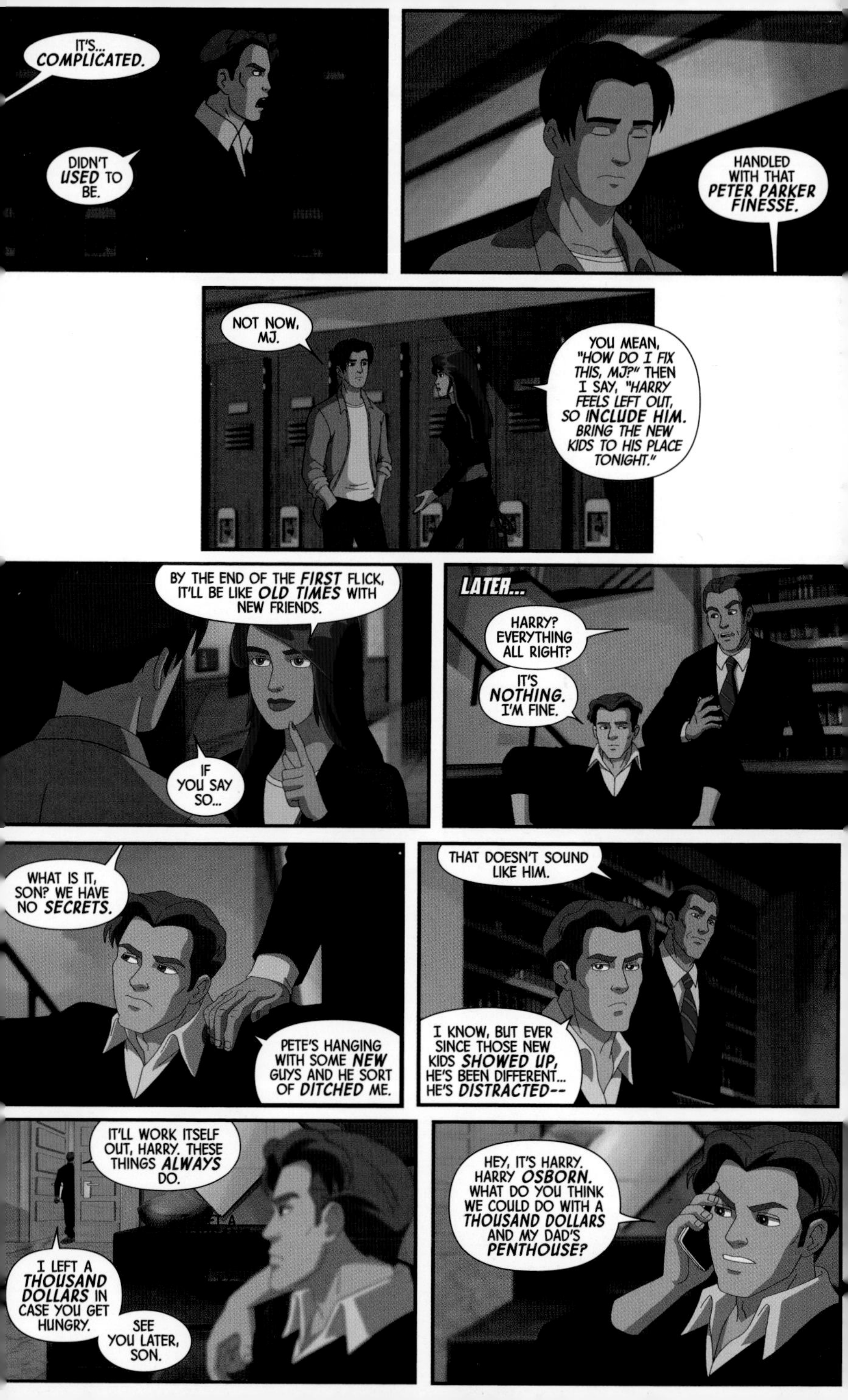
IT'S... COMPLICATED.
DIDN'T USED TO BE.
HANDLED WITH THAT PETER PARKER FINESSE.
NOT NOW, MJ.
YOU MEAN, "HOW DO I FIX THIS, MJ?" THEN I SAY, "HARRY FEELS LEFT OUT, SO INCLUDE HIM. BRING THE NEW KIDS TO HIS PLACE TONIGHT."
BY THE END OF THE FIRST FLICK, IT'LL BE LIKE OLD TIMES WITH NEW FRIENDS.
IF YOU SAY SO...
LATER...
HARRY? EVERYTHING ALL RIGHT?
IT'S NOTHING. I'M FINE.
WHAT IS IT, SON? WE HAVE NO SECRETS.
PETE'S HANGING WITH SOME NEW GUYS AND HE SORT OF DITCHED ME.
THAT DOESN'T SOUND LIKE HIM.
I KNOW, BUT EVER SINCE THOSE NEW KIDS SHOWED UP, HE'S BEEN DIFFERENT... HE'S DISTRACTED--
IT'LL WORK ITSELF OUT, HARRY. THESE THINGS ALWAYS DO.
I LEFT A THOUSAND DOLLARS IN CASE YOU GET HUNGRY.
SEE YOU LATER, SON.
HEY, IT'S HARRY. HARRY OSBORN. WHAT DO YOU THINK WE COULD DO WITH A THOUSAND DOLLARS AND MY DAD'S PENTHOUSE?

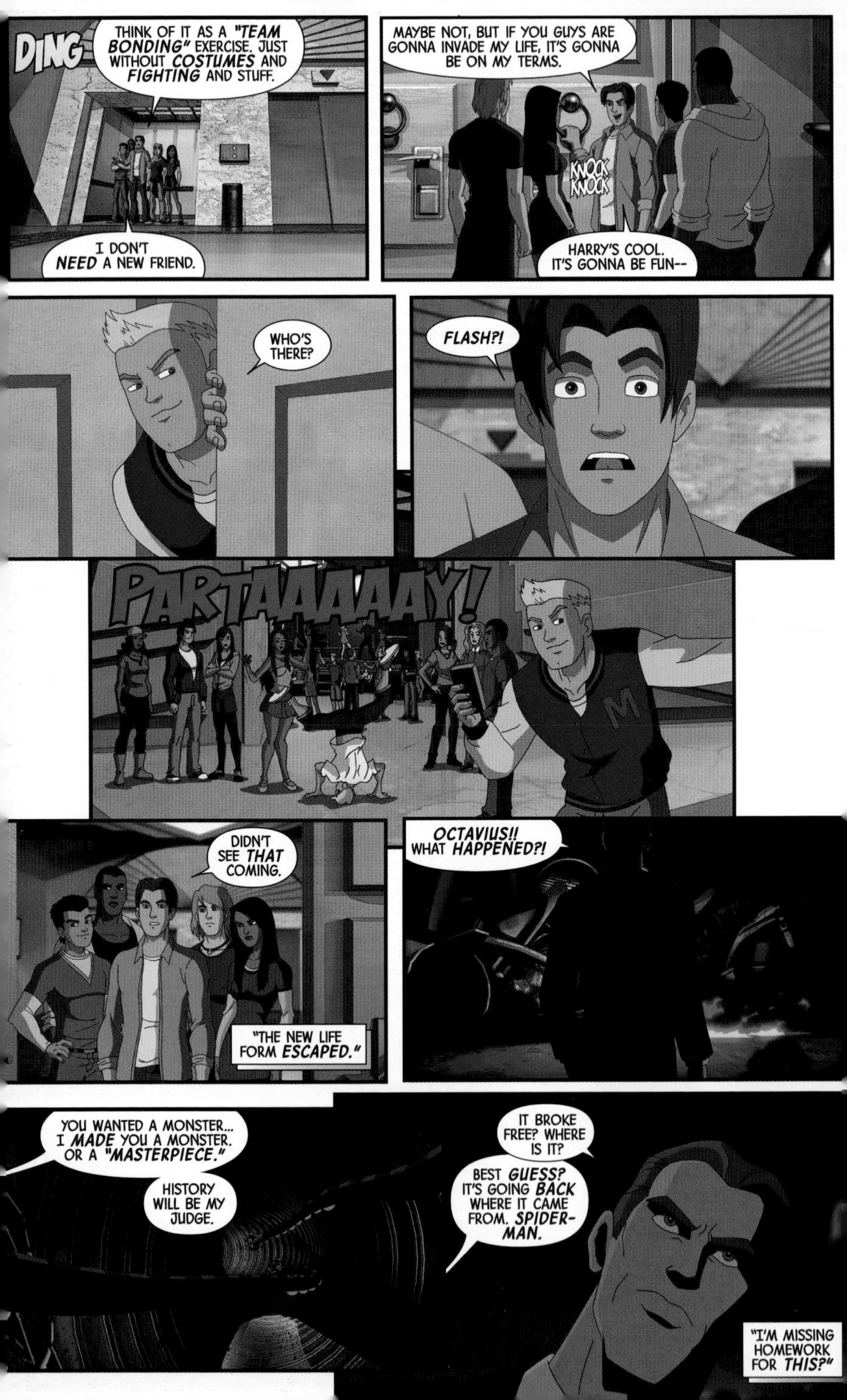
DING
THINK OF IT AS A "TEAM BONDING" EXERCISE. JUST WITHOUT COSTUMES AND FIGHTING AND STUFF.
I DON'T NEED A NEW FRIEND.
MAYBE NOT, BUT IF YOU GUYS ARE GONNA INVADE MY LIFE, IT'S GONNA BE ON MY TERMS.
KNOCK KNOCK
HARRY'S COOL. IT'S GONNA BE FUN--
WHO'S THERE?
FLASH?!
PARTAAAAAY!
M
DIDN'T SEE THAT COMING.
"THE NEW LIFE FORM ESCAPED."
OCTAVIUS!! WHAT HAPPENED?!
YOU WANTED A MONSTER... I MADE YOU A MONSTER. OR A "MASTERPIECE."
HISTORY WILL BE MY JUDGE.
IT BROKE FREE? WHERE IS IT?
BEST GUESS? IT'S GOING BACK WHERE IT CAME FROM. SPIDER-MAN.
"I'M MISSING HOMEWORK FOR THIS?"

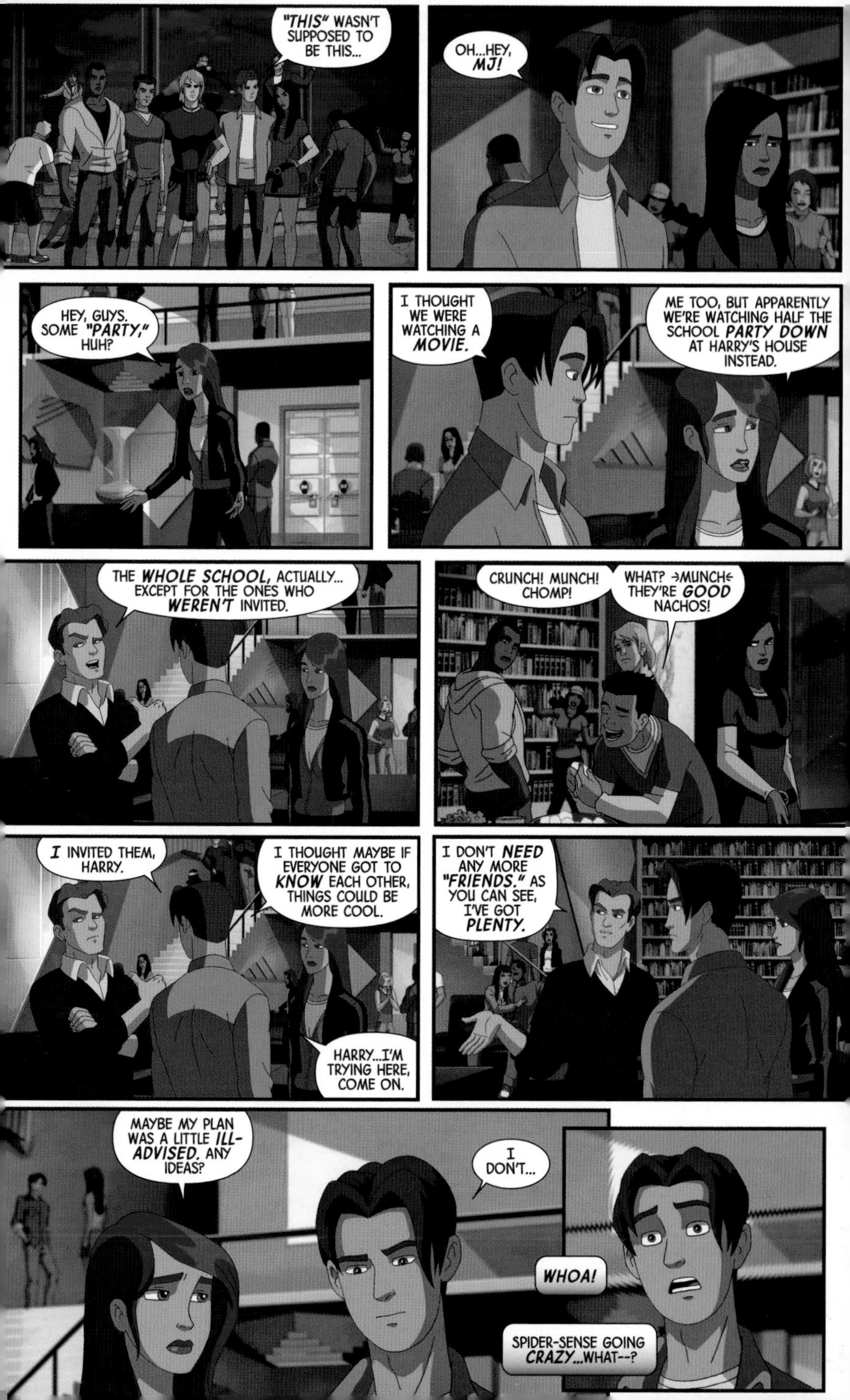
"THIS" WASN'T SUPPOSED TO BE THIS...
OH...HEY, MJ!
HEY, GUYS. SOME "PARTY," HUH?
I THOUGHT WE WERE WATCHING A MOVIE.
ME TOO, BUT APPARENTLY WE'RE WATCHING HALF THE SCHOOL PARTY DOWN AT HARRY'S HOUSE INSTEAD.
THE WHOLE SCHOOL, ACTUALLY... EXCEPT FOR THE ONES WHO WEREN'T INVITED.
CRUNCH! MUNCH! CHOMP!
WHAT? →MUNCH← THEY'RE GOOD NACHOS!
I INVITED THEM, HARRY.
I THOUGHT MAYBE IF EVERYONE GOT TO KNOW EACH OTHER, THINGS COULD BE MORE COOL.
HARRY...I'M TRYING HERE, COME ON.
I DON'T NEED ANY MORE "FRIENDS." AS YOU CAN SEE, I'VE GOT PLENTY.
MAYBE MY PLAN WAS A LITTLE ILL-ADVISED. ANY IDEAS?
I DON'T...
WHOA!
SPIDER-SENSE GOING CRAZY...WHAT--?

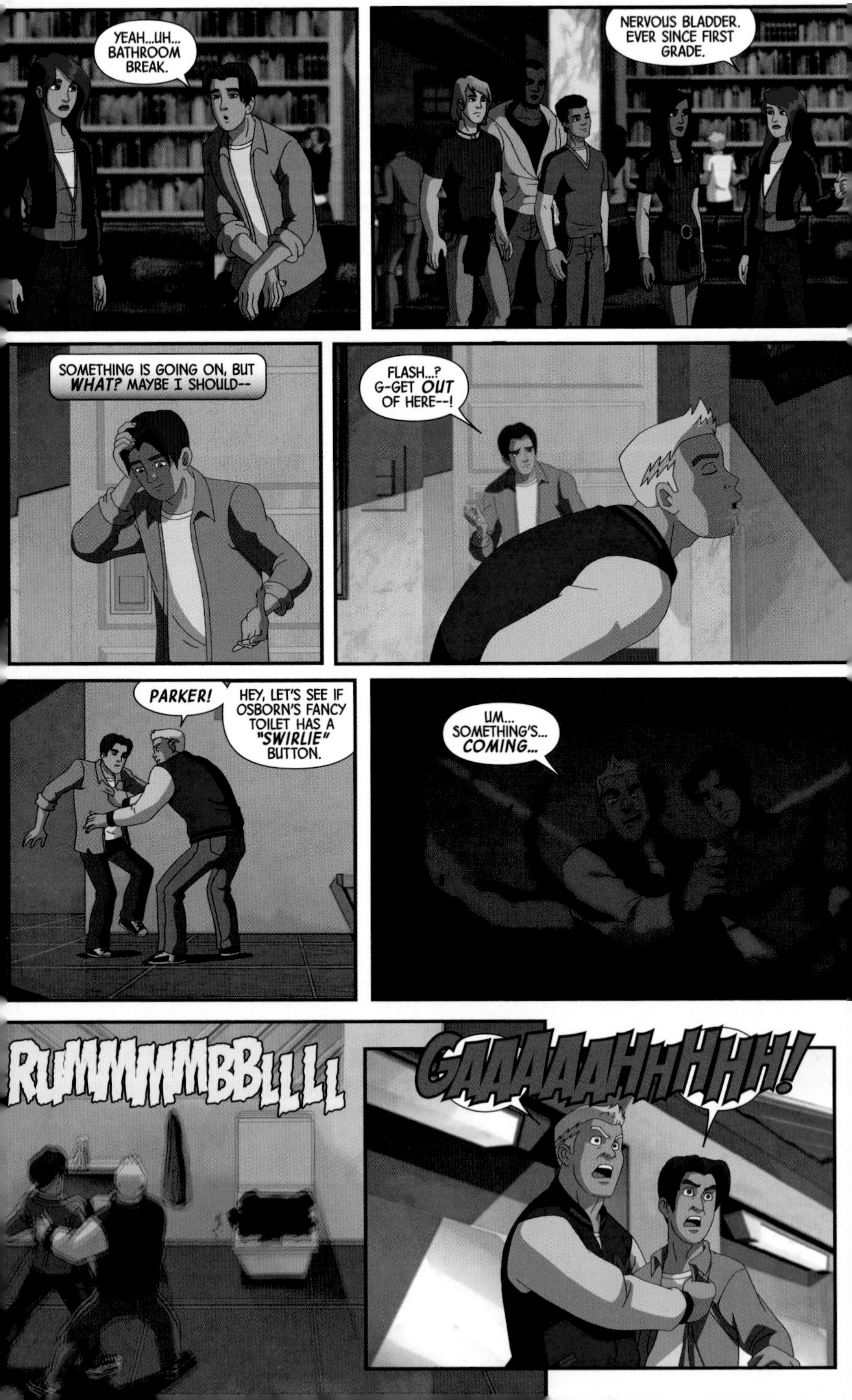
YEAH...UH... BATHROOM BREAK.
NERVOUS BLADDER. EVER SINCE FIRST GRADE.
SOMETHING IS GOING ON, BUT *WHAT?* MAYBE I SHOULD--
FLASH...? G-GET *OUT* OF HERE--!
PARKER!
HEY, LET'S SEE IF OSBORN'S FANCY TOILET HAS A *"SWIRLIE"* BUTTON.
UM... SOMETHING'S... *COMING...*
RUMMMMBBLLLL
GAAAAAHHHHH!

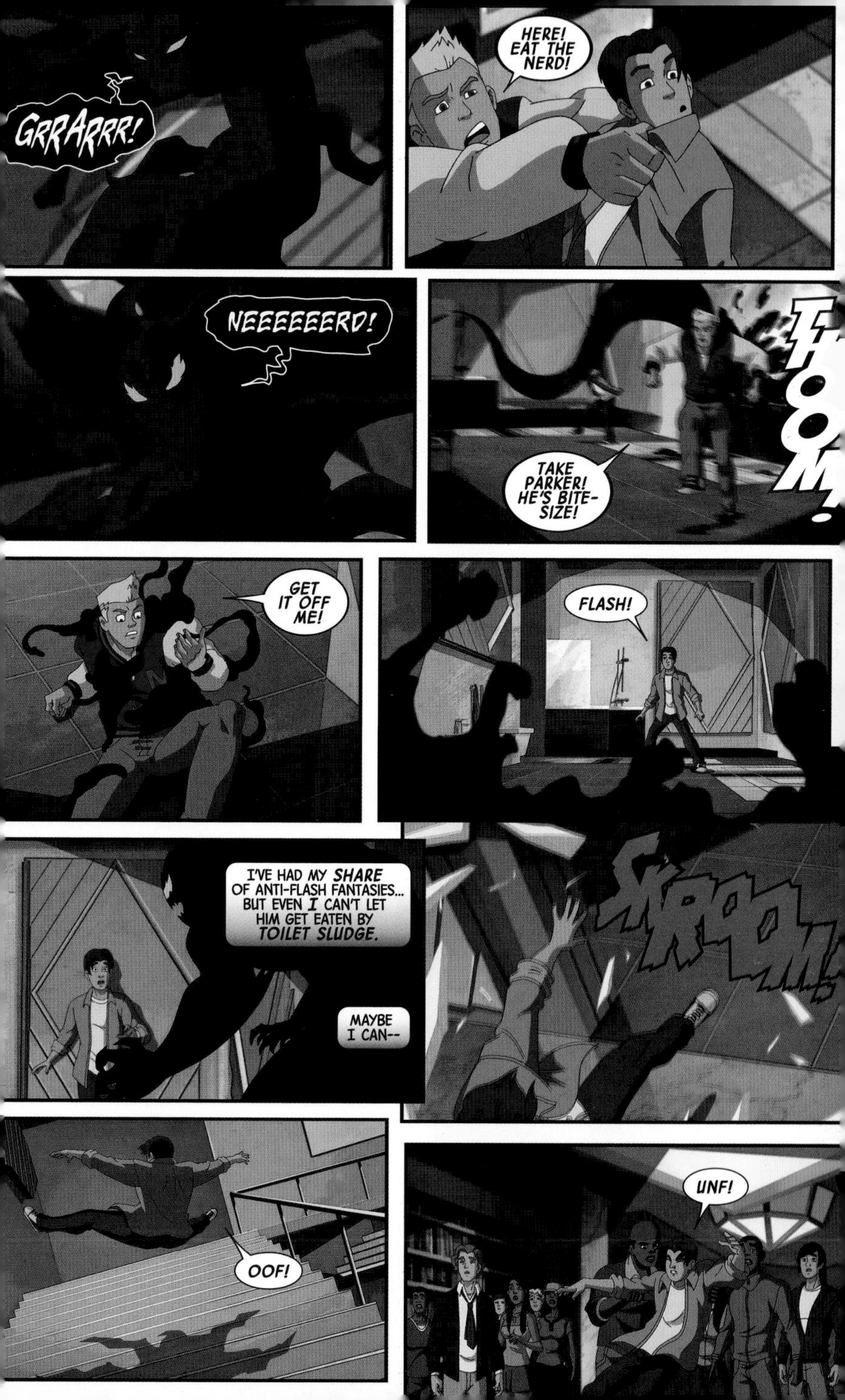
GRRARRR!
HERE! EAT THE NERD!
NEEEEEEERD!
TAKE PARKER! HE'S BITE-SIZE!
FOOM!
GET IT OFF ME!
FLASH!
I'VE HAD MY SHARE OF ANTI-FLASH FANTASIES... BUT EVEN I CAN'T LET HIM GET EATEN BY TOILET SLUDGE.
MAYBE I CAN--
SPROOM!
OOF!
UNF!

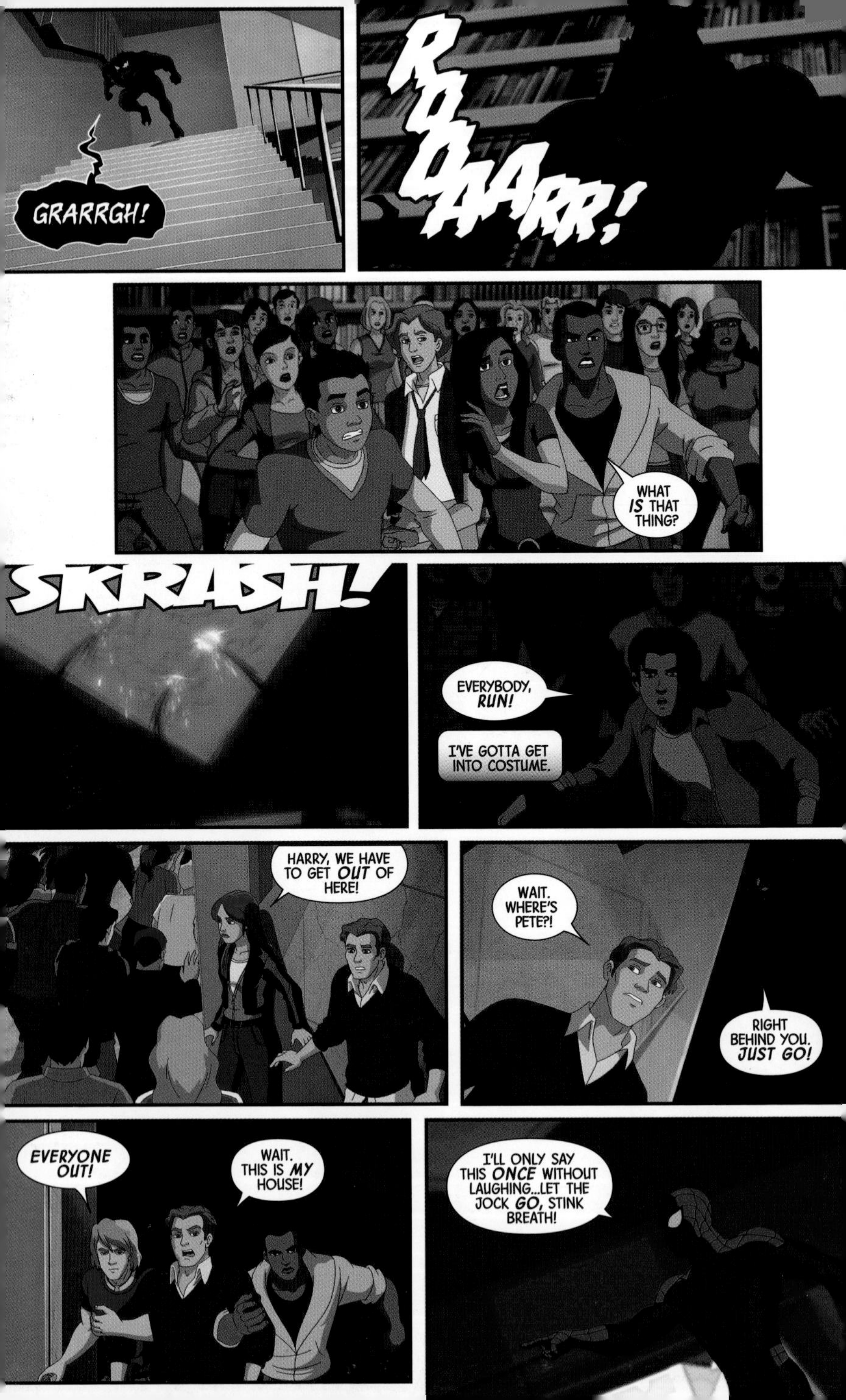
GRARRGH!
ROOAARR!
WHAT IS THAT THING?
SKRASH!
EVERYBODY, RUN!
I'VE GOTTA GET INTO COSTUME.
HARRY, WE HAVE TO GET OUT OF HERE!
WAIT. WHERE'S PETE?!
RIGHT BEHIND YOU. JUST GO!
EVERYONE OUT!
WAIT. THIS IS MY HOUSE!
I'LL ONLY SAY THIS ONCE WITHOUT LAUGHING...LET THE JOCK GO, STINK BREATH!

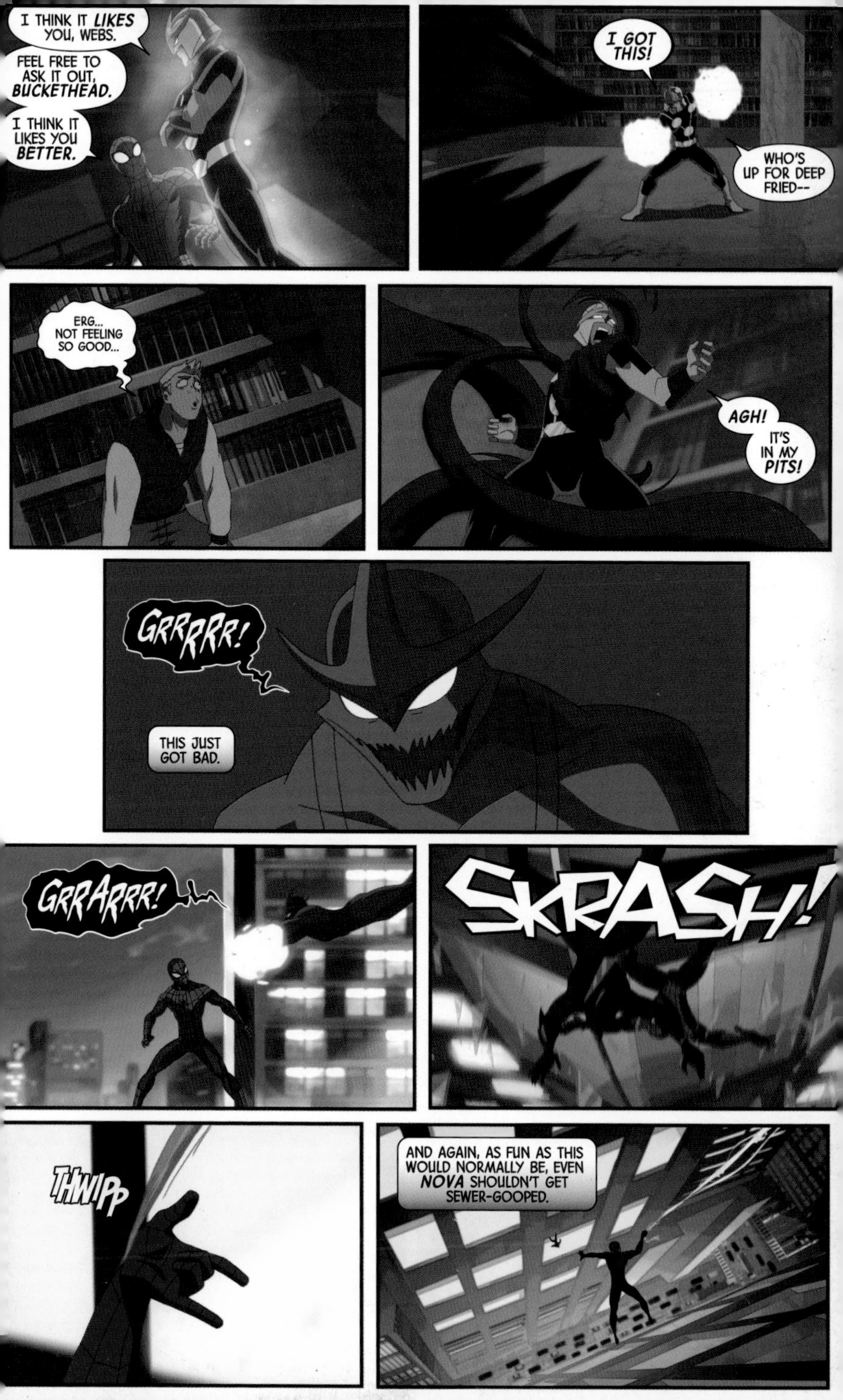
I THINK IT LIKES YOU, WEBS.
FEEL FREE TO ASK IT OUT, BUCKETHEAD.
I THINK IT LIKES YOU BETTER.
I GOT THIS!
WHO'S UP FOR DEEP FRIED--
ERG... NOT FEELING SO GOOD...
AGH!
IT'S IN MY PITS!
GRRRRR!
THIS JUST GOT BAD.
GRRARRR!
SKRASH!
THWIPP
AND AGAIN, AS FUN AS THIS WOULD NORMALLY BE, EVEN NOVA SHOULDN'T GET SEWER-GOOPED.

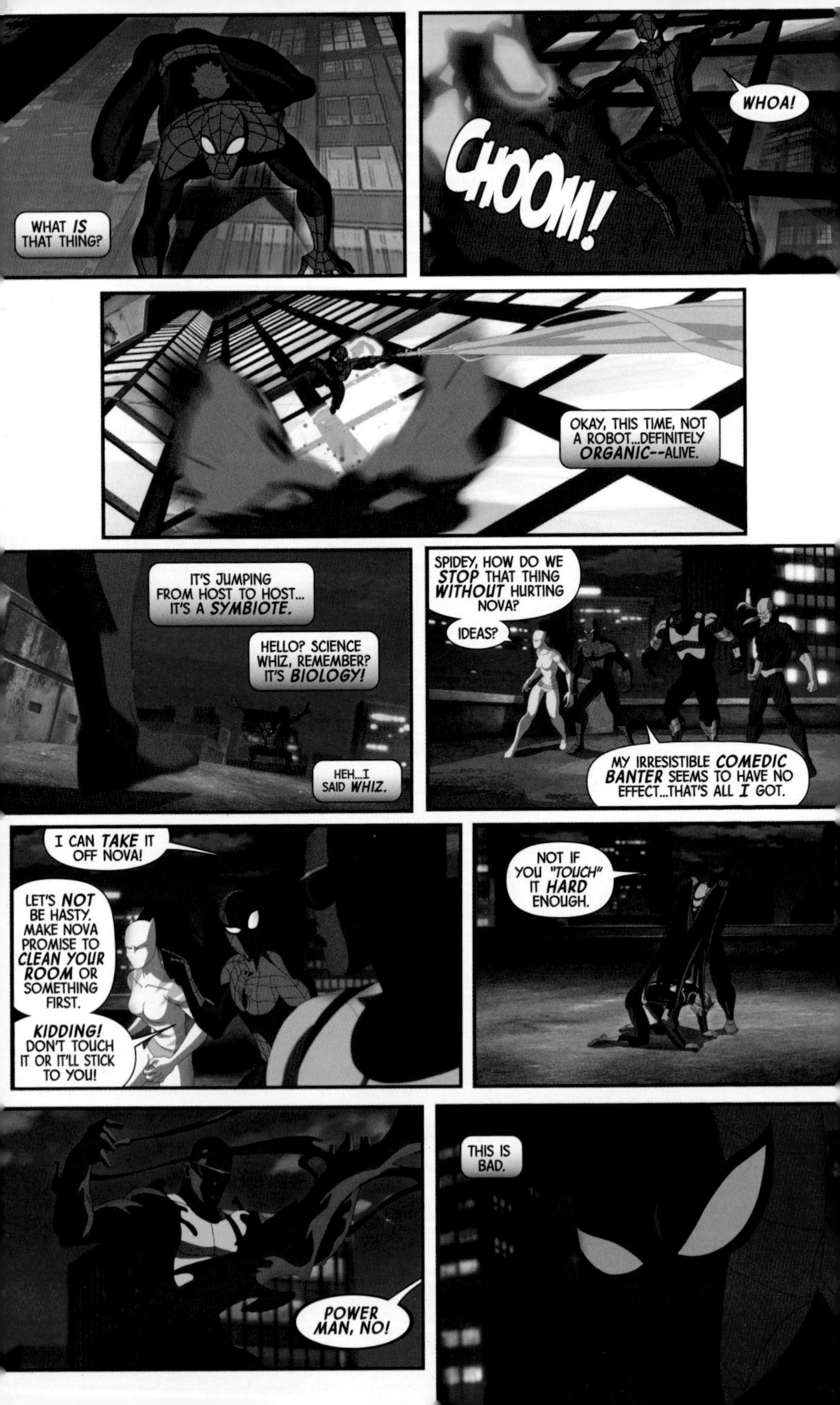
WHAT *IS* THAT THING?
WHOA!
CHOOM!
OKAY, THIS TIME, NOT A ROBOT...DEFINITELY *ORGANIC*--ALIVE.
IT'S JUMPING FROM HOST TO HOST... IT'S A *SYMBIOTE.*
HELLO? SCIENCE WHIZ, REMEMBER? IT'S *BIOLOGY!*
HEH...I SAID *WHIZ.*
SPIDEY, HOW DO WE *STOP* THAT THING *WITHOUT* HURTING NOVA?
IDEAS?
MY IRRESISTIBLE *COMEDIC BANTER* SEEMS TO HAVE NO EFFECT...THAT'S ALL *I* GOT.
I CAN *TAKE* IT OFF NOVA!
LET'S *NOT* BE HASTY. MAKE NOVA PROMISE TO *CLEAN YOUR ROOM* OR SOMETHING FIRST.
KIDDING! DON'T TOUCH IT OR IT'LL STICK TO YOU!
NOT IF YOU *"TOUCH"* IT *HARD* ENOUGH.
POWER MAN, NO!
THIS IS BAD.

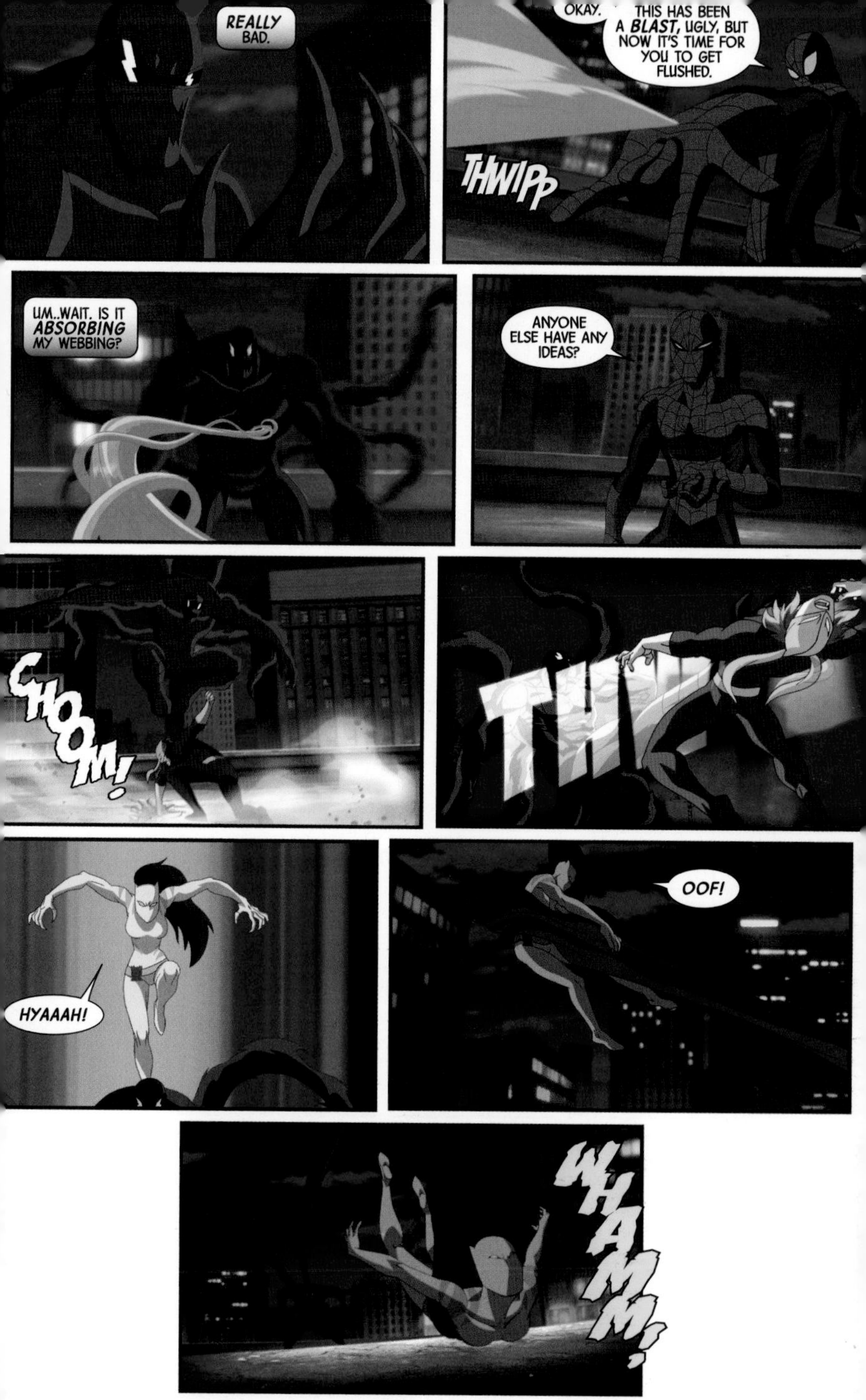
REALLY BAD.
OKAY.
THIS HAS BEEN A BLAST, UGLY, BUT NOW IT'S TIME FOR YOU TO GET FLUSHED.
THWIPP
UM..WAIT. IS IT ABSORBING MY WEBBING?
ANYONE ELSE HAVE ANY IDEAS?
CHOOM!
THHH
HYAAAH!
OOF!
WHAM!

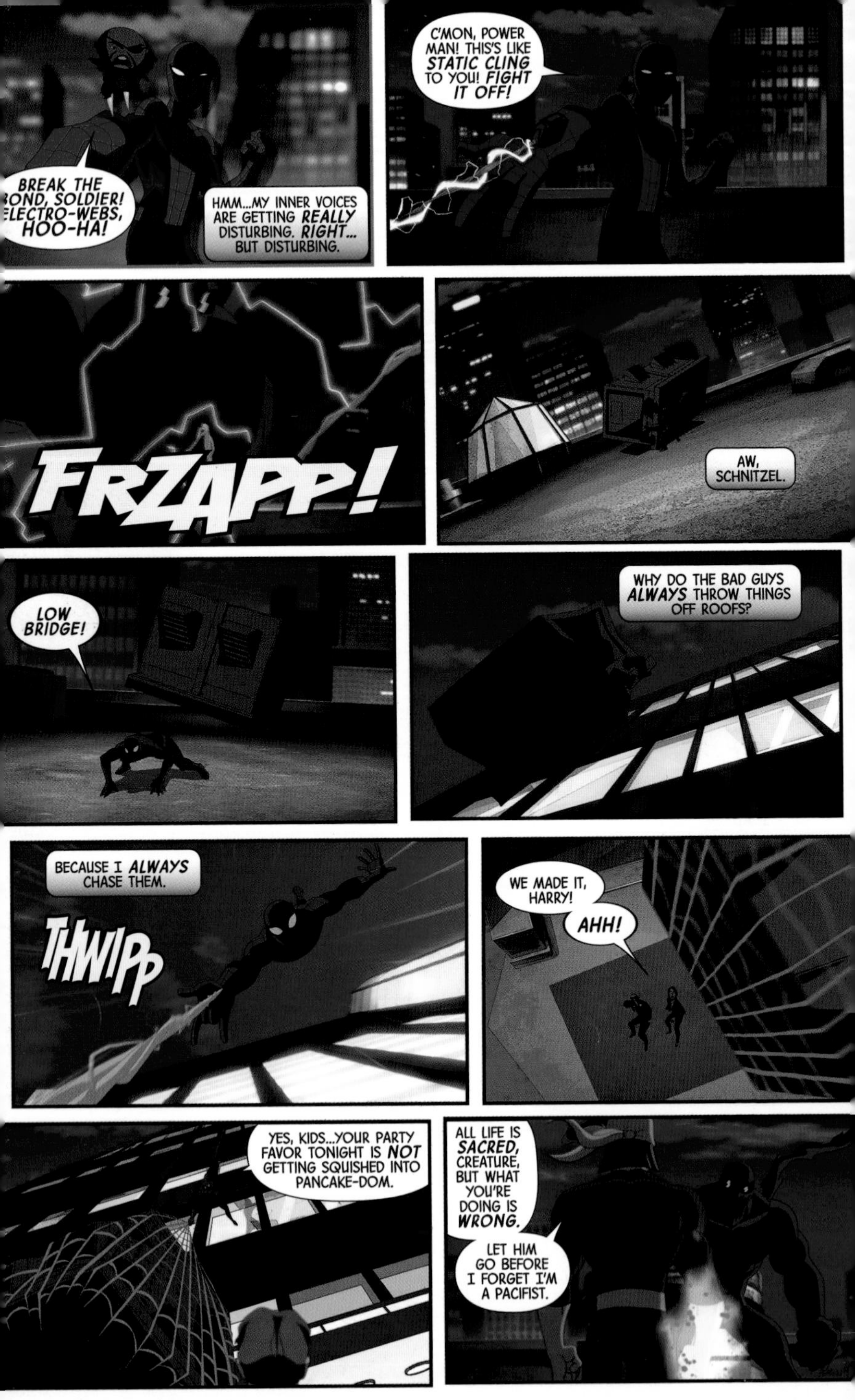
BREAK THE BOND, SOLDIER! ELECTRO-WEBS, HOO-HA!
HMM...MY INNER VOICES ARE GETTING REALLY DISTURBING. RIGHT... BUT DISTURBING.
C'MON, POWER MAN! THIS'S LIKE STATIC CLING TO YOU! FIGHT IT OFF!
FRZAPP!
AW, SCHNITZEL.
LOW BRIDGE!
WHY DO THE BAD GUYS ALWAYS THROW THINGS OFF ROOFS?
BECAUSE I ALWAYS CHASE THEM.
THWIPP
WE MADE IT, HARRY!
AHH!
YES, KIDS...YOUR PARTY FAVOR TONIGHT IS NOT GETTING SQUISHED INTO PANCAKE-DOM.
ALL LIFE IS SACRED, CREATURE, BUT WHAT YOU'RE DOING IS WRONG.
LET HIM GO BEFORE I FORGET I'M A PACIFIST.

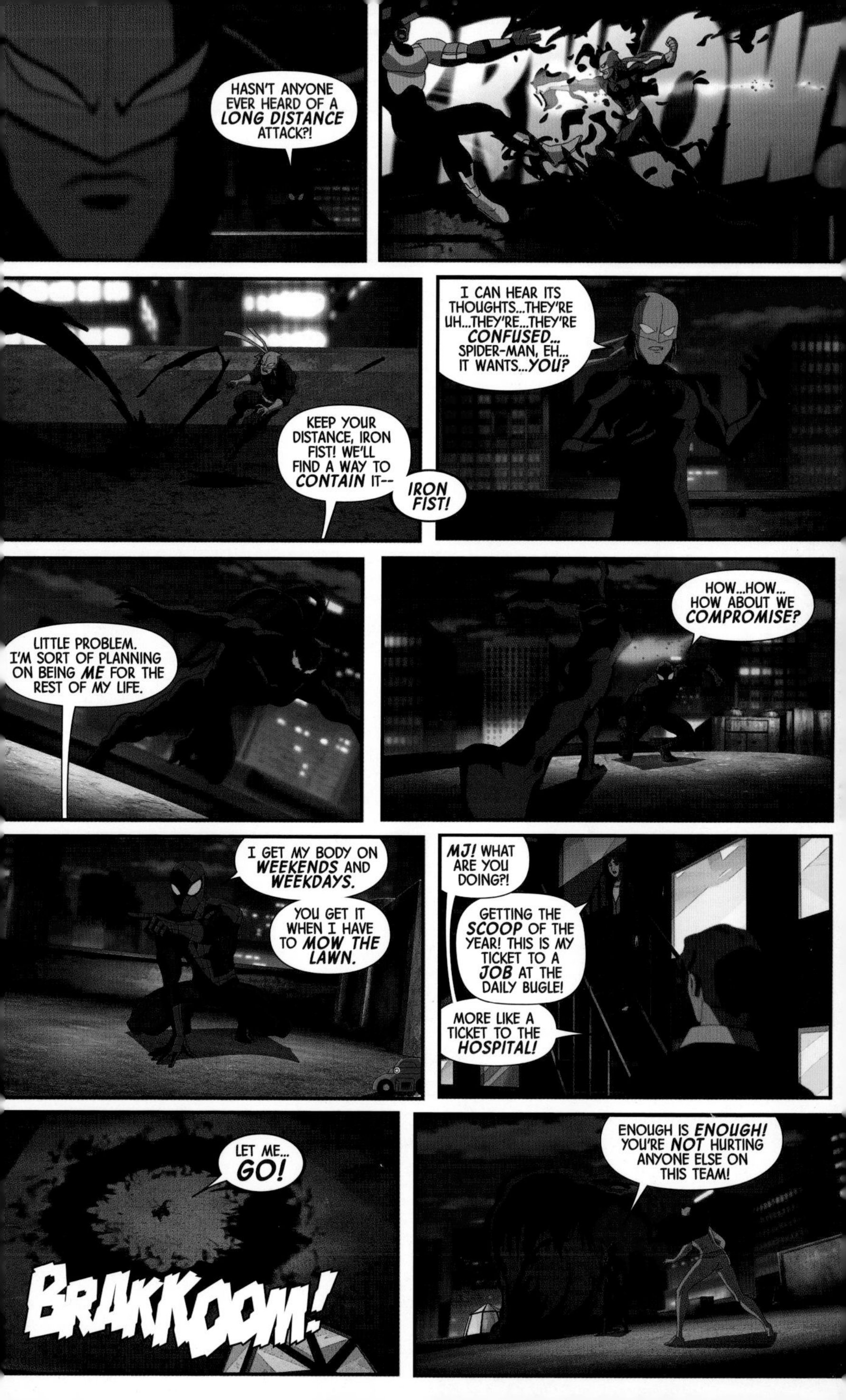
HASN'T ANYONE EVER HEARD OF A LONG DISTANCE ATTACK?!
KEEP YOUR DISTANCE, IRON FIST! WE'LL FIND A WAY TO CONTAIN IT--
IRON FIST!
I CAN HEAR ITS THOUGHTS...THEY'RE UH...THEY'RE...THEY'RE CONFUSED... SPIDER-MAN, EH... IT WANTS...YOU?
LITTLE PROBLEM. I'M SORT OF PLANNING ON BEING ME FOR THE REST OF MY LIFE.
HOW...HOW... HOW ABOUT WE COMPROMISE?
I GET MY BODY ON WEEKENDS AND WEEKDAYS.
YOU GET IT WHEN I HAVE TO MOW THE LAWN.
MJ! WHAT ARE YOU DOING?!
GETTING THE SCOOP OF THE YEAR! THIS IS MY TICKET TO A JOB AT THE DAILY BUGLE!
MORE LIKE A TICKET TO THE HOSPITAL!
LET ME... GO!
BRAKKOOM!
ENOUGH IS ENOUGH! YOU'RE NOT HURTING ANYONE ELSE ON THIS TEAM!

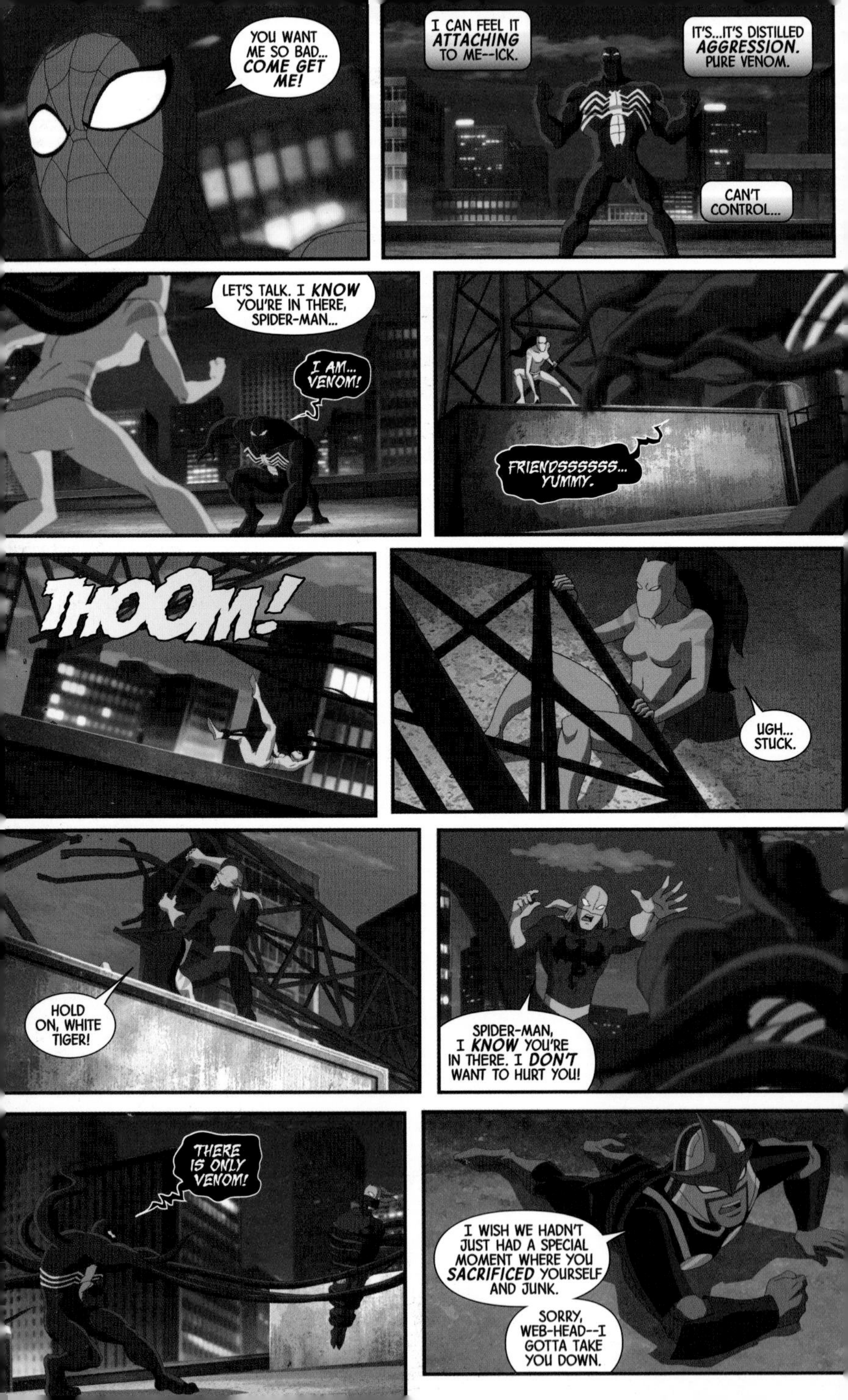
YOU WANT ME SO BAD... COME GET ME!
I CAN FEEL IT ATTACHING TO ME--ICK.
IT'S...IT'S DISTILLED AGGRESSION. PURE VENOM.
CAN'T CONTROL...
LET'S TALK. I KNOW YOU'RE IN THERE, SPIDER-MAN...
I AM... VENOM!
FRIENDSSSSSS... YUMMY.
THOOM!
UGH... STUCK.
HOLD ON, WHITE TIGER!
SPIDER-MAN, I KNOW YOU'RE IN THERE. I DON'T WANT TO HURT YOU!
THERE IS ONLY VENOM!
I WISH WE HADN'T JUST HAD A SPECIAL MOMENT WHERE YOU SACRIFICED YOURSELF AND JUNK.
SORRY, WEB-HEAD--I GOTTA TAKE YOU DOWN.

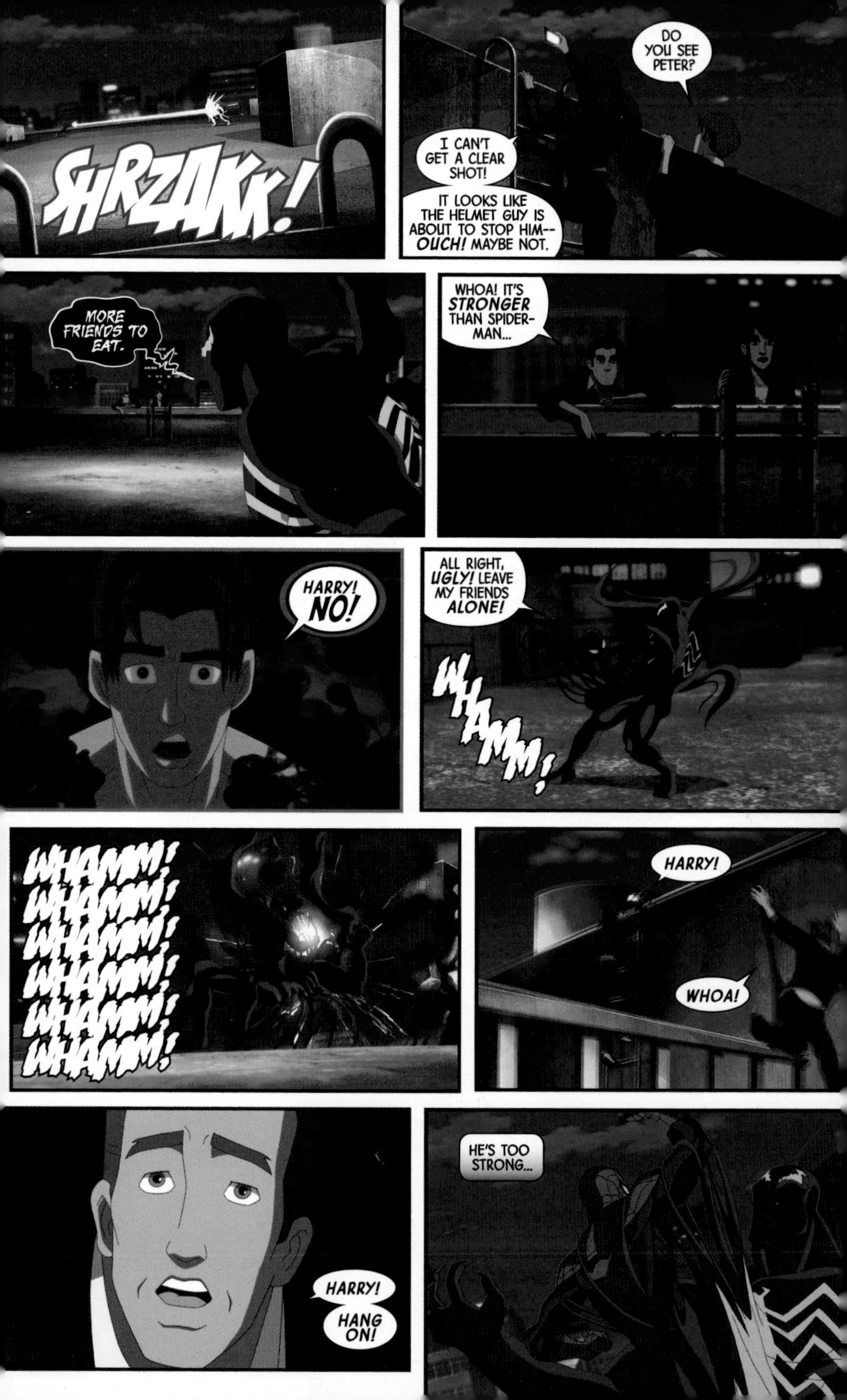
SHRZAKK!
DO YOU SEE PETER?
I CAN'T GET A CLEAR SHOT!
IT LOOKS LIKE THE HELMET GUY IS ABOUT TO STOP HIM-- *OUCH!* MAYBE NOT.
MORE FRIENDS TO EAT.
WHOA! IT'S *STRONGER* THAN SPIDER-MAN...
HARRY! NO!
ALL RIGHT, *UGLY!* LEAVE MY FRIENDS *ALONE!*
WHAMM!
WHAMM! WHAMM! WHAMM! WHAMM! WHAMM! WHAMM!
HARRY!
WHOA!
HARRY!
HANG ON!
HE'S TOO STRONG...

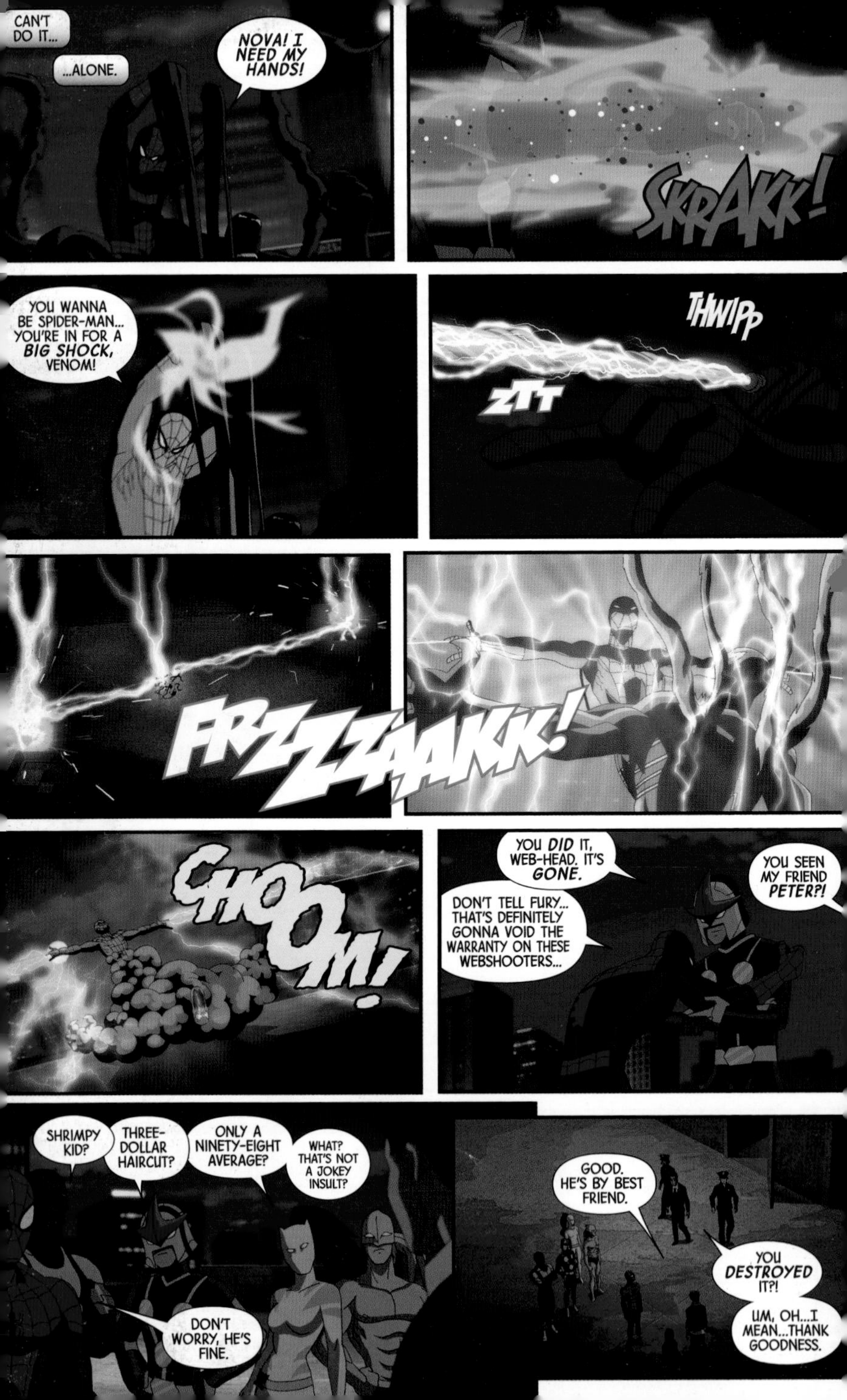
CAN'T DO IT...
...ALONE.
NOVA! I NEED MY HANDS!
SKRAKK!
YOU WANNA BE SPIDER-MAN... YOU'RE IN FOR A BIG SHOCK, VENOM!
THWIPP
ZTT
FRZZZAAKK!
CHOOM!
YOU DID IT, WEB-HEAD. IT'S GONE.
DON'T TELL FURY... THAT'S DEFINITELY GONNA VOID THE WARRANTY ON THESE WEBSHOOTERS...
YOU SEEN MY FRIEND PETER?!
SHRIMPY KID?
THREE-DOLLAR HAIRCUT?
ONLY A NINETY-EIGHT AVERAGE?
WHAT? THAT'S NOT A JOKEY INSULT?
DON'T WORRY, HE'S FINE.
GOOD. HE'S BY BEST FRIEND.
YOU DESTROYED IT?!
UM, OH...I MEAN...THANK GOODNESS.

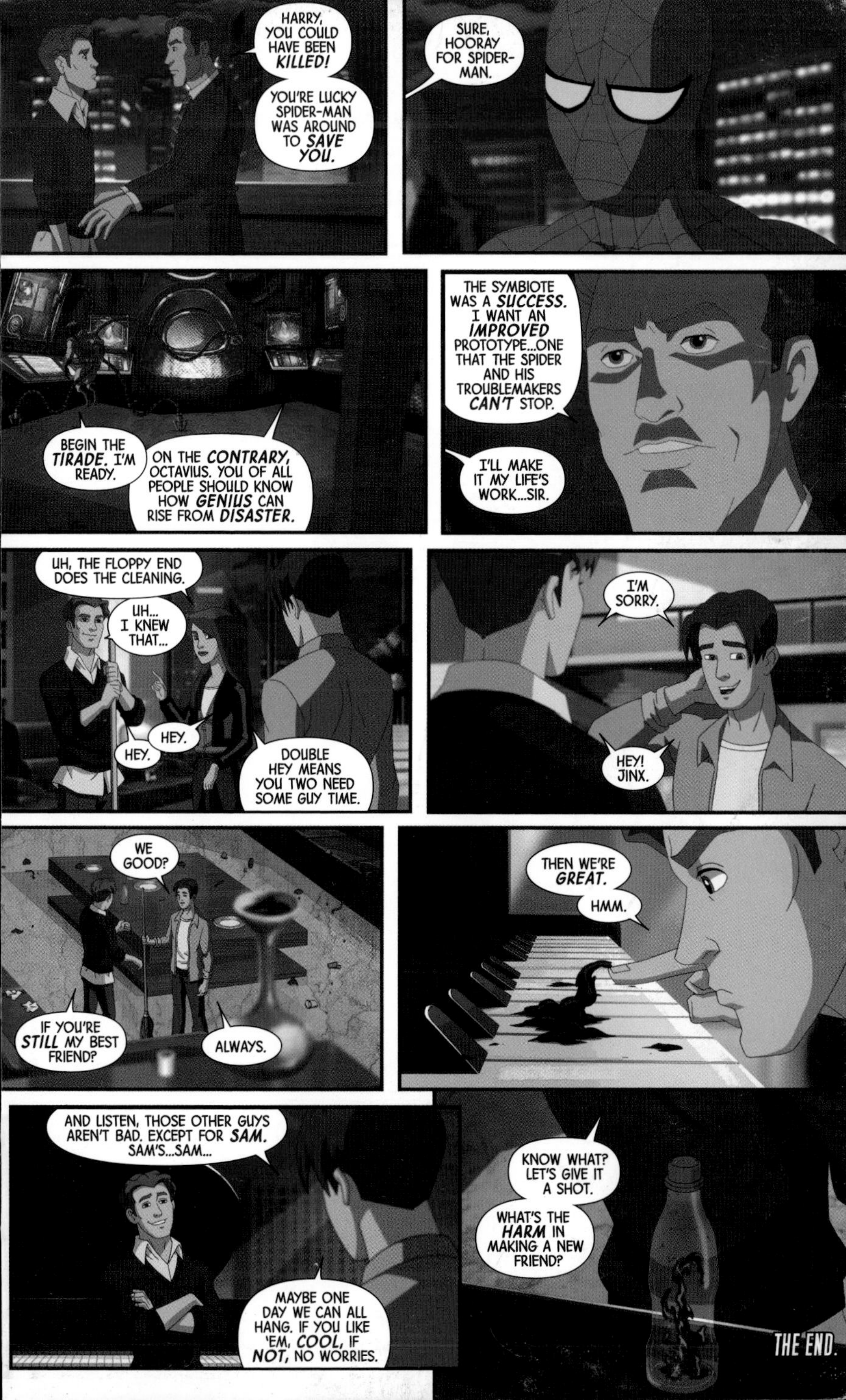
HARRY, YOU COULD HAVE BEEN KILLED!
YOU'RE LUCKY SPIDER-MAN WAS AROUND TO SAVE YOU.
SURE, HOORAY FOR SPIDER-MAN.
BEGIN THE TIRADE. I'M READY.
ON THE CONTRARY, OCTAVIUS. YOU OF ALL PEOPLE SHOULD KNOW HOW GENIUS CAN RISE FROM DISASTER.
THE SYMBIOTE WAS A SUCCESS. I WANT AN IMPROVED PROTOTYPE...ONE THAT THE SPIDER AND HIS TROUBLEMAKERS CAN'T STOP.
I'LL MAKE IT MY LIFE'S WORK...SIR.
UH, THE FLOPPY END DOES THE CLEANING.
UH... I KNEW THAT...
HEY.
HEY.
DOUBLE HEY MEANS YOU TWO NEED SOME GUY TIME.
I'M SORRY.
HEY! JINX.
WE GOOD?
IF YOU'RE STILL MY BEST FRIEND?
ALWAYS.
THEN WE'RE GREAT.
HMM.
AND LISTEN, THOSE OTHER GUYS AREN'T BAD. EXCEPT FOR SAM. SAM'S...SAM...
MAYBE ONE DAY WE CAN ALL HANG. IF YOU LIKE 'EM, COOL, IF NOT, NO WORRIES.
KNOW WHAT? LET'S GIVE IT A SHOT.
WHAT'S THE HARM IN MAKING A NEW FRIEND?
THE END.

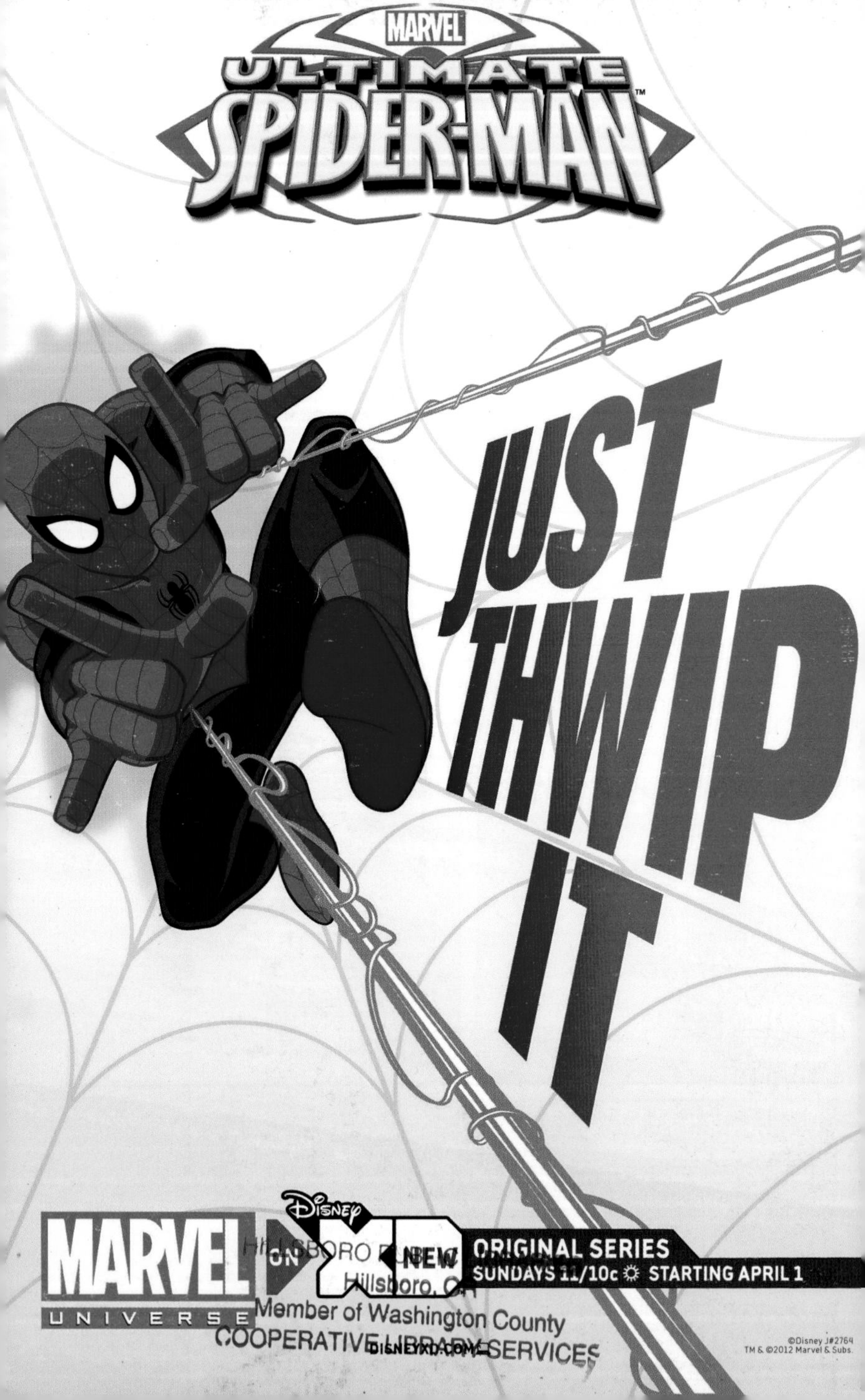
MARVEL
ULTIMATE
SPIDER-MAN™
JUST
THWIP
IT
MARVEL
UNIVERSE
ON
DISNEY
XD
NEW
ORIGINAL SERIES
SUNDAYS 11/10c ☼ STARTING APRIL 1
DISNEYXD.COM
©Disney J#2764
TM & ©2012 Marvel & Subs.